Using Newspapers in the Classroom

Paul Sanderson

CAMBRIDGE
UNIVERSITY PRESS

PUBLISHED BY THE PRESS SYNDICATE OF THE UNIVERSITY OF CAMBRIDGE
The Pitt Building, Trumpington Street, Cambridge, United Kingdom

CAMBRIDGE UNIVERSITY PRESS
The Edinburgh Building, Cambridge CB2 2RU, UK   http://www.cup.cam.ac.uk
40 West 20th Street, New York, NY 10011–4211, USA   http://www.cup.org
10 Stamford Road, Oakleigh, Melbourne 3166, Australia
Ruiz de Alarcón 13, 28014 Madrid, Spain

First published 1999
Reprinted 1999

Printed in the United Kingdom at the University Press, Cambridge

Typeset in Sabon 10.5/12pt   [CE]

A catalogue record for this book is available from the British Library

Library of Congress Cataloguing in Publication data
Sanderson, Paul.
Using newspapers in the classroom / Paul Sanderson.
    p.   cm. – (Cambridge handbooks for language teachers)
Includes bibliographical references (p.   ) and index.
ISBN 0–521–64526–3 (pbk.)
1. Newspapers in education.   2. Language arts.
I. Title.   II. Series.
LB1044.9.N4S24   1999
371.33–dc21   98–44354   CIP

ISBN 0 521 64526 3 paperback

To J.A.S.

Contents

Contents

Contents

Acknowledgements

My thanks are due to a number of people: to David Hill, Jackie Smith, John Morgan, Seth Lindstromberg and Silvia Stephan for commenting on earlier versions of activities in this book; to David Harrison, Sarah Ellis and Nina Nad for their support, enthusiasm and encouragement; to Denny Packard for his technical assistance; to Jane Clifford for her practical editorial support; to Julia Harding for her meticulous editorial work; to Penny Ur for her invaluable advice and guidance.

The author and publishers are grateful to the authors, publishers and others who have given permission for the use of copyright material identified in the text. It has not been possible to identify the sources of all the material used and in such cases the publishers would welcome information from copyright owners.

pp. 42 and 86 extracts from the *Express on Sunday* and the *Express*, Express Newspapers plc; *p.* 42 extract from the *Europa Times*, Het Laatste Nieuws, Belgium; *pp.* 56 and 241 (item 9) extracts from the *Sunday Telegraph* and the *Daily Telegraph* © Telegraph Group Limited, London 1998; *pp.* 77, 86 and 186–187 extracts from the *Mirror* and the *Sunday People*, Mirror Syndication International; *p.* 86 extract from the *Sun*, News International Newspapers Limited; *p.* 109 photo by Jeremy Pembrey; *pp.* 112–113 and *pp.* 132–133 extracts from the *Hastings and St Leonards Observer*; *p.* 132 advert from Rainbow Recruitment; *p.* 132 advert from Medical Emergency Relief International; *p.* 154 appeal from Brainwave; *p.* 154 appeal from Help the Aged; *p.* 155 appeal from NSPCC; *p.* 155 appeal from Shelter; *pp.* 167–183 earlier versions of these activities appeared in *Modern English Teacher*, 3/4, October 1994; *pp.* 198, 204, 208, 209 and 218 'I don't believe it', 'Up and running' and 'Mahood' cartoons and weather extract from the *Daily Mail*, Solo Syndication Limited; *p.* 204 'Garfield' cartoon © 1998 Paws Inc; *p.* 208 'Dog & Duck' cartoon from the *Sun*, News International Newspapers Limited and Terry Fulham; *p.* 208 'Austin' cartoon from the *Guardian*, © David Austin; *p.* 208 'Steve Bell' cartoon from the *Guardian*, © Steve Bell; *pp.* 212–213 an earlier version of this activity first appeared in *Standpoints*, 35, December 1994, reproduced by kind permission of *Standpoints*; *p.* 214 weather forecast © The Press Association Limited 1998; *p.* 240 (item 5) the Ty-phoo tea trademark is reproduced by permission of Premier Beverages; *p.* 241 (item 6) The Royal Ballet, (item 7) Sporting Pictures (UK) Ltd., (item 10) Stanley Stewart; *p.* 254 extracts from *The Universal Journalist* by David Randall, published 1996 by Pluto Press, London; *p.* 258 extracts from *The Newspaper Handbook* by R. Keeble © Routledge, 1994.

Introduction

The aims of the book

It should be made clear from the outset that the aims of *Using Newspapers in the Classroom* are neither to prepare students to become journalists, nor to teach them how to write in a newspaper style. Instead, this book attempts to achieve other important aims:

Meeting teachers' needs

To provide teachers with practical and creative ideas which exploit all the different sections of newspapers.

Meeting students' needs

To enable teachers to meet the diverse needs and interests of their students, using newspaper materials which engage and challenge them.

Developing language skills

To provide students with purposeful and valuable language practice through newspaper-based activities and tasks which develop reading, writing, speaking and listening skills.

Fostering positive attitudes

To instil in students a positive and comfortable attitude towards working with English-language newspapers, and towards reading generally in English, both inside and outside the classroom.

Encouraging reading

To promote extensive reading by giving students the confidence, the motivation and the ability to continue their reading outside the classroom.

The importance of using newspapers in the classroom

There are a number of very strong arguments in favour of using newspapers in the language classroom:

General educational value

Newspapers help keep us informed about what is happening in the world, thereby extending our knowledge and deepening our understanding. For this reason, they are of general educational value and importance to students.

As language teachers, we are also educators. Particularly in the case of language teachers working within the school system, this means that we are also responsible for the development and general education of our students, rather than merely the restrictive aim of improving their language skills.

Cultural information

Language and culture are inextricably linked, and the newspapers of a given target community reflect its culture through the language they contain. At one level, culture permeates language through references to the people, places, institutions, customs and traditions of that community. However, at a much deeper level, this is achieved through the cultural associations of words, and the shared experiences, knowledge, values, beliefs, emotions and attitudes that a writer assumes. Newspapers are an invaluable source of such information, and the more widely students read, the greater their understanding of this socio-cultural meaning will be.

Language change

Newspapers reflect changes in the language, and, in so doing, help students (and teachers) keep abreast of such changes. With their fingers on the pulse of language development, newspapers are linguistically topical and up-to-date, and provide valuable linguistic data.

Varieties of English

Newspapers contain a wide variety of text types and language styles not easily found in conventional language-learning materials (e.g. general coursebooks), and students need to become familiar with such language forms. Newspapers provide a natural source of many of the varieties of written English that become increasingly important to students, and valuable for language study as they progress.

Reader interest

The enormous variety of subject-matter in newspapers means that any one newspaper will invariably contain something of value or concern to every reader. This makes them interesting and motivating for students to work with. Newspapers report real-life events, and this arouses our natural curiosity about the world around us and our fellow human beings.

Reading for pleasure

For countless people worldwide, reading newspapers is already an enjoyable and popular pastime. Newspaper-based activities in the language classroom become, for such people, simply an extension of this interest, and one which teachers can capitalise on. For others, who do not read newspapers in their own language, there is the para-pedagogic benefit that working with English-language newspapers may even encourage them to do so.

Reading inside the classroom can help students discover their own tastes and interests. This in turn can play an important role in the process of motivating them to read of their own accord outside the classroom, thereby extending their contact with English. A judicious and sensitive teacher can encourage this by engaging students in enjoyable activities using varied and stimulating newspaper materials.

Authentic materials

Newspapers are an invaluable source of authentic materials, and their use in the language classroom is very much in keeping with current thinking and practice in teaching pedagogy. Indeed, for many students, the ability to read and understand English-language newspapers for work purposes represents a very real and tangible goal to aim for. Using newspaper materials in the classroom will also be particularly helpful for those students who may go to live or work in the target-language community.

Subject-specific materials

The diversity of information in newspapers enables teachers of English for Specific Purposes, as well as teachers of General English, to choose current materials to suit the precise needs and interests of their students.

Using newspapers in the classroom

This is especially important to teachers of specialist subjects in their search for suitable materials. Even a cursory glance through a newspaper and the special interest sections and supplements will reveal a wealth of material for those involved in teaching law, business, tourism, political studies, catering, journalism (of course) and numerous other subjects. People learn through reading, and reading about interesting new things in one's specialist subject undoubtedly helps motivation.

Teaching materials

English-language newspapers are readily available in most countries throughout the world, and there is a constant, on-going supply which is replenished with new content on a daily basis. As such, they provide language teachers with a limitless supply of teaching materials which can be used to develop their students' language skills.

Multi-level

Newspapers can be used effectively with a wide range of levels from Elementary to Advanced. In addition, you will find activities in this book which have a degree of open-endedness built into them; some, where a personal opinion or reaction is called for; others, where there is quite simply no one correct answer. This means that they are particularly suitable for mixed-ability classes, and that the stronger students in the class will have little or no advantage.

Lesson planning

Newspaper items are conveniently self-contained units which vary in length from a short paragraph to a complete page or more. This is a particularly helpful feature for teachers, in that it offers them a great deal of flexibility when planning lessons and selecting materials to meet certain criteria, e.g. the length of the newspaper item(s), the complexity of the language, the density of information, the subject-matter and content, the lesson time available and the level of the students.

This feature of newspapers is also helpful to students, who can measure and increase their reading tolerance, progressing from very short items, perhaps for detailed study, to much longer ones for extensive reading. As such, they offer students tangible, on-going targets to aim for in their reading.

Access to newspapers

English-language newspapers are becoming increasingly available throughout the world, and today, more than eighty non-English-speaking countries produce at least one English-language newspaper.

Some teachers using this book may be fortunate enough to be working in an English-speaking environment, with easy, regular access to newspapers. For others, this may not be the case, and the cost of English-language newspapers will be higher, and access to them more restricted. For these teachers in particular, I would like to suggest a number of ways that they may more easily obtain newspapers:

Cost-sharing with colleagues

With a small group of colleagues, you can club together and buy newspapers. This keeps the cost comparatively low, and this collaborative approach means that you can share the material, and perhaps even share the lessons you prepare.

Local organisations

Large hotels, airlines, international companies and banks often receive English-language newspapers on a regular basis. These are potential sources of free newspapers, and it is worth contacting local organisations such as these and explaining why you need them. Your request may fall on sympathetic ears.

Inter-school newspaper exchange

You may be able to arrange a newspaper exchange with a school in an English-speaking country. This should be easy if your school already has overseas links for educational and cultural exchanges. Indeed, if your school does arrange such visits, your next trip would be an ideal opportunity to stock up with a good supply of newspapers.

School subscription

Another possibility is to ask your school (or Parents' Association) if they would approve a special budget to pay for a subscription to a newspaper. This can reduce the cost per issue considerably, and should be substantially cheaper than buying individual copies from a newsagent.

Twin towns

Many towns (especially in Europe) are twinned with towns in English-speaking countries. If your own town is part of this scheme, you may be able to persuade the local organisers to help you obtain English-language newspapers for your students.

Overseas penfriends

If any of your students have penfriends in English-speaking countries, you might suggest that they enclose their next letter inside the pages of a newspaper from your country. They can then ask their penfriend to return the favour. The cost of sending this by surface mail should not be prohibitively high.

Overseas holidays

Holiday periods are an ideal opportunity to ask friends, family, colleagues, and your students going abroad to English-speaking countries, to buy newspapers on their way home. On some international flights, newspapers are given out free to passengers. It is also worth asking your students if their parents ever travel abroad on business to English-speaking countries. If they do, they may be willing to bring back one or two copies of newspapers.

Local English-speakers

English-language speakers living in your area are another potential source of English-language newspapers, and they may be quite willing to pass them on to you once they have read them. One teacher I met decided to contact English-speakers by advertising locally and requesting old copies of newspapers for her students. She was overwhelmed with offers, and was amazed to discover just how many English-speakers there were living nearby. She now has a constant, on-going supply of English and American newspapers.

Your own students

You can also ask your own students to help share the cost of buying newspapers. They are, after all, the very people who will benefit from working with them in the classroom. You might, for example, suggest that a different student buy a newspaper each week. This will be a co-operative and collective effort, and you will soon amass a wealth of material.

The Internet

Finally, but not least important, we find ourselves in a period of rapid technological changes in mass communications, with a global network of interconnected computers. Through the Internet, we are now able to access thousands of newspapers worldwide, and this figure is increasing daily. Although this technology is not yet available to all teachers, it is already being exploited by a growing number. It is quite clear that the Internet will increasingly become a major source of newspapers for language teachers, and those who already have access to the Internet will find a list of useful web sites in Appendix 2 of this book.

Collecting newspaper materials

Even with relatively few newspapers, you should find suitable materials for the majority of activities in this book quite easily and quickly. To save you time, however, a number of activities are provided with ready-made, photocopiable materials which you can use immediately, or supplement with your own.

Materials collection is an on-going process, but it is well worth devoting some time during the long school holidays (and long winter evenings) to collecting and filing specific categories of newspaper extracts (e.g. weather forecasts, short articles, advertisements, head-lines). This will ensure that you have a good supply of the materials you need when you wish to use the activities in class.

When you are searching for materials, it is helpful to keep several activities in mind that you wish to try out at a future date. It is also worth enlisting the help of family, friends and colleagues (as well as your students) to keep on the look-out for specific newspaper items such as Problem Page letters and cartoons.

The key points with materials collection are to plan in advance, and to throw nothing away until you are absolutely sure it is of no use. Fortunately, you will find activities throughout the book which will allow you to use almost every scrap of newsprint you find.

Choosing newspaper materials

In choosing suitable newspaper materials to use with your students, it is helpful to ask yourself a number of important questions:

Will my students find the materials interesting?

As language teachers, we are clearly concerned with the development of our students' language skills. However, we should not overlook the fact that students invariably respond far more positively and favourably towards materials they find interesting. Our students' motivation is crucial to the success of the lesson, and it can be a fruitless and frustrating task to try to make them work with materials they simply do not like.

Are the materials appropriate for my students in terms of their existing knowledge?

The ability to integrate new information with one's existing knowledge (e.g. cultural knowledge, general knowledge of the world, subject-specific knowledge) is part of the process of successful learning. If there is too great a mismatch between the conceptual difficulty of the materials you choose, and your students' ability to understand the materials, they will soon become discouraged. It can help considerably if you choose materials which contain at least some information your students already understand.

Are the materials appropriate for my students in terms of language level?

If an activity calls for a detailed and in-depth understanding of the language in the materials you choose, students can soon lose motivation and interest if the language is simply too difficult for them to understand. Although this point is dealt with more fully in a later section (see *Language difficulty in newspapers* on page 12), we can say briefly here that there are several options for teachers to consider: give your students adequate help and preparation to work with more challenging materials; choose materials where the language level is suited to the level of your students; choose tasks which are achievable by your students at their level.

Should I use only materials from today's newspapers?

Although it would seem preferable to use the news of the day in newspaper-based lessons, this is not always practical from the teacher's point of view – teachers have busy schedules, news can date quickly, and lessons take time to prepare. Without wishing to avoid topical items, it is worth mentioning that most activities in this book work extremely well with 'eternal' news items, or what is called in newspaper jargon, 'soft' news. These are news stories which are usually not head-line news, and are extremely difficult to put a date on. For this reason, newspapers frequently use such items as fillers. The advantage to you is that materials you prepare using such items can be used over and over again. This will obviously reduce your workload and the amount of preparation needed. In choosing such materials, a helpful tip is to avoid using items which include dates or the names of well-known personalities or topical events.

Can I use newspaper materials which are not from English-language newspapers?

As stated earlier, an important aim of this book is to instil in students a positive and comfortable attitude towards working with English-language newspapers, and towards reading generally in English inside (and outside) the classroom. It is clear, therefore, that presenting texts to students in their own language will deny them this opportunity. In spite of this, the possibility of using materials taken from newspapers from your own country is not completely ruled out. The key point to bear in mind when making this decision is to be perfectly clear about your lesson objectives and the skill(s) you wish to give your students practice in.

Many of the photograph-based activities from Chapter 3, for example, could undoubtedly be used with such materials, and would involve little (if any) adaptation, or deviation from the objectives of the lessons. In addition, many activities in this book use newspaper texts as a springboard for practising other important language skills, and this aim should still be achievable using non-English newspaper materials.

However, for other activities, particularly those which focus on certain genres of text or deal with specific features of English-language newspapers, any other materials would be quite simply unusable.

All of the above factors clearly interrelate, and the selection of suitable newspaper materials will be very much a compromise decision.

Organising newspaper materials

Once you begin the search for appropriate newspaper materials, it should not be long before you have amassed a formidable collection. The danger here is that unless you have a system to organise this bank of materials, it can too easily become unmanageable and inaccessible. Nothing is more frustrating than knowing you have just the article you need for tomorrow's lesson, but not being quite sure where you last saw it. It is therefore important to devise and implement a system of organisation which suits you, to ensure that materials are to hand when you need them. There are a number of possible ways you might choose to do this:

Newspaper sections

Perhaps the easiest system of materials organisation, and a good starting-off point, is to use the chapter titles of this book (e.g. *Articles, Horoscopes, Problem Page letters*), as category titles under which you can classify your materials.

Themes and topics

As your collection of materials grows, you will almost certainly want to subdivide each category to create more narrowly defined classifications. One way of doing this is to sort your materials into the major themes and topics you intend to work on with your students, e.g. sport, politics, crime, technology, health, and environmental issues. Even Problem Page letters can be classified into specific types of problem, such as letters which deal with health problems, problems between parents and children, relationship problems, and so on.

Language skills

Some teachers may prefer a system which classifies materials according to the main language skill they will be used to practise, i.e. Reading Skills, Writing Skills or Speaking Skills. Each of these categories can later be more precisely subdivided according to the particular sub-skill or strategy being practised, e.g. Reading Skills can be subdivided into fast reading, predicting and anticipating content, intensive reading, and so on.

Language systems

You may also wish to classify materials according to the language focus of the activities you wish to use them with, e.g. activities whose main aim is to practise vocabulary or structure and grammar.

Language level

Some teachers may prefer to organise materials according to the level of the students with whom they intend to use the materials. This is a very practical way of organisation, particularly if you are using newspaper materials to supplement a class coursebook.

Many teachers may find it convenient to use a combination of the above systems to organise their materials. As you continue using newspapers with your students, you will soon develop the system which works best for you.

Preparing newspaper materials

It is important to remember that the presentation and appearance of teaching materials can play a significant role in motivating students to read. Technical details such as the use of photographs and illustrations, the print size and the layout all combine to help make students want to read, and to enjoy what they read. It is therefore worth taking the time to produce materials which are as attractive and inviting as possible.

From your own point of view, when you are preparing materials for one class, you should do so with the intention of using them with other suitable classes in the future. This way, you will build up a bank of high-quality, reusable materials, and this will ultimately reduce your day-to-day preparation time.

Few teachers would disagree that preparing materials can involve a considerable investment in terms of time and effort. For many, there is undeniably a certain degree of satisfaction to be had from looking at an attractive piece of material they have produced. However, even the most conscientious and dedicated teacher would think twice about making such an effort if they thought that at the end of one lesson, they would have to prepare exactly the same of set materials for the next. Yet for a number of reasons, teachers can easily find themselves in exactly this situation: they have given away their last copy of lesson material; the only copy they have left is unreadable; their last copy has been spoilt during the lesson; they have simply mislaid or lost the materials.

The end result is that the teacher will either have to start all over again and make up a duplicate set of materials, or – sadly – will abandon all idea of using the lesson ever again, denying future students an enjoyable activity and the opportunity of working with interesting materials.

This situation can easily be avoided by following a few guidelines concerning materials preparation:

Making master-copies

Always make a master-copy of every item of material you prepare. From this, you will be able to make clean copies for your students.

Labelling master-copies

Label all your master-copies clearly, perhaps by drawing a small, brightly coloured circle in the top right- or left-hand corner. You can also explain to your students that if (by accident) you give them a copy of material marked in this way, they should return it to you immediately.

Storing master-copies

Store all your master-copies in a safe place, and avoid taking them into class, where they may get used, damaged, lost, or taken accidentally.

Protecting original materials

Never use your original materials in class if you can avoid it. However, if you must do so (e.g. in the case of original photographs), try to protect them in some way, perhaps by laminating them or putting them inside plastic covers.

NB **You must ensure that you have the right to make multiple copies of the material involved or seek the necessary permission to do so from the copyright holder.**

Language difficulty in newspapers

Many teachers avoid using newspapers with Pre-Intermediate students because they feel that the language is simply too difficult for such students to cope with. It is true, of course, that newspapers contain language which is in no sense graded – they are, after all, authentic. However, teachers should be aware of the importance of using newspaper materials at early stages of learning, even if they do appear to be difficult.

This concern over language difficulty is perhaps the single most common reason why so many students are denied the opportunity of working with newspapers until they reach an Intermediate or Advanced level of English. Yet this need not be the case, and there are several ways that teachers can make newspaper materials more accessible to Pre-Intermediate students. In the next section, you will find a number of suggestions for doing this.

If materials are selected solely on the basis of their linguistic complexity, there are a number of risks:

1 Teachers may reject materials which would, because of their students' interest in the subject-matter, encourage those students to overcome any inherent problems of language. Often, students will want to read difficult materials because they interest them, and they will continue to read because they find them enjoyable. It is not simply the linguistic difficulty of materials that teachers should judge, but also how motivated their students are to read them. We should not forget that motivation is a key factor in successful reading.

2 Teachers can sometimes develop lower expectations of students than is appropriate, and choose correspondingly low-level materials which do not challenge them sufficiently. Yet it can be extremely rewarding and encouraging for students to find that they can cope quite successfully with 'difficult' materials. We should not deny our students this success.

3 Students are able to understand language at a level far higher than they are able to produce. Selecting materials according to our students' level of language production rather than their level of comprehension is an easy trap to fall into.

4 Teachers may choose bland materials which do not meet the needs or interests of their students, simply because the vocabulary and grammar is controlled. This denies students the opportunity of a positive learning experience using stimulating materials.

If we take these factors into consideration, we can go a long way towards compensating for any inherent linguistic difficulties in the materials.

Making newspaper materials accessible to Pre-Intermediate students

There are four key ways teachers can successfully use newspaper materials with Pre-Intermediate students:

1 pre-activity preparation;
2 careful selection of materials;
3 careful design of tasks;
4 recycling materials.

1 Pre-activity preparation

Pre-activity preparation involves familiarising students with the content of the materials you are using, and preparing students for any difficult language they contain, before they read them. This can make students feel confident about working with newspaper materials, and enable them to participate fully in the lesson.

Pre-activity preparation techniques such as those listed below can be used in combination with one another.

1 Give your students the materials before the lesson and ask them to look up any problem vocabulary for homework.
2 Explain any key vocabulary in the materials.
3 Summarise the newspaper item.
4 Chat to your students about the general theme or topic of the newspaper item.
5 Ask your students to brainstorm everything they know about the subject of the newspaper item.
6 Let your students read a newspaper report, watch a video news report, or listen to a radio broadcast in their own language before they read the English-language version.
7 Before your students read a newspaper item, tell them the headline or title, and show them any accompanying photograph or illustration. Ask them to call out in their own language the vocabulary they think the item will contain, and then provide the English translations.
8 Before reading, write on the board and explain (or translate) key vocabulary from the newspaper item, and ask your students to predict the story-line.

These are only a few of the possible ways in which we can prepare less advanced students to work with newspaper materials before they read them. Teachers reading this book will undoubtedly have many ideas of their own to add to this list.

In addition, there are several other things teachers can do to help students during the course of the activity itself:

1 When preparing materials, add a gloss (an explanation or a translation) to deal with anticipated vocabulary and language problems.
2 Allow your students to use dictionaries during an activity to look up difficult vocabulary.
3 Explain any problem vocabulary as it arises during the lesson.
4 Encourage your students to go for the overall meaning of a text, rather than trying to understand every word. This will, of course, depend on the nature of the task involved.
5 Generally encourage your students to bring to their reading their own world knowledge and their expectations of the text content and genre ('top-down' processes). Too often, students approach reading with no expectations, and try to extract meaning only through word-by-word decoding of the text itself ('bottom-up' processes). It is generally agreed that successful reading involves a combination of both processes.

2 Careful selection of materials

As Nunan (1989) explains, the degree of difficulty of a text is affected by a number of factors. These include the grammatical complexity of the text, the density of information, the degree of information recycling, the amount of low-frequency vocabulary, the explicitness of the information, the discourse structure, and whether or not information is presented in chronological order. All this applies equally to newspaper materials.

However, it is important to remember that not all newspaper materials are difficult. Clearly, some texts are easier than others, and, as they stand, present little difficulty to Pre-Intermediate students. This is particularly true in the case of short newspaper items such as News in Brief articles, where only two or three words may need explaining to make the texts fully understandable. This can easily be achieved by adding a gloss to the materials you prepare, or by pre-teaching difficult vocabulary at the beginning of the activity.

Generally speaking, many students can find it quite tiring and discouraging to have to read a long, and perhaps complicated, newspaper article from beginning to end. Also, the longer the article you use, correspondingly greater will be the risk that a number of the factors mentioned above will combine to make the text inaccessible to Pre-Intermediate students. For these reasons, the majority of activities in this book recommend the use of relatively short newspaper items. This can be helped further by using the minimum number of materials suggested for an activity.

3 Careful design of tasks

'Grade the task – not the material' is a well-known maxim in language teaching. In practice, very low-level students can work with difficult texts, provided the task we set is suited to their level and demands less-than-complete reading of the text in order for it to be completed successfully. This in itself is a powerful argument against rejecting materials solely on the basis of their linguistic difficulty.

The issue of task design is an extremely complex one, and there are too many factors which impinge on task difficulty to discuss this issue here in any detail. It may be helpful, however, to consider a few reading tasks which can be used with lower-level students even with the most difficult reading materials:

1 Students circle or underline all the words they understand in the text.
2 Students circle or underline all the words in a text connected with a particular topic.

3 Students skim a text to identify the general subject-matter, e.g. sport, business, crime or politics.

4 Students scan a text to answer specific information questions (e.g. Yes/No questions and Wh-questions) to retrieve factual details from the text.

In devising tasks for Pre-Intermediate students working with newspaper materials, teachers can use the activities in this book as frames for their own activities, and as stimuli for their own creative variations and new ideas. In addition, many stimulating ideas for tasks can be found in publishers' series of (multi-level) resource books, as well as in specific-skills practice books and general coursebooks at Pre-Intermediate level.

4 Recycling materials

Another way we can make newspapers accessible to Pre-Intermediate students is by taking the materials we have used for one activity, and using them again, but with another activity. There are a number of advantages in recycling newspaper materials:

1 Different activities require different ways of working with materials, and this can offer students a new and fresh point of entry to materials which they may previously have found difficult.

2 A new activity with familiar materials can give students valuable practice in different skills and strategies without the language in the materials causing difficulty.

3 Recycling materials helps deepen students' understanding of the language they contain, and this can increase their confidence in working with them.

From the teacher's point of view, there is also the added advantage that using the same materials for more than one activity involves little, if any, extra preparation.

Choosing newspaper activities

This is not a book which is intended to be read from cover to cover, but one for teachers to dip into as and when they need to. *Using Newspapers in the Classroom* is divided into the following ten chapters:

1 Headlines
2 Articles

Each chapter deals with one particular feature of newspapers that teachers commonly use in their lessons. This organisation is intended to cater for the different approaches teachers adopt in their lesson planning, enabling them to use as a starting-point in their lesson preparation either the activities in this book (i.e. a task-driven approach), or newspapers themselves (i.e. a materials-driven approach).

In practice, this means that some teachers will find a newspaper item which interests them and will then refer to the relevant chapter in this book for a suitable activity to help them exploit this material. For example, if you have found a newspaper article of interest, you should read Chapter 2 on articles and select an appropriate activity. Alternatively, if you find an activity in a particular chapter which appeals to you, you can then look through a newspaper to find suitable materials to use for the activity.

In addition, as teachers are well aware, it is relatively unusual to practise any one language skill in complete isolation; even the most basic reading-comprehension exercise can involve integrated practice in reading, writing, speaking and listening skills. So it is with the activities in this book, which involve practice in a combination of skills.

However, for those teachers who wish to select activities which focus on more specific points, they will find it helpful to consult the index at the back of this book. This lists activities under entries such as 'creative writing', 'dictation', 'fast reading' and 'grammar'.

Cross-references

A helpful feature of *Using Newspapers in the Classroom* is the use of activity cross-references throughout the book. Two types of cross-reference are indicated:

1 Combination activities, i.e. references to activities which can be used in combination with other activities, either as a lead-in or as a follow-up activity.

2 Combination materials, i.e. references to activities which differ in their task design but use the same materials.

As an example of this last type, exactly the same materials used in 1.4 *Ask the right question* (where students have to anticipate the content of articles) can later be used for 2.17 *Ranking articles* (where students have to rank articles according to their own chosen criteria).

1 Headlines

1.1 Words

Writing sentences using headline words

Level: Elementary–Intermediate

Preparation

Select a number of headlines from a broadsheet and/or a tabloid newspaper (see note below) and cut them into individual words. Use these to compile a sheet of headline words in a jumbled order, and make one copy of this sheet for each pair of students in the class.

In class

1 Pair students, give each pair a copy of the words sheet and tell your students that the words have all been taken from newspaper headlines. Deal with any problem vocabulary at this stage of the activity.
2 Tell your students that they should try to use as many of these words as they can to make up sentences, but make it absolutely clear that they do not need to use all the words on the sheet.
3 Explain that their sentences can be as long or as short as they wish, and tell them that they can add grammatical words (e.g. auxiliary verbs, linking words, pronouns and articles) which do not appear on the sheet to help them make their sentences grammatically correct. This is a good opportunity to point out to your students the elliptical nature of headlines by writing two or three headlines on the board and showing the kind of words that are commonly deleted (refer to Appendix 1).
4 Tell your students that as they use a word, they should tick it on the sheet and not use that word again. They should write out in a list all the sentences they make, adding the appropriate punctuation (e.g. full stops, commas, question marks).
5 As each pair finishes, ask them to exchange their list with another pair to check the sentences they have each produced.
6 Finally, ask pairs to read out their lists of sentences, and discuss their

19

accuracy with the class. Deal with any language problems as they arise.

Extensions

You can use this same sheet in future lessons for a variety of tasks:

1 Look for examples of prefixes or suffixes.
2 Look for different types of collocation (e.g. noun + noun, as in *price rise*, or adjective + noun, as in *private word*).
3 Make a list of all the words that contain a particular sound (e.g. /æ/).
4 Classify the words into nouns, verbs, adjectives, adverbs, and so on.
5 Find words which can be a verb as well as a noun (e.g. *hand, page, stone*).
6 Find different pronunciations for a particular letter of the alphabet (e.g. Y – *try, system, country*), or for a combination of letters (e.g. OO – *good, flood, poor*).
7 Classify words according to the sense (i.e. smell, taste, touch, hearing, sight) with which students associate them.
8 Find words belonging to the same lexical group (e.g. words connected with *family*).

Variation

Instead of asking your students to make complete sentences, tell them to use the words to make newspaper headlines of any length, and allow these to have grammatical words omitted. The headlines can be discussed with the whole class, and students asked to make up stories which relate to the headlines.

Comment

An open-ended activity of this type is particularly well-suited to mixed-ability classes, in that it allows all the students in the class to produce language at their own level of proficiency. Higher-level students are challenged to produce more linguistically complex sentences, whilst even the students in the class with the least English will achieve a measure of success.

Note

Broadsheets (or broadsheet newspapers) are large-sized newspapers, and are printed on a size of paper known as broadsheet, hence this term. They are sometimes referred to as *the qualities*, or *the heavies* (referring to the weekend editions of certain broadsheets which contain so many pages that they are physically quite heavy to carry). Broadsheets are considered to be informative and objective, keeping news and opinion or comment firmly apart. They present the reader with serious news, which is supported with detailed and informed analysis and comment on economic, political, social and world events. Such newspapers in Britain include *The Times*, the *Daily Telegraph*, the *Financial Times*, the *Independent* and the *Guardian*.

Tabloids (or tabloid newspapers) are newspapers whose pages are about half the size of broadsheet newspapers. All popular newspapers in Britain are tabloids, far exceeding the broadsheets in their sales. Typically, tabloids contain many photographs, attention-grabbing headlines and sensational stories, often concerning scandal involving prominent figures and personalities in the public eye. They are considered to be more entertaining than informative in terms of their news coverage, so much so that *tabloid* is frequently used in a pejorative sense when talking about the press collectively. Such newspapers in Britain include the *Sun*, the *Daily Mirror*, the *Daily Star* and the *Daily Express*.

Cross-references

A quick oral version of 10.4 can serve as a suitable lead-in activity. The headlines used in most of the other activities in this chapter can be recycled in this activity.

1.2 Headline halves

Matching halves of newspaper headlines

Level: Post-Elementary–Intermediate

Preparation

MAIN ACTIVITY

Compile a list of between eight and ten headlines, each of which should consist of six or more words. The meanings of the headlines should be transparent, i.e. there should be no word play or ambiguity.

EXTENSION

Paste the accompanying articles (without the headlines) onto a sheet of paper, numbering them for ease of reference. Deal with any vocabulary or language problems by adding a gloss (a translation or an explanation), and make one copy of this sheet for each student in the class. Keep the matching headlines for the final stage to check your students' answers.

In class

1 On the left-hand side of the board, write the beginnings of the headlines you have chosen. On the other side of the board, write the endings of these headlines, but in a jumbled order. Deal with any vocabulary or language problems at this stage of the activity.

2 Explain to your students that the headline endings on the right complete the beginnings on the left, but that they are in a jumbled order. Tell them that they should try to find as many possible matching endings for each headline beginning as they can. Their complete headlines should have meaning, and they should form grammatically possible combinations (allowing for the elliptical nature of many headlines).

3 Begin the activity. When your students are ready, ask them to compare and discuss their complete headlines with a partner.

4 To check your students' answers, ask them to call out their complete headlines, and discuss each one with the class in terms of its grammatical acceptability and whether it has meaning. To check this last point, ask your students to briefly tell the stories behind their headlines.

5 Finally, tell your students the original (complete) headlines.

Extension

After Stage 4 of the activity, give each student a copy of the articles sheet, and tell them that they should read the articles and try to re-create the original headlines from the headline beginnings and endings on the board.

When your students are ready, ask them to read aloud the headline(s) they wrote for each article. Finally, deal with any articles for which your students had problems finding a suitable headline.

Cross-references

The same headlines can later be used in 1.1, 1.10, and 1.16.

1.3 **Headline hangman**

Playing 'Hangman' to discover newspaper headlines

Level: Post-Elementary–Advanced

Preparation

Select three or four short articles with headlines containing two or more words. Remove the headlines and paste the articles onto a sheet of paper, numbering them for ease of reference. Make one copy of this sheet for each student in the class. Keep the headlines safe, as these will later serve as your answer key.

In class

1 Give each student in the class a copy of the articles sheet and tell them to read the first article. Deal with any language or vocabulary problems as they arise.
2 On the board, for each word in the headline of the first article, draw a short line, and explain to your students that each line represents one word.
3 Tell your students that to discover the original headline, they should call out individual words they think are in the headline. If a word is correct, you will write it in its correct position on the board. If a word is not correct, you will draw one part of the well-known hangman diagram.
4 Begin the activity, and continue play until your students have guessed the whole headline correctly, or have used up all their guesses and are 'hanged'.
5 Continue this procedure for each of the remaining articles.

Extension

In a future lesson, ask your students to find short newspaper articles and make up their own headline hangman game to play in class with a partner.

Comment

This activity is a fun way for your students to discover important structural and stylistic features of headlines, and you may even wish to select headlines which all focus on one particular feature (refer to Appendix 1).

Cross-references

This can serve as a suitable lead-in to 2.6, 2.14, 2.15, 2.19, 2.22 and 2.24. The same headlines can be used in 1.1, 1.10, and 1.16.

1.4 Ask the right question

Writing and answering questions about newspaper headlines

Level: Pre-Intermediate–Post-Intermediate

Preparation

Select a number of newspaper articles covering a range of subject-matter, making sure that you choose articles with headlines that are easy to understand. You will need as many articles as you have students in the class, plus one other (with its corresponding headline) to demonstrate the activity. Remove the headlines, and paste (or copy) each one onto a separate sheet of paper, leaving plenty of space below for writing. Display these headline sheets around the classroom, on walls or desktops. Paste each article onto a separate sheet of paper and add a gloss (a translation or an explanation) where necessary to deal with key vocabulary. Keep the articles for the final stages of the activity.

In class

1 To demonstrate the activity, write your sample headline on the board and ask your students to imagine what information an article with this headline might contain. Tell them to put their ideas in the form of questions. Write their questions on the board (e.g. *What's the boy's name? How old is he? Where did it happen?*).

2 When they have exhausted their ideas, answer as many of their questions as you can by referring to the original article. Your students may be quite surprised to see how many of their questions the article answers.

3 Pre-teach any problem vocabulary in the headline sheets on display, then ask your students to read all the sheets, and each choose a different one.

4 Tell your students that they should now go from sheet to sheet and, on each one, write a question which they think an accompanying article would answer. They should write clearly, and leave room for an answer to be written.

5 When there are several questions on each of the headline sheets, ask your students to claim the headline they first chose. Give each student their matching article and explain that everyone should now read their articles and try to answer any questions they can.

6 When all your students have done this, ask them to display their articles and headline sheets together on walls or desktops. Tell everyone to circulate and check to see if their questions have been answered.

7 Finally, explain to your students that it is often possible to predict or anticipate a certain amount of information to be found in an article if we understand the headline. This can help us in our reading of a text.

Cross-references

This can serve as a suitable lead-in to 2.5, 2.6, 2.9, 2.11, 2.14, 2.15, 2.18, 2.22 and 2.24. The same headlines can be used in 1.1, 1.10 and 1.16. The same materials can be used in 2.17.

1.5 Frames

Writing progressively longer headlines

Level: Intermediate–Advanced

Preparation

Choose three or four short articles which you feel would interest your students, cut off the headlines, and paste each article at the bottom of a sheet of paper. Add a gloss (a translation or an explanation) to deal with problem vocabulary or language where necessary. Make enough copies of each article for several pairs of students to have the same article. Keep the headlines for the final stage of the activity, and make a note of which articles they accompany.

In class

1 Pair students and give each pair one of the articles, making sure that several pairs have copies of the same article in order to cross-check their answers later.

2 Explain that each pair should read their article carefully, discuss its contents and then write one (or more) suitable one-word headline(s) at the top of the page. Below this, they should then write one (or

more) suitable two-word headline(s), then headlines with three words, and then four words, and so on until they have written the longest possible headline they can to accompany their article.

3 When your students have written as many headlines as they can, put two pairs with the same article together, and ask them to compare their work. They should look for identical headlines they have written, and comment on the appropriacy of any different ones.

4 After this checking stage, work with the whole class and discuss any particularly interesting headlines your students wrote, focusing on any which seem inappropriate within the context of the article, and any which are grammatically unacceptable.

5 Finally, show your students the original headlines which accompanied their articles.

Comment

Before trying this activity, your students should already be familiar with different types of headline (refer to Appendix 1).

Cross-references

This can serve as a suitable follow-up to 1.8. The same headlines can be used in 1.1, 1.10 and 1.16.

1.6 One step at a time

Progressively changing one headline into another

Level: Post-Intermediate–Advanced

Preparation

MAIN ACTIVITY

Find two headlines where the only common feature is the number of words – between three and six words is the optimum number.

EXTENSION

Make copies of the two accompanying articles for your students to read at the end of the activity.

In class

1 Write the two headlines on the board, pair students and ask each pair to copy them – the first at the top of a sheet of paper, the other at the bottom of the sheet.
2 Explain that by changing only one word at a time, they should progressively change the first headline into the second headline. Each time they do this, they should write the new headline below the previous one. Their aim is to reach the second headline with as few new headlines as possible.
3 Point out that each new headline they make will tell a different story, and that they should be able to make up suitable stories to match their new headlines.
4 Begin the activity. Circulate to help your students if they get stuck, and to give encouragement.
5 When your students are ready, put two pairs together and ask them to compare their work. Tell them that each pair should briefly tell the stories behind the new headlines they have made.
6 At the end of the activity, find out which pair(s) managed to change the first headline into the second in the minimum number of moves, and tell them to write their headlines on the board.
7 If you wish, you can allow the class to challenge any doubtful headline by asking to hear the story behind the headline.

Extension

Give your students a copy of the original articles for them to read.

Comment

This activity is based on a popular word game in newspapers where the player has to convert one word (e.g. *said*) into another word with the same number of letters (e.g. *tell*) in the minimum number of moves.

Cross-references

The same headlines can be used in 1.1, 1.10 and 1.16.

1.7 Unlocking headlines

Understanding tabloid headline words through synonyms in the article

Level: Pre-Intermediate–Post-Intermediate

Preparation

Cut out several short articles from tabloid newspapers (see note in 1.1) with headlines containing examples of *tabloidese* (also called *journalese*) – short, sensational and often exaggerated words (see note below). You should make sure that each of the articles you choose contains a synonym (the more usual word) in the text which corresponds to the headline tabloidese word – this is invariably the case (see Box 1 for example headlines and texts). Paste each article onto a separate sheet of paper, underline the tabloidese word in each headline, and number each sheet for ease of reference.

In class

1 Write the list of tabloidese words on the board and ask your students to copy them. While they are doing this, display the article sheets around the classroom.
2 Explain to your students that all the words on the board have been taken from newspaper headlines and that such headlines can be difficult to understand. An important reason for this is that newspapers often try to sensationalise news, and powerful headline words have a greater impact on the reader. In addition, headline space is limited, and tabloidese words are usually shorter than their more everyday synonyms.
3 Explain to your students that they should look at each article, find the underlined tabloidese word there in the headline, and look for a synonym in the accompanying article. Because these tabloidese words are often difficult, you should allow your students to look them up in a dictionary. They should write the synonym next to the corresponding tabloidese word on their list. They should then read the headline again, replacing the tabloidese word with the synonym, to see if the headline now makes (more) sense and is easier to understand.
4 When your students have finished, ask them to compare their answers with a partner.
5 Check the answers with the whole class and ask if they found the headlines easier to understand with the help of the synonyms.

6 Finally, discuss the use of the tabloidese word and its synonym in each article with your students to discover which of the two words is the most accurate and appropriate. Bring out the point clearly that the restriction of space in headlines, and the headline writer's attempt to grab the public's attention with short, expressive, sensational words, may lead to headlines being exaggerated and distorted. Fortunately, the truth of the matter is invariably revealed soon into the body of the article.

Box 1 **Example texts**

Garage blast kills driver

An elderly man was killed yesterday in an explosion on a garage forecourt ...

BT to slash calls cost

British Telecom announced plans yesterday to reduce the price of international calls by ...

PM woos reject Tories

In a surprise move to win the support of Conservative MPs who lost their seats in the General Election, Prime Minister ...

Comment

The problem of vocabulary in newspaper headlines is a significant factor in discouraging teachers and students from working with newspapers at early stages of learning. This activity can help to show that headlines containing examples of tabloidese are less intimidating than they seem.

Note

In order to make the greatest possible impact on the reader, journalists have created their own particular jargon, often referred to as *tabloidese* or *journalese*. This is the use of short, powerful words intended for effect, e.g. *rap*, *slam*, *axe*, *chaos*, *crusade*, *dash*, and many more. For language students, this use of language can present a major obstacle to understanding English-language newspaper headlines.

This is hardly surprising for, as Keith Waterhouse (1993,

29

pp. 229–230) points out, this genre of language is not one that people actually use in normal, everyday speech: 'Why, if these words are now so common, are they not in common use? Why do we not hear housewives at bus-stops saying, "Our Marlene used to be a till girl at that blaze superstore" or "Did I tell you about young Fred being rapped after he slammed his boss? He thinks he's going to be axed."'

Although tabloidese is now ingrained in the British tabloid press, and leaving aside the fact that it bears no resemblance to the language people use in real life, there are other important arguments against its use: a headline such as *Judge slams shock jury decision* includes a value judgement made by the journalist writing the article, but it is presented under the guise of legitimate description. Here, it is the journalist's opinion that the decision is 'shocking', yet the job of a journalist is to present news and let the readers judge for themselves whether a particular news item is sensational, dramatic, disturbing or, indeed, shocking.

Also, many headlines containing examples of tabloidese are quite simply gross exaggerations of the reality, and quite misleading. Every disagreement becomes a 'dispute', bad luck becomes a 'curse', and a traffic jam becomes 'road chaos'.

Tabloidese today can be considered almost as a fossilised genre, and it is so over-used that it now has little, if any, impact on the reader. It is, however, here to stay, and is slowly influencing the headline-writers of broadsheet newspapers.

Cross-references

The same headlines can be used in 1.1, 1.10 and 1.16.

1.8 Headline features

Finding stylistic and structural headline features

Level: Intermediate–Advanced

Preparation

From Appendix 1, choose one or more stylistic (and/or structural) features used in newspaper headlines which you feel would be suitable for the level of your students. In addition, bring to class a supply of newspapers, pairs of scissors, sheets of A3 paper, and glue.

In class

1 Give a short explanation to your students of the newspaper headline feature(s) you have chosen, using examples from Appendix 1, and/or any others you can find yourself.
2 Write the name of each feature on a separate sheet of A3 paper and place these on different tables around the room.
3 Tell your students that their task is to find as many examples of these features as they can in the headlines in the newspapers you have brought in. Tell them that they should cut out their examples and place them on the appropriate sheet.
4 When your students have collected several examples of each feature, bring the class together and ask them to comment on the correctness of the examples on each sheet. If they are correct, paste them down. If not, ask your students to decide which headline feature they do exemplify.
5 These sheets can then be displayed around the classroom walls, added to in future lessons, and used with other groups.

Extension 1

If you are working in a non-English-speaking country, ask your students for homework to look for parallel headline features in their own newspapers, and bring examples of these to the next lesson.

Extension 2

In future lessons, deal progressively with other features of headlines to give your students a more complete overview.

Comment

This activity helps show students that newspaper headlines constitute a genre in their own right, and contain stylistic and structural features which are typical of this genre.

Cross-references

The same headlines can be used in 1.1, 1.10 and 1.16. For a suitable follow-up activity, see 1.5.

1.9 Ambiguity

Rewriting ambiguous headlines to make their meanings clear

Level: Post-Intermediate–Advanced

Preparation

From Box 2 below, choose between five and ten examples of ambiguous headlines.

In class

1 Write one of the ambiguous headlines on the board (e.g. *Kids make nutritious snacks*) and ask your students to explain the meaning of this headline. If your students fail to see the double meaning, tell them that the headline has two meanings (i.e. it is ambiguous). The amusing interpretation (i.e. that eating children is a nutritious way to appease your hunger) is almost certainly not the one the headline writer intended.
2 Now ask your students to suggest ways the headline could be rewritten to make its intended meaning clear. The simplest solution is to change the verb *make* to *prepare* to produce *Kids prepare nutritious snacks*.
3 Put your students into groups of three, write several other ambiguous headlines on the board and ask your students to copy them. Make it clear that all these headlines have double meanings.
4 Explain that each group should try to find the double meanings in the headlines and then rewrite each headline with the meaning the headline writer probably intended, making the minimum number of changes to the original headline. Allow your students to use dictionaries to look up any problem vocabulary.
5 When your students are ready, check the answers with the whole class. Establish the two meanings of each headline and ask groups to call out their rewritten versions for the intended meaning of each headline. Write these on the board and discuss their appropriateness with your students.

Extension 1

Ask each group to choose one of the ambiguous headlines and write a short News in Brief item for their headline, but based on the amusing, unintentional meaning.

Extension 2

With an advanced class, ask your students to try to identify and explain the cause of the ambiguity in the headlines. There may be a number of causes, including ambiguous word order, ambiguous grammatical structure, lack of hyphens (e.g. *Squad helps dog-bite victim*) or other punctuation (e.g. *Teacher strikes – idle kids*), polysemy and homonyms.

Cross-references

The same headlines can be used in 1.1, 1.10, 1.14 and 1.16.

Box 2   **Sample ambiguous headlines**

Kids make nutritious snacks

Squad helps dog bite victim

Miners refuse to work after death

Hospitals are sued by 7 foot doctors

Panda mating fails; veterinarian takes over

Lung cancer in women mushrooms

Eye drops off shelf

Safety experts say school bus passengers should be belted

Teacher strikes idle kids

US President wins on budget, but more lies ahead

Shot off woman's leg helps golfer to 66

Juvenile court to try shooting defendant

Stolen painting found by tree

Drunken drivers paid $1000

Red tape holds up new bridge

Chef throws his heart into helping feed needy

Arson suspect is held in Massachusetts fire

Local high school dropouts cut in half

New vaccine may contain rabies

Include your children when baking cookies

1.10 Categories

Categorising newspaper headlines

Level: Intermediate–Advanced

Preparation

Compile a sheet of complete newspaper headlines of varying lengths, make one copy for each group of three students in the class, and cut each sheet into individual headlines to make sets. Store each set in an envelope for safe-keeping.

In class

1 Put students into groups of three and give each group one set of headlines. Ask them to read the headlines. Deal with any vocabulary or language problems at this stage of the activity.
2 Explain to your students that they should try to put all these headlines into three or more different categories. Tell them that they can categorise the headlines in any way they wish, with one exception – they cannot group headlines according to the number of words they contain.
3 Begin the activity. When your students are ready, put two groups together and ask them to explain their categories to each other.
4 Allow a few minutes for this exchange, then, working with the class together, ask groups to call out different ways they categorised the headlines, and discuss these with your students.

Comment

This activity is open enough to allow students to categorise the head-lines in a number of ways, e.g. according to the particular stylistic and/or structural features they contain (refer to Appendix 1), their internal structure, the meanings behind the headlines, and also your students' personal reactions to them.

Cross-references

The same headlines can be used in 1.2. The headlines used in most of the other activities in this chapter can be recycled in this activity.

1.11 Me in headlines

Exchanging personal information using headline collages

Level: Pre-Intermediate–Advanced

Preparation

Before the lesson, make up a collage which gives personal information about yourself using only newspaper headlines – complete headlines, phrases and even individual words (see Box 3 for author's personal collage). You should feel comfortable about explaining anything in your collage to your students. In addition, bring to class several newspapers, pairs of scissors, sheets of A3 paper, and glue.

In class

1 Show your students your headline collage and explain how the words and phrases relate to you personally. Encourage your students to discover information by asking you questions about anything they do not immediately understand.
2 Tell your students that they are going to make up similar collages containing information about themselves, also using words and phrases taken from newspaper headlines.
3 Put glue, scissors, paper and newspapers at everyone's disposal, and begin the activity. While your students are working, circulate to deal with any vocabulary and language problems as they arise.
4 When your students have finished their collages, ask them to work with a partner to explain and discuss their collages. Allow a few minutes for this first exchange, and then ask your students to change partners.
5 Continue this procedure of exchanging collage information with different partners for as long as your students' interest and energy holds.
6 Finally, ask your students to display their collages around the classroom walls. This is an attractive and decorative way of personalising their classroom.

Cross-references

See 10.11 for an expanded version of this activity using a mixture of newspaper items.

Box 3 **Author's personal collage**

1 Coffee, croissant, and a splash of Sartre

6 **Cable car disaster**

4 mobile phones

8 Get fit to stay ahead

9 SOCCER FAN

3 1001 uses for your old Amstrad

7 home for Christmas

2 Stand up for Britain

5 in your living room

10 **Pictures worth taking**

Explanatory notes

1 Early morning breakfasts in Paris, sitting in a café and watching people hurry to work. Something I adore.

2 I'm constantly trying to defend English cuisine. Yet even before I begin, I know it's a lost cause, especially when I'm talking to people from France, or Italy, or Spain, or . . .

3 My first computer was an Amstrad, and it made preparing lessons so much simpler and a lot more fun. It was a faithful servant for several years. I gave it away to a computerless friend one Christmas.

4 I hate them! It drives me to distraction if someone receives a call when I'm with them and they ignore me for the next fifteen minutes. I feel like getting up and going.

5 My living room is the room I like most in my flat. It's bright and warm and cheerful, with lots of plants and pictures. It's a room where I can really relax.

6 I find the thought of this really quite horrific. I don't think I'm particularly afraid of heights, but I do have a fear of falling from a high building or from the edge of a cliff.

7 I rarely go home to Britain for Christmas, but last year I did. I had a fantastic time with a wonderful group of friends, and I think I was struck by how much I missed Christmas in my own country. It made me feel very homesick.

8 I'm ashamed to say that I haven't done any sport for years, and walking up five flights of stairs to my flat makes me very conscious of this – sometimes very unconscious!

9 This is something I'm definitely not! I really dislike football, and haven't watched a match for more than twenty years.

10 I'm a keen photographer, and I always look for an unusual angle on what seems like a rather bland subject.

1.12 Personal connections

Explaining personal reactions to headlines

Level: Intermediate–Advanced

Preparation

You will need to try this activity yourself before the lesson, in order to find headlines with which you feel a strong personal connection, or to which you react strongly. Very importantly, you should be able to explain very precisely why you feel these different reactions. For example, while looking through a recent newspaper, I found these two headlines:

Fast-food restaurants at Stonehenge?
WHEN IT'S BETTER TO TELL A LIE

These headlines provoked in me quite different thoughts and reactions, including:

'Oh, no! That would be a disaster.'
'That reminds me of the time I . . .'

In addition, you should bring to class two or three newspapers separated into individual pages.

In class

1 Tell your students that, while looking through a newspaper, you found a number of headlines (not the articles themselves) that you felt a personal connection with or reaction towards.

2 Write your sample headlines on the board, and explain as fully as you can to your students what these reactions were, and the reasons behind them. If you wish, allow your students to discuss their own reactions (if any) to these headlines and to question you about yours.

3 Tell your students that they should now look through the newspaper pages to find headlines that they also feel a strong personal connection with or reaction towards. Tell them that they should copy out the headlines onto a sheet of paper.

4 Begin the activity. Circulate to deal with any vocabulary or language problems as they arise.

5 When everyone has found at least two headlines, form groups of three students and ask them to read their chosen headlines to their partners, and explain why they chose them.

6 If you wish, you can invite students to read aloud any headlines they felt particularly strongly about and which they would like to discuss with the class.

Comment

It is difficult to understand all the factors that attract us towards one particular article before, or instead of, another. However, the degree of personal identification with the headline which the reader experiences clearly plays an important role.

1.13 Headline combinations

Creating headlines and inventing matching stories

Level: Pre-Intermediate–Intermediate

Preparation

MAIN ACTIVITY

Find six very short news items with headlines containing two words only – a total of twelve words. Copy out the six headlines for your own reference. It is worth noting that several types of two-word collocation are commonly found in newspaper headlines: *missing link*, *murder charge, cold comfort, wounded pride, inflation falls* are just a selection I found on three pages of one newspaper. Such headlines would be particularly useful for this activity.

EXTENSION

Remove the headlines from the articles and paste the articles onto a sheet of paper, numbering them for ease of reference. Make one copy of this sheet for each student in the class.

In class

1 On the board, write the twelve headline words in a jumbled list (avoiding using initial capital letters) and explain any problem vocabulary. Tell your students that these words come from six two-word headlines.
2 Tell your students that they should use the twelve words in different combinations to make as many two-word headlines as they can. They can use each word as many times as they wish.
3 Stop your students when they seem to be running out of ideas and ask them to compare their headlines with a partner. Tell them that if they have a headline which their partner does not have, they should explain briefly what the story is about.
4 Allow a few minutes for this exchange, then invite your students to call out some of their headline combinations. You should accept any doubtful combinations if your students can justify them by making up possible story-lines, however fantastic they might be.
5 Finally, tell your students what the original six headlines were, and ask them to check if they had formed these headlines themselves.

Extension 1

Do not tell your students the original headlines (Stage 5), but give each student a copy of the articles sheet and ask them to read the articles and try to re-create (and match) the six original headlines using the twelve headline words.

When your students are ready, ask them to compare their answers with a partner, and then check the results with the whole class.

If you wish to avoid making photocopies of the articles, read each one aloud to the class, and ask your students to call out the original headline.

Extension 2

Ask your students to select two or three of their own original headlines and write one-line News in Brief items.

Comments

(a) This activity brings home the importance of word order in very short headlines, and the different meanings that can be created. A headline such as *Danger money* will accompany a completely different story to one with the headline *Money danger*.

(b) If you have chosen headlines which comprise two-word collocations, some may be worth teaching as lexical items. This activity may thus provide a useful opportunity to make your students aware of the existence of collocations in English, and of the value and importance of learning vocabulary this way.

Cross-references

The same headlines can later be used in 1.1, 1.10 and 1.16. The complete articles can be used in many of the activities in Chapter 2.

1.14 Call my bluff

Inventing stories and listening to stories to decide which are true

Level: Intermediate–Advanced

Preparation

Select four or five short newspaper items (see Box 4 for sample texts) with headlines that could have more than one possible meaning. For example, *Queen to visit China* would be too transparent, whereas *Catch of the day* is open to several interpretations; this could be a story about someone catching a prize-winning fish, or perhaps a story about a catch in cricket which helped a team win an important match. Make enough copies of the articles for each group of three students in the class to have one news item, although you can use each article with several groups. You will need one other suitable news item to introduce the activity.

In class

1 Demonstrate the activity by writing your example headline on the board and telling the class three different (plausible) accompanying stories – one of which is the original story and two others which you

have made up yourself. Ask the class to vote on which they think is the true story.

2 Now form groups of three students and give each group one of the articles with its accompanying headline. With lower-level students, you may wish to add a gloss of key vocabulary to each article.

3 Explain that each group should prepare a short oral summary of their article. They should also make up two other possible stories which could accompany the headline. Allow them to make brief keyword notes for their three summaries, but avoid letting this turn into a writing exercise.

4 When your students are ready, put two groups together and explain that one group should tell the other their newspaper headline and then tell the three possible stories which accompany it. The other group should then decide which of the three stories they have heard is true.

5 When the listeners have made their choice, the story-tellers should tell them if they have guessed correctly or not. The groups should then reverse roles.

6 Finally, ask partner groups to exchange articles to read.

Variation

If you are working with a small class of up to twelve students, you can invite each group to challenge the class as you did in your demonstration of the activity.

Cross-references

The same headlines can be used in 1.1, 1.10 and 1.16. The complete articles can be used in many of the activities in Chapter 2. The headlines used in 1.9 can be used in this activity.

Box 4 **Sample texts**

Spreading the word

LIBRARIES were opening in some parts of the country for a trial run today — the first time on a Sunday.

The Library Association says branches in Surrey and London already experimenting with Sunday opening are popular with readers and traders.

Anti-Sunday trading campaigners condemned the move.

from the *Express on Sunday*

Final bedtime

Lima, Peru - "The poor man just didn't have the strength to free himself", said Lima police of 81-year-old Eduardo Aveza, who died of starvation after being trapped in his hideaway wall-bed when it slammed shut. Although neighbors called at his house, they "had no idea" that Aveza was trapped in the fold-up bed. *(Het Laatste Nieuws)*

from the *Europa Times*

Counter attack

Kent, England- "It's not funny, although some people seem to find it amusing", said a police constable, after his police station's counter bell had been stolen. This is the second time in only one month that the counter bell has been stolen from Sevenoaks police station, but the embarrassed officers have a plan: "We'll get a buzzer", said the constable, "then we will see who's laughing". *(London Independent)*

from the *Europa Times*

A hole lot fresher

A NEW label which will take the worry out of frozen or chilled food safety is being launched in the New Year.

Fresh Check labels are programmed to a specific time and temperature so if the food is no longer safe to eat, the consumer knows immediately. As time passes or the temperature rises, a small hole on the packaging gradually fills in.

from the *Express*

1.15 Headline charades

Miming newspaper headlines

Level: Pre-Intermediate–Post-Intermediate

Preparation

MAIN ACTIVITY

Select a number of headlines with four or more words in each. You should make sure that the headlines you choose contain vocabulary your students already know. Paste (or copy) the headlines onto small, individual cards to make them easier to handle. You will need one different headline for each pair of students in the class.

EXTENSION

Using the articles from which you took the headlines, paste each one onto a separate sheet of paper, and display these sheets around the classroom on walls or desktops.

In class

1 If this is the first time your students have done a miming activity where they have to mime individual words, explain and demonstrate (and perhaps practise with your students) techniques and gestures used in the parlour game charades (see Box 5).
2 When your students are comfortable with these techniques, pair students and tell them that each pair is to mime a newspaper headline to another pair.
3 Explain that one pair of students (the mimers) should begin to mime their first headline word to another pair (the guessers), who should call out words (and continue doing so) until they have found the exact word that is being mimed. The miming pair should confirm a correct guess clearly. The mimers should then mime the remaining words. When the guessers have successfully found the complete headline, they should write it, and pairs should then reverse roles.
4 When your students are clear about these instructions, give each pair one of the headlines. A miming activity of this type should be spontaneous, so do not allow more than a few moments for pairs to prepare their mimes.
5 When they are ready, put two pairs of students together and begin the activity.
6 At the end of the activity, ask if your students found any words

particularly difficult to mime, and ask for volunteers in the class to show how they would mime them.

Extension

Ask each pair to find the article which matches the headline they saw being mimed from those displayed around the classroom.

Variation

Instead of displaying complete matching articles, you can display an accompanying photograph with its caption, the caption or photograph alone, or one or two key sentences from each article copied onto a sheet of paper.

Comment

This can be used as a warm-up exercise with a class who are already comfortable with mime and drama activities. It can also help sensitise students to how headlines are constructed.

Cross-references

The same headlines can be used in 1.1, 1.10 and 1.16. The complete articles can be used in many of the activities in Chapter 2.

Box 5 Charades: miming techniques

- The number of fingers shown indicates the number of words in the headline.
- Showing the same number of fingers but touching one of the fingers indicates which word (i.e. the first, second, third, etc.) you intend to mime.
- The thumb and index finger held one or two inches apart indicates a small, grammatical word (e.g. *a, an, the, but, and, this*, etc.).
- The number of fingers held on the forearm indicates the number of syllables in the word to be mimed (each syllable is then mimed).
- Touching the ear means that the word (or syllable) sounds like another word (perhaps easier to mime), which is then mimed.
- An extended hand shaken quickly means that the word guessed is nearly correct.
- A 'thumbs-up' sign indicates the correct word has been guessed.

1.16 Headline fantasy

Using newspaper headlines for story-telling

Level: Pre-Intermediate–Advanced

Preparation

Compile a sheet of ten or more 'interesting' newspaper headlines. As far as possible, try to use headlines which contain fixed expressions and collocations (e.g. *A disaster **from beginning to end**, Scientists **break new ground***) which would be of general learning value to your students. Make one copy of this sheet for each pair of students in the class. Alternatively, to avoid photocopying, write the headlines on the board.

In class

1 Pair students, give each pair a copy of the headlines sheet and deal with any vocabulary or language problems.
2 Explain that each pair should use as many of the headlines as they can to make up a story. They should make only minimal changes to the headlines themselves (e.g. to make them grammatically correct), but they are allowed to add as much extra language as they wish to link headlines together, e.g. **When** *scientists break new ground,* **it is often** *a disaster from beginning to end.*
3 Tell your students that they should not write the story but should prepare it orally.
4 When they are ready, invite pairs to tell their stories to the class. You should ensure that the story-telling is shared equally, with each student in the pair taking their turn at telling part of the story.
5 At the end of the activity, ask the class to vote on which story they considered to be the most imaginative they heard.

Extension 1

Ask each pair to write their story, either during class-time or for homework.

Extension 2

In the next lesson, revise and help fix the language contained in the headlines by writing the headline beginnings on the board and their endings alongside, but in a jumbled order. Ask your students to match the two halves.

Cross-references

The headlines used in most of the other activities in this chapter can be used in this activity.

2   Articles

2.1 Categorising articles

Categorising articles according to subject-matter

Level: Elementary–Pre-Intermediate

Preparation

Compile a sheet of News in Brief or Stop Press items covering a wide variety of subject-matter. Number each article for ease of reference and add a gloss (a translation or an explanation) to deal with any vocabulary or language problems. Make one copy of this sheet for each group of three students in the class, and cut up each sheet into (a set of) individual articles. Store each set in an envelope for safe-keeping.

In class

1 Elicit from your students as many different themes and topics dealt with in newspaper articles as they can think of (e.g. crime, sport, politics, natural disasters, education, and so on) and write their ideas on the board.
2 To demonstrate the activity, read two or three of the articles aloud to the class, and ask your students to decide which categories from the list on the board the articles belong to. If an article does not fall neatly under one of these categories, ask your students to try to name the category which the article does belong to, and add this new name to the list.
3 Now put your students into groups of three and give each group a set of the articles.
4 Tell your students that these articles cover a number of different areas of news. Explain that they should read the articles, decide on their general content, and then put the articles into groups of the same news category. They should make a note of the numbers of the articles in each category, as well as the category name for each group of articles.

5 When they are ready, ask each group to compare their categories with another group, and discuss any differences they find.

6 Finally, invite one group to record their results on the board, writing the category names and the numbers of the articles they grouped under each one. Use this set of answers as a basis for discussion about other groups' answers. Any differences can be resolved on the spot by everyone reading carefully the article in question and deciding on the most suitable category.

Cross-references

The same materials can be used in 2.3, 2.19 and 2.20. A quick oral version of 10.4 can serve as a suitable lead-in or follow-up activity.

2.2 What, who, where, when, how, why?

Finding factual information in introductory paragraphs to articles

Level: Post-Elementary–Intermediate

Preparation

Compile a sheet with the introductory (i.e. the first) paragraph plus the headline from several 'hard news' articles – news of the day which deals with quotations and factual details, and which contains little description, journalistic comment, or analysis. Number each paragraph for ease of reference and make one copy of this sheet for each student in the class.

In class

1 Write the following questions on the board and explain to your students that the introductory paragraph of a newspaper article will usually answer several of these questions:

What happened?
Who did it involve?
Where did it happen?
When did it happen?
How did it happen?
Why did it happen?

You can add that answering all the above questions in the first paragraph would overload it with words and information, but the rest of the story will almost certainly go on to answer other questions. You can also mention that very short, one-sentence articles rarely attempt to answer all these questions.

2 Now write the following introductory paragraph on the board:

Schoolgirl tragedy

A 14-year-old schoolgirl drowned
in a swimming-pool yesterday
while she was on work experience
at a holiday camp.

3 Ask your students to read the paragraph and answer as many of the questions on the board as they can. Tell your students to call out their answers. Write their answers on the board. This particular paragraph answers the following questions:

Who? (a 14-year-old schoolgirl)
What? (drowned)
Where? (in a swimming-pool at a holiday camp)
When? (yesterday)
When? (while she was on work experience)

4 Give each student a copy of the paragraphs sheet and explain that these are the introductory paragraphs to several articles. Tell them that they should read each one and try to answer as many of the six questions on the board as they can.
5 Begin the activity. Deal with any vocabulary or language problems as they arise.
6 When your students are ready, ask them to compare their answers with a partner.
7 Finally, check the answers with the whole class and ask your students to say which questions they were able to answer for each introductory paragraph.

Note

The introductory paragraph of an article is one of the few major focal points for the newspaper reader as s/he surveys the page; it has the crucial function of having to grab the reader's attention. As Richard Keeble (1994, p.109) explains, the introductory paragraph is the most difficult for a journalist to write and yet is the most important 'since it has to draw the reader into the story by creating a sense of urgency and exciting their interest. It should highlight the main theme or angle of the story and set the tone.'

Cross-references

This can be used in combination with 2.3. A quick oral version of 10.4 can serve as a suitable lead-in activity.

2.3 Unpacking sentences

Understanding information-packed sentences

Level: Pre-Intermediate–Intermediate

Preparation

For each pair of students in the class, find a News in Brief or Stop Press news item which is only one sentence long and which contains twenty-five words or more.

In class

1 Write the following article on the board:

TV presenter blames tablets for tumble

Children's television presenter Simon Kirk blamed an accidental overdose of the painkillers he is taking for a shoulder injury for being found lying in the road yesterday by police officers while attending a television awards ceremony in Blackpool.

2 Ask your students what facts they learn from this article and write their ideas on the board in the form of short, complete sentences. You should end up with a similar list to this:

Simon Kirk is a children's television presenter.
He was attending a television awards ceremony.
The ceremony was in Blackpool.
He was found lying in the road.
He was found by police officers.
He has a shoulder injury.
He is taking painkillers for his shoulder injury.
He took an overdose of painkillers.

The overdose was accidental.
He blames the overdose for being found in the road.
This all happened yesterday.

3 Point out that this one-sentence, thirty-eight-word article contains a lot of information. The length of the sentence and the density of the information can make it seem complicated, and can make it difficult to understand all the relevant facts.
4 Now pair students and give each pair one of the articles. Tell them that they should read their article and make a list of all the facts the article contains.
5 When they have finished, ask each pair to exchange articles and lists with another pair. Tell them that they should read each other's articles and check the lists of facts to see if they are complete. They should add any new facts they find and correct any they think are wrong.

Extension

With a higher-level group, ask pairs to exchange lists of facts and headlines only. Tell them that each pair should try to write a one-sentence article based on their headline, incorporating all the facts. These can later be compared with the original articles.

Note

News in Brief items with sentences containing thirty words are not at all uncommon, and the introductory sentence in some articles in broadsheet newspapers (see note in 1.1) can contain nearly fifty words. This is generally longer than the introductory sentences in articles found in tabloid newspapers and local newspapers, which average between sixteen and twenty words.

For language students, sentence length can be an obstacle to understanding. If you add to this the fact that many such sentences can be very densely packed with information, it is not surprising that they have to be read very carefully for the reader to extract all the facts.

Cross-references

This can be used in combination with 2.2. The same materials can be used in 2.1, 2.19 and 2.20.

2.4 Forming groups

Forming groups by matching different parts of news items

Level: Post-Elementary–Post-Intermediate

Preparation

Select several articles, each of which has an accompanying photograph with caption. From each individual article you will need four items: the headline, the photograph, its accompanying caption and the opening paragraph. Together, these four items make up one set of material and you will use them to form a group of four students.

Make up enough sets of material from the remaining articles to match the number of groups (of four students each) you wish to form.

In class

1 Jumble up all the headlines, photographs, captions and opening paragraphs and give one item to each student in the class. Tell them not to show these to each other.
2 Explain that each student has to find their three partners, e.g. if they have an opening paragraph, they need to find three other students with a matching headline, a matching photograph and a matching caption.
3 Tell your students that those with headlines, captions or paragraphs can read them aloud, and students with photographs should describe them.
4 Ask all your students to come into the middle of the room and begin the activity. You should circulate to help with vocabulary and language problems as they arise.
5 When all your students have found their matching partners, and groups have been formed, tell each group to look at their headline, photograph, caption and paragraph together to check that they do, indeed, make a set.
6 When all the groups have been formed correctly, ask each group to study their four items together and identify the elements which link them.

Variations

1 To form pairs, use an article and its accompanying photograph.
2 To form groups of three students, use an article plus its headline and accompanying photograph.

3 To form larger groups of five or six students, use additional paragraphs from each article.

2.5 News flash

Answering comprehension questions – with restricted access to the article

Level: Elementary–Advanced
Special equipment: overhead projector (OHP)

Preparation

Choose an article which you feel will be of general interest to your students, and prepare an OHP transparency of it, enlarging it if necessary to ensure that it can be seen easily from the back of the class. In addition, prepare a set of questions (suited to the level of your students) based on the content of the article. For lower-level students, you should make sure that your questions follow the order of the article. Make one copy of the question sheet for each student in the class.

In class

1 Give each student a copy of the question sheet and read through this with your students to deal with any vocabulary or language problems.
2 Explain to your students that you will use the OHP to show them the newspaper article on which the questions are based. You will show them this for about twenty seconds only. You will then take away the transparency for a short time, and they should write answers to any questions they can and read other questions they have yet to answer.
3 Tell them that you will continue this procedure of showing and then removing the transparency until someone in the class has managed to answer all the questions. Tell your students that they do not need to write their answers as full sentences – keyword answers will be enough.
4 Begin the activity, increasing or decreasing the viewing time and the time allowed for answering questions according to how well your students are doing.
5 Finally, check the answers with the whole class. Focus on any parts of the article which caused difficulty and on any questions your students were unable to answer.

Extension

If your questions follow the order of the key information given in the article, at the end of the activity, your students will have the main points of the article. Ask them to use this to help them write a brief summary of the article, in class or as a homework assignment.

Variation 1

There are several ways to use this activity to challenge higher-level students:

1 Reduce the length of time the transparency is on view.
2 Reduce the length of time your students have for answering questions.
3 Limit the number of times your students actually see the transparency.
4 Write your questions in a jumbled order, i.e. not following the order of the information given in the article.

Variation 2

Before your students see the article, ask them to invent their own answers to the questions, and then use the article to confirm or correct their answers. This can help to focus their reading and they will be more motivated to read the article to discover if any of their invented answers are correct.

Comment

Fast-reading exercises in published materials often fail to achieve their aims, simply because the material is on view for too long and many students pore over it trying to understand every word. This activity eases this problem by allowing the teacher to control the length of time during which students have access to the text.

Cross-references

This can serve as a suitable lead-in to 2.6. For a suitable lead-in activity, see 1.4. For a suitable follow-up activity see 2.15. If the article you choose has an accompanying photograph and caption, 3.1 and 3.2 can serve as suitable lead-ins. A quick oral version of 10.4 can also serve as a suitable follow-up activity.

2.6 Strip cloze

Reconstructing a text using a variable cloze technique

Level: Elementary–Advanced
Special equipment: overhead projector (OHP)

Preparation

Select an article you think will interest your students and make an OHP transparency of this. You should ensure that it can be seen easily from the back of the class. In addition, cut out several long strips of thin card of different widths – wide enough to cover one, two, three, four or five letters. The wider the strip you use, the more difficult the activity becomes.

In class

1 Show your students the transparency of the article and allow them enough time to read it through from beginning to end. Deal with any vocabulary or language problems at this stage of the activity. If you wish, you can discuss the content and/or the theme of the article with your students.
2 Now place one of the strips of card on the transparency – either vertically or at an angle (see Box 6 for example text). Begin reading the article aloud, but stop before the first word (partly) concealed by the strip. Ask your students to call out the word, spelling it if you think this is necessary. Check their answer by continuing reading to the end of the line and then moving the strip down one line to reveal the correct solution on the line above. Continue this procedure for the rest of the article.
3 When you have worked through the whole article, place the strip on the article in a new position, pair students and ask them to work through the article together.
4 Finally, point out to your students that this is an activity they can easily do alone with a text for follow-up language practice.

Extension

If you wish, you can repeat the procedure at the end of your first reading by moving the strip to another position on the transparency, by using two strips at different angles, or by using a wider strip.

Cross-references

This can serve as a suitable follow-up to 2.5, 2.9 and 9.2. For suitable lead-in activities, see 1.3, 1.4 and 6.1. A quick oral version of 10.4 can serve as a suitable lead-in activity. For a suitable follow-up activity, see 2.15. If the article you choose has an accompanying photograph and caption, 3.1 and 3.2 can serve as suitable lead-ins.

Box 6 **Example text**

Welsh fight to keep English language

by JOHN GASKELL

PAREN... in South Wales, furious ...r plans to make Welsh ... pulsory in nursery clas... are fighting to keep E...ish as a first language...

A petiti... of more than 700 signatur... has been collected in ...aker's Yard, Merthyr ...il, a borough where Engl... is the predominant langu... "This is just the lates... ureaucratic attempt to s... Welsh down people's thr...s," said one resident, And...y Felton.

The petitio... o be sent to the Welsh Off... is part of a campaign to t...rt plans by the local coun... o stop English being the ...t language in Woodland, ... village's nursery. Th... council describes the p...nt situation as "a glarin...omaly".

But Carol Hou... who has six grandchildre... the village, said: "It is ...that we are anti-Welsh but we don't want our children learning Welsh as a first language.

"We have been told it will be an advantage for our children. But mothers don't want them to learn Welsh."

Parents think the move is designed to counter falling rolls at Welsh-speaking schools. The council claimed there was "a great deal of justified frustration... on the part of parents unable to access bilingual nursery provision at the school".

Original proposals recommended an all-Welsh nursery but a bilingual option is now being considered following protests.

Dewi Jones, the education chief in Merthyr Tydfil, said the nursery was part of a Welsh-speaking school. "It makes it difficult for the head to organise activities and cultural events. Pupils will be given a bilingual education. I think parents will see that as an advantage."

from the *Sunday Telegraph*

2.7 Putting it back together

Reconstructing an article from memory using jumbled phrases

Level: Post-Elementary–Pre-Intermediate

Preparation

Select a short newspaper article which you think will interest your students, divide it into short, natural phrases and copy these onto a sheet of paper but in a jumbled order. Make one copy of this sheet for each pair of students in the class. Alternatively, to reduce photocopying, you can write the jumbled phrases on the board.

In class

1 Write the headline of the article you have chosen on the board, explain it if necessary, and then ask your students to speculate on the content of the article.
2 Pre-teach any key vocabulary in the article, then read the article aloud to your students at normal speed. After this first reading, discuss with them how close their predictions were.
3 Read the article aloud a second time, but, as you do so, pause from time to time before the next word (or even after the first syllable of a word) to allow your students the chance to remember this word.
4 Read the article aloud once more, at normal speed.
5 Now pair students and give each pair a copy of the jumbled phrases sheet. Tell them that this is the article you read aloud, but that it is now divided into phrases which are in a jumbled order. Their task is to use all the phrases to reconstruct the original article.
6 Begin the activity. When they are ready, ask each pair to compare their version with another pair.
7 Finally, read the article aloud for your students to check their versions. Allow them time to correct their work as you read.

Acknowledgement

This activity is based on *Piecing it together* in *Dictation*, by P. Davis and M. Rinvolucri, Cambridge University Press (1988).

Cross-references

If the article you choose has an accompanying photograph and caption, 3.1 and 3.2 can serve as suitable lead-ins.

2.8 Mastermind

Memorising information in newspaper articles

Level: Pre-Intermediate–Advanced

Preparation

Compile a sheet containing three short newspaper articles of about the same length which you think will interest your students. Number each article, make one copy of this sheet for each student in the class and cut each sheet into the three individual articles.

In class

1 Put your students into groups of three, pre-teach any problem vocabulary or language in the first article, then give each student a copy of this article. Allow your students a few moments to read it, and then ask two or three questions to check their general understanding.
2 Assign a number (1, 2, or 3) to each of the three students in each group and tell your students that they will have exactly five minutes to read this article. Explain that during this time, Student 1 should try to memorise as much of the information in the article as s/he can. Students 2 and 3 should prepare questions based on the information in the article to test Student 1's memory.
3 Begin the activity. At the end of five minutes, tell Student 1 in each group to turn over the article. Tell Students 2 and 3 to begin asking their questions and to keep a note of how many correct answers are given. Their aim is to find the 'Mastermind' in the group.
4 Repeat exactly the same procedure using the other two articles for Students 2 and 3 in each group. This should include pre-teaching any problem vocabulary, allowing your students a few moments to read the articles and asking two or three questions to check their general understanding.
5 At the end of the third round, ask your students to add up their scores to find the 'Mastermind' in each group.

Extension

This activity can be extended to run as a knockout competition to find the class 'Mastermind'. Students who have been eliminated in earlier rounds can still participate by asking questions.

Variation

This activity can also be done with lower-level classes using articles from newspapers in your students' own language. The important point here is that your students ask and answer questions in English.

Comment

This activity works well in mixed-ability classes where you can give the higher-level students longer, more difficult articles, and lower-level students shorter, easier articles.

Cross-references

The same materials can be used in 2.16, 2.17, 2.26 and 2.28. These activities can also serve as suitable lead-ins or follow-ups.

2.9 Three-minute warning

Reproducing a newspaper article from memory

Level: Intermediate–Advanced
Special equipment: overhead projector (OHP)

Preparation

Select an article about three hundred words long which you think will be of interest to your students. Make an enlarged OHP transparency of the article, ensuring that it is clearly visible from the back of the class.

In class

1 Before you show the article, write the headline on the board, check that your students understand it, and then pre-teach any key vocabulary or language from the article.
2 Explain to your students that you will show them the article for exactly three minutes (or other suitable time limit). They should use this time to read the article and try to remember as much as they can.
3 Show the transparency for exactly three minutes (or your agreed time limit), then turn off the projector.
4 Ask your students to come into the middle of the room with pen and paper, and explain that they should talk to everybody and exchange

any information they can remember and make a note of it. Tell them that they have ten minutes to exchange and collate information.

5 Begin this information exchange stage. Stop it promptly at the end of the time limit.

6 Pair students and explain that each pair should now combine their notes to help them rewrite their own version of the article.

7 When they have finished, ask each pair to exchange their article with another pair for them to read and comment on it.

8 Finally, collect in all the articles to read and to correct language mistakes.

Variation

Before your students begin the writing stage of the activity, you may wish to show them the article again (for perhaps a further three minutes) to give them an opportunity to check the information they have collected from other members of the class.

Cross-references

For a suitable lead-in activity, see 1.4. If the article you choose has an accompanying photograph and caption, 3.1 and 3.2 can serve as suitable lead-ins. For suitable follow-up activities, see 2.6 and 2.15. A quick oral version of 10.4 can also serve as a suitable lead-in or follow-up activity.

2.10 Exchanging the news

Retelling newspaper stories

Level: Intermediate–Advanced

Preparation

Bring to class a selection of recent newspapers – if possible, one copy for each student in the class.

In class

LESSON I

1 Begin the lesson by telling your students about a newspaper story you have read recently which interested you. You should also explain why

it interested you. Allow your students to ask you questions if they wish.

2 Spread out the newspapers you have selected and ask your students to each choose one.
3 Explain that for homework, they should look through their newspapers and find one story which particularly interests them. They should read this carefully and come to the next lesson ready to tell other students their story. Tell them they should use dictionaries to look up any key vocabulary.

LESSON 2

4 Pair students and ask them to tell each other their stories (without referring to their newspapers) and to explain why they chose them.
5 When they have exchanged stories, tell them to change partners and retell their stories. This stage can be repeated with several other partners.
6 At the end of the activity, ask your students to comment on any story they heard which interested them enough to want to read it themselves. Let them take home the newspapers which contain these articles to read.

Variation

If you do not have enough newspapers for each student to have their own, the activity can be made into a rotating homework with one storyteller (who takes a newspaper home to read) and the whole class as listeners. In subsequent lessons, each student can take the role of storyteller.

2.11 Predictive listening

Predicting missing words

Level: Pre-Intermediate–Advanced

Preparation

Select a newspaper article which you think will interest your students. Go through the article carefully to find places in the text where you could stop before a particular word, and your students could try to guess what this word might be.

When selecting which words (i.e. answers) you want your students to guess, there are two possible types of answer you can choose: you can stop before obvious 'right/wrong' or limited-possibility answers, e.g. the final word of collocations, fixed expressions, or grammatical constructions. Alternatively, you can stop before answers where a number of more creative, open answers would be possible. This requires your students to use their imaginations; their offering plausible answers here shows that they are following the story as it unfolds.

In class

1 Write the headline of the article you have chosen on the board and check that your students understand it. Then tell your students a brief summary of the article and, as you do so, pre-teach any key vocabulary in the text, but none that is contained in the 'answers' you want your students to guess.
2 Explain to your students that you are going to read the newspaper article aloud to them, but that you will stop in several places before the next word. When you stop, they should call out what they think the next word will be in the context of the story.
3 Begin reading the article aloud up to the first point where your students have to suggest the next word, and make a clear gesture to your students that they should begin calling out their ideas.
4 Let your students continue doing so until they have exhausted all their ideas, then tell them the correct solution.
5 If your students are giving you answers which are clearly going in the wrong direction, this is an indication that they have misunderstood something or have been unable to follow. In this case, reread the previous section, explaining it if necessary.
6 Continue this procedure for the rest of the article.
7 Point out to your students that during reading, we are subconsciously predicting and anticipating language, based on our knowledge of language as well as our understanding of the text. This can help us in our reading, for we are reading to confirm our expectations.

Comment

An important aim of this activity is not for your students to always get the 'right' answer, but for your students to follow the story and suggest plausible answers. For this reason, unknown vocabulary in the 'answers' should not be pre-taught.

Acknowledgement

My thanks to Silvia Stephan, who suggested this activity.

Cross-references

For a suitable lead-in activity, see 1.4. If the article you choose has an accompanying photograph and caption, 3.1 and 3.2 can serve as suitable lead-ins.

2.12 Margins of error

Completing deleted beginnings and endings of lines

Level: Pre-Intermediate–Advanced

Preparation

Choose an article which you think will be of general interest to your students. If the article is printed in one column, you will need to cut it in half and re-position it on a sheet of paper so that you have two columns, side by side. Before you paste it down, cut off a strip with two or more letters from the beginning of each line in the left-hand column. Also cut off a strip with the last few letters from the end of each line in the right-hand column. Make one copy of this sheet for each student in the class. Keep a copy of the original complete text, as this will later serve as your answer key.

In class

1 Give each student a copy of the article and allow them a few moments to read it. They will soon see that the lines are incomplete and letters are missing. Deal with any other vocabulary or language problems at this stage.
2 Tell your students how many letters are missing from each line and explain that they should try to complete each line by writing in the missing letters. This will involve writing the beginnings or endings of words; in some cases, they may need to supply a complete word.
3 Tell your students they are allowed to use dictionaries, and begin the activity. They will find dictionaries particularly helpful to complete the endings of words in the right-hand column.
4 When your students have done as much as they can, ask them to check their answers with other students.
5 Finally, check your students' answers by reading the article aloud, pausing for them to call out the incomplete words.

Variation

With a higher-level group, you can increase the difficulty of the exercise by removing more letters, or a different number of letters each time, from the words.

Comment

This activity is a useful and enjoyable variation on the standard 'cloze' technique, and losing letters or words from a text can actually happen when we photocopy material too hastily or without due care.

Acknowledgement

My thanks to Rob Jamieson, who reminded me how much fun and how useful this type of activity can be for students, who have to work at sentential and supra-sentential levels to complete the task.

Cross-references

If the article you choose has an accompanying photograph and caption, 3.1 and 3.2 can serve as suitable lead-ins. A quick oral version of 10.4 can serve as a suitable lead-in activity.

2.13 Pay-offs

Reconstructing the ending of a newspaper article

Level: Pre-Intermediate–Advanced

Preparation

Select a short news item (see Box 7 for sample text), preferably an amusing one, where the last sentence contains the pay-off (i.e. the punchline) of the story.

In class

1 Begin the activity by writing the headline of the article on the board and discussing the theme of the article with your students.
2 Pre-teach any problem vocabulary, then begin reading the article aloud to the class, checking their understanding as you go along.

When you reach the final sentence, stop reading, and ask your students to guess or predict the conclusion to the story. Do not confirm or reject any of their suggestions at this stage.

3 When your students have run out of ideas, write the words of the concluding sentence to the story in a jumbled order on the board.

4 Pair students and explain that the conclusion to the story is contained in the jumbled words on the board. Tell them that together they make one complete sentence, and that in order to discover how the story ends, they have to reconstruct this sentence.

5 If your students are finding the task difficult, give them just enough help to encourage them to continue looking for the correct solution.

6 Finally, check to see which pairs have successfully reconstructed the sentence and found the conclusion to the story. Invite one of the pairs to write their sentence on the board.

Cross-references

If the article you choose has an accompanying photograph and caption, 3.1 and 3.2 can serve as suitable lead-ins.

Box 7 Sample text

Comforting words

British Rail's attempts to 'reach new heights of customer satisfaction' by keeping travellers 'better informed' suffered a setback yesterday when they added yet another gem to their list of memorable excuses for a frequently poor service. Exhausted and frustrated commuters waiting vainly on a bleak platform in Essex heard this immortal station announcement:

the	an	Rail	to	this	which	train,
of	lateness	excess	is		'British	
due	of	apologise	for		passengers.'	

(Answer: British Rail apologise for the lateness of this train, which is due to an excess of passengers.)

2.14 **Putting in the paragraphs**

Inserting missing paragraphs into their correct position in an article

Level: Intermediate–Advanced

Preparation

Select an article which contains at least ten paragraphs and cut it into individual paragraphs. Remove two complete paragraphs, each one from a different place in the article, then paste all the remaining paragraphs back in order onto a sheet of paper, numbering them for ease of reference. At the bottom of the sheet, paste the two paragraphs you have removed. Add a gloss (a translation or an explanation) to deal with vocabulary or language problems where necessary, and make one copy of this sheet for each student in the class.

In class

1 Give each student a copy of the article, ask them to look through it quickly, and then discuss with them the general theme of the article and their reactions to it.
2 After this familiarisation stage, explain to your students that the paragraphs at the bottom are missing from the article. Tell them that their task is to decide where the two paragraphs best fit in.
3 Begin the activity. When your students are ready, ask them to compare their answers with a partner.
4 Finally, with the whole class, discuss where they placed the missing paragraphs. Although there may be more than one possible position for a paragraph, any clearly wrong answers your students give will result in the article losing coherence and cohesion. A very fruitful part of this discussion phase will be to focus on your students' wrong answers.

Cross-references

This can serve as a suitable lead-in to 2.22. For suitable lead-in activities, see 1.3 and 1.4. A quick oral version of 10.4 can serve as a suitable lead-in activity. If the article you choose has an accompanying photograph and caption, 3.1 and 3.2 can serve as suitable lead-ins. For a suitable follow-up activity, see 2.15.

2.15 Crossheads

Writing suitable paragraph headings

Level: Intermediate–Advanced

Preparation

From a broadsheet newspaper (see note in 1.1), select a newspaper article which you think will interest your students and which consists of five or more paragraphs. Cut the article into individual paragraphs and paste them onto a sheet of paper in their original order, but leaving a space between each one for your students to write a line. Number each paragraph for ease of reference, and make one copy of this sheet for each student in the class.

In class

1 Pre-teach any problem vocabulary or language in the article, and then give each student a copy of the article. Ask your students two or three questions to check their general understanding of the article, and, if you wish, further questions to check their detailed understanding.
2 Explain to your students that you have rearranged the original layout of the article to allow a space between each paragraph – this space is for them to write a suitable heading for each paragraph.
3 Tell them that they should read through the complete article carefully, and then write a suitable heading for each paragraph in the space provided. Point out that the headings they write should be short and concise – one or two words only – and should reflect the key point of the paragraph.
4 Begin the activity. When your students are ready, put them into pairs or small groups, and ask them to compare their work, explaining and justifying their choice of paragraph headings. Each pair or group should try to agree on one set of suitable paragraph headings.
5 Finally, with the whole class, deal with the article paragraph by paragraph. Ask your students to call out the different headings they have written for each paragraph and invite discussion and comments from the class. If you wish, draw a grid on the board and ask students to write in the headings they gave to each paragraph. This will make it easier to compare all your students' answers during this discussion stage.

Comment

The ability to write suitable headings for the paragraphs of an article is a clear demonstration of your students' understanding of the intended message of the writer and of the meaning or impact of the text.

Note

Crossheads is the journalistic term for paragraph headings, and, as Keith Waterhouse (1993, pp. 82–85) explains, they are used almost exclusively by tabloid newspapers rather than by the broadsheets. Indeed, Waterhouse criticises the tabloids for their indiscriminate and unsystematic use of crossheads, the original purpose of which was to break up long, unending columns of grey text.

Waterhouse points out that the standard crosshead should be one word containing seven or eight characters (letters), and a set of crossheads within one article should not stray from one word class to another. Furthermore, he suggests that there should be some clear and logical connection between crossheads, and he gives examples of what he considers to be successful sets of crossheads, grouped by feature or word class:

1 using alliteration (*Hot, Hazy, High*)
2 using word association (*Faith, Hope, Charity*)
3 using adjectival forms (*Good, Better, Best*)
4 using abstract nouns that relate to human behaviour (*Sorrow, Theft, Attack*) in preference to other types of abstract noun
5 using verbs and adjectives in preference to nouns

Cross-references

This can serve as a suitable lead-in to 2.22. This can serve as a suitable follow-up to 2.5, 2.6, 2.9 and 2.14. For suitable lead-in activities, see 1.3 and 1.4. If the article you choose has an accompanying photograph and caption, 3.1 and 3.2 can serve as suitable lead-ins. A quick oral version of 10.4 can serve as a suitable lead-in activity.

2.16 Order of preference

Ordering newspaper articles according to personal preferences

Level: Pre-Intermediate–Advanced

Preparation

Cut out between six and ten short articles, each one from a different page of the same edition of one newspaper. Paste the articles onto a sheet of paper in a jumbled order, add a gloss (a translation or an explanation) to deal with problem vocabulary or language and make one copy of this sheet for each student in the class. For your own reference, make a note of which pages the articles actually appeared on.

In class

1 Explain to your students that the work of a newspaper editor involves deciding which articles will appear in the newspaper, how long they should be and which pages they should appear on. Tell your students that they are going to be newspaper editors for this activity.

2 Give each student a copy of the articles sheet and explain that they should read the articles and decide in which order they should appear in the newspaper. Their decision should be determined exclusively by their own interest in the stories, and they should number them from 1 onwards (i.e. the most interesting to the least interesting).

3 Begin the activity. When your students are ready, form groups of three or four students and ask them to compare their orders, explaining the reasons for their decisions.

4 Finally, show your students the newspaper from which the articles were taken and tell them the order in which they actually appeared.

Extension

Lead a class discussion on editorial decision-making concerning the ordering of items in a newspaper. Use the articles and their original order as the starting-point for your discussion, looking for the possible reasons why they appeared in this order. Your discussion should lead to a consideration of why major sections (e.g. Home News, International News, Business, Sport, etc.) appear in the order they do. You may even wish to compare several newspapers to look for regular underlying patterns in the ordering of particular newspaper sections.

Cross-references

The same materials can be used in 2.8, 2.17, 2.26 and 2.28. These activities can also serve as suitable lead-ins or follow-ups. For a suitable lead-in activity, see 4.1. A quick oral version of 10.4 can serve as a suitable lead-in activity.

2.17 Ranking articles

Ranking articles in different ways

Level: Intermediate–Advanced

Preparation

Compile a sheet of between five and eight short articles covering a variety of subject-matter. Number each article and add a gloss (a translation or an explanation) to deal with vocabulary or language problems where necessary. Make one copy of this sheet for each pair of students in the class, and cut each sheet into individual articles to make a set for each pair. This will make them easier to handle during the activity.

In class

1 Pair students and give each pair a set of the articles.
2 Explain that each pair should read the articles and then rank them in as many ways as they can think of. To clarify what your students should do, suggest one or two possible ways of ranking the articles (e.g. the longest to the shortest), but tell them not to include your examples – they should think of different ways (see Box 8 for other suggestions).
3 Tell your students that they should make a note of their different ranking orders on a sheet of paper, and the reasons why they have ranked the articles in these ways.
4 When your students have several different ranking orders, put two pairs together. Tell them that one pair should lay out their articles on the table in one of their ranking orders, and their partner pair should try to guess the reason why they ranked the articles in this way. Both pairs should continue this procedure for all their different ranking orders.
5 Allow a few minutes for this exchange and then, finally, with the whole class, invite your students to explain some of the different ways they ranked the articles.

Variation 1

With a small class, each pair can challenge the class by writing one of their ranking orders on the board for the whole class to guess the reason for this order.

Variation 2

This activity need not be confined to newspaper articles but can easily be used with photographs, headlines, advertisements, cartoons, and even with a combination of newspaper items. This can produce very interesting results.

Comment

This is a very open activity, with no one correct answer. As such, it can be used with mixed-ability classes, with each student working at his/her own linguistic level.

Cross-references

The same materials can be used in 1.4, 2.8, 2.16, 2.26 and 2.28. These activities can also serve as suitable lead-ins or follow-ups. A quick oral version of 10.4 can serve as a suitable lead-in activity.

Box 8 Example criteria for ranking articles

The longest article ↔ The shortest article
The most important event ↔ The least important event
The most detailed article (i.e. the amount of information / number of facts given) ↔ The least detailed article
The most interesting article ↔ The least interesting article
The event nearest to here ↔ The event furthest away from here
The highest number of people involved ↔ The lowest number of people involved
The greatest impact on my life ↔ The least impact on my life
The easiest (language) to understand ↔ The most difficult to understand
The most recent event ↔ The least recent event
The most positive event ↔ The most tragic event
The most shocking/surprising event ↔ The least shocking/surprising event
The event I would most like to have attended ↔ The event I would least like to have attended

---

2.18 Real-life interviews

Interviewing the teacher and writing an article about a real-life incident

Level: Pre-Intermediate–Post-Intermediate

Preparation

Think of a real-life incident that happened to you and summarise it in the form of a headline, e.g. *Teenager on school trip saved from drowning*.

In class

1 Write your headline on the board and tell your students that this is a headline about an incident that really happened to you. Tell them that they should ask you questions to get the full story about the incident, which they will later write as a short article. Explain that the interview takes place shortly after the incident, i.e. you will answer as the teenager you were when it happened.

2 Allow your students to prepare for the interview by giving them a few minutes to think of suitable questions to ask you.

3 When they are ready, invite questions from the 'journalists' and tell everyone to make notes of your answers. Tell them that they can also write down anything you say which they could use as a direct quote (e.g. 'I really thought that was the end. I can't thank Jim enough.'). You may need to slip in information towards the end of the interview to cover any important information they have overlooked in their questions.

4 At the end of the interview, form pairs or groups of three students and ask them to pool their information and then write a short article about the incident using the headline on the board or their own headline.

5 Finally, ask groups to exchange their articles to read. If possible, find and photocopy a photograph of yourself from that period of your life, and give a copy to each group to 'print' with their article.

Extension

In future lessons, repeat the activity but with your students taking the role of interviewees and being interviewed about an incident from their own lives. The resulting articles can all be put together to produce a class newspaper for the group.

Cross-references

For a suitable lead-in activity, see 1.4.

2.19 Press conference

Expanding short newspaper articles

Level: Pre-Intermediate–Post-Intermediate

Preparation

From a national newspaper, select a News in Brief item which you think will interest your students. Very little information and few details should be given in the story you choose.

In class

1 Copy the article you have chosen onto the board and explain any key vocabulary or language. Spend a few minutes discussing the general theme of the article with your students, as well as the story itself and your students' reactions to it.
2 Point out that very little information is given in this particular (national) newspaper's account, but that a local newspaper in the area where the incident happened would give a lot more information.
3 Tell your students that they are going to expand on the story by interviewing the people in it. Ask for volunteers from the class to play the roles of these people.
4 Put the rest of the class into pairs or groups of three students and tell them that each group is a team of journalists representing a local newspaper. Tell them that they should think of a name for the newspaper they represent, and explain that they should prepare questions to interview the people in the story to get as much extra information as they can.
5 Tell the interviewees that while the journalists are preparing their questions, they should work together to prepare and agree on the background of their characters and the details of the story.
6 When the journalists and interviewees are ready, begin the press conference, with the journalists asking their questions and the inter-viewees at the front of the class answering them. Tell the journalists that they should make a note of the answers and any important quotations.

7 When the journalists have had all their questions answered, ask each team of journalists to compare their notes and then write their article, expanding on the board version. They can also use direct quotes, and they should write the name of their newspaper and add a byline – this is the line usually under the headline (or at the end of an article) which gives the name(s) of the journalist(s) who wrote the article. Tell the interviewees that they should also work together to write their own (full) account of the story.

8 When each team have finished writing their article, ask them to display their work around the room for other students to read. Ask everyone to look for and try to identify any discrepancies between the different versions.

9 Finally, ask the interviewees if they think the articles are a true and fair account of the story they told.

Cross-references

The same materials can be used in 2.1, 2.3 and 2.20. For a suitable lead-in activity, see 1.3.

2.20 Filling in the gaps

Adding missing information to short articles

Level: Pre-Intermediate–Advanced

Preparation

Cut out a number of News in Brief items covering a variety of subject-matter. Paste each one onto a separate sheet of paper, leaving plenty of space for your students to write. Add a gloss (a translation or an explanation) to deal with problem vocabulary or language where necessary. You will need one article for each student in the class.

In class

1 Give each student one of the articles, form groups of between six and eight students and ask each group to sit together in a circle.

2 Tell your students that they should first read their own article and write one question on the sheet to ask about information which the article does not give, simply because it is so short.

3 When all the students have written their questions, they should pass their article to the person on the right. Again, this student should read the article and write a question which it does not answer.

4 When all the articles have done a complete circle and are back with their owners, ask them to read all the questions and choose one of the other students' questions (not their own) to answer. They should imagine a possible answer to the question and write this next to the question.

5 When your students have all answered one question, they should pass their sheet to the person on their right, who again should write an answer to another student's question.

6 Continue this procedure until all the articles have done a complete circle and are back with their owners with all the questions answered.

7 Finally, ask each student to rewrite their story, incorporating as many of the answers to the questions as they can. These can then be put on display for everyone to read and see how their answers have been included in the new versions of the articles.

Cross-references

The same materials can be used in 2.1, 2.3 and 2.19.

2.21 Fleshing out text

Grammaticalising lexis to reconstruct a short newspaper article

Level: Intermediate–Advanced

Preparation

Select a short article which you think will be of general interest to your students. Rewrite the article (see Box 9 for sample text), making the following types of change to the text:

- omit grammatical words (e.g. *a*, *the*, *in*, *to*, *is*, *was*)
- omit grammatical changes to the ends of words (e.g. *'s* or *s'* to indicate possession, *-r* or-*er* to form the comparative of certain adjectives)
- delete verb inflections (e.g. *-s*, *-es*, *-d*, *-ed*, *-ing*)

You should, however, retain all the punctuation and all the keyword vocabulary.

In class

1 Introduce the article by writing the headline on the board and asking your students to speculate on the content of the article.

2 To demonstrate the activity, write the first skeleton keyword sentence on the board and work with the class to help them reconstruct the original sentence. When they have done this, remind them of the type of changes you made to the original sentence.

3 Write the rest of the skeleton article on the board. Ask your students to read through it quickly and make sure they are able to understand the general content. Even though the language is ungrammatical, the content should still be clear from the keywords.

4 Deal with any vocabulary or language problems in the skeleton article and tell your students that they should now try to grammaticalise the rest of the text to reconstruct the original article.

5 Begin the activity. When your students are ready, put them into pairs and ask them to compare their versions and discuss any differences they have with their partner. Tell them that they should try to agree on one final version.

6 Finally, write the original article on the board and ask pairs to check their own versions against this. Tell your students to call out any alternative answers they have written. Discuss the acceptability and correctness of these with the whole class.

Comments

(a) This activity is easily adapted to different levels and mixed-ability classes by simply varying the amount of information you delete. With lower-level students, you can omit fewer words, and indicate where, and how many, words are missing, as well as where grammatical inflections (e.g. *'s* for possession) need to be added to keywords.

(b) This activity is intended to raise students' awareness of language by asking them to formulate correct language with the keywords – but within the framework of a story to achieve a coherent and cohesive whole.

Cross-references

If the article you choose has an accompanying photograph and caption, 3.1 and 3.2 can serve as suitable lead-ins.

Box 9 **Sample text**

Original text

Jinxed Alan's lucky 13th

BRITAIN'S most accident-prone man counted himself lucky last night after surviving another Friday the 13th.

Alan Room's grandmother warned he would be 'trouble' when he was born in the middle of a thunderstorm on September 13, 1968 – a Friday.

And she was right. Aircraft worker Alan, 25, has survived two stabbings, a couple of car crashes, a gunpoint robbery and a ruptured kidney. He's also suffered a damaged heart, a broken leg, and a lung that collapsed when he laughed too much at a comedy show.

'My friends are convinced I'm the unluckiest man alive', said Alan, from Horsham, Sussex. 'I just seem to be in the wrong place at the wrong time.'

But new research suggests Friday the 13th really is unlucky. It's the day when there are more admissions to hospital due to transport accidents than any other day of the year.

from the *Daily Mirror*

Skeleton text

Jinxed Alan's lucky 13th

BRITAIN most accident-prone man count himself lucky last night after survive another Friday the 13th.

Alan Room grandmother warn he be 'trouble' when he born middle thunderstorm September 13, 1968 – Friday.

And she be right. Aircraft worker Alan, 25, survive two stabbings, couple car crashes, gunpoint robbery and ruptured kidney. He also suffer damaged heart, broken leg, and lung that collapse when he laugh too much comedy show.

'My friends be convince I be unlucky man alive', say Alan, from Horsham, Sussex. 'I just seem be wrong place wrong time.'

But new research suggest Friday the 13th really be unlucky. It be day when there be more admissions hospital due transport accidents than any other day of year.

2.22 News in brief

Shortening a long newspaper article

Level: Intermediate–Advanced

Preparation

Select one fairly long newspaper article which you think will interest your students. Add a gloss (a translation or an explanation) to deal with any vocabulary or language problems and make one copy of this article for each pair of students in the class.

In class

1 Pair students and give each pair a copy of the article.
2 Tell your students that, in its present form, the article is too long for publication because of lack of space. Their task, therefore, is to reduce it to exactly fifty words for publication as a News in Brief item. Their rewritten version must be an accurate summary of the original article, containing all information which is of central importance.
3 Tell pairs that they should write their new version on a clean sheet of paper. Before they begin, emphasise again that their rewritten version must be precisely fifty words – no longer, no shorter.
4 Begin the activity. When your students are ready, put two pairs together and ask them to exchange their rewritten versions to read. They should decide if their partner pair's News in Brief item is a true and accurate summary of the original article.

Cross-references

For suitable lead-in activities, see 1.3, 1.4, 2.14 and 2.15. A quick oral version of 10.4 can also serve as a suitable lead-in activity. If the article you choose has an accompanying photograph and caption, 3.1 and 3.2 can serve as suitable lead-ins.

2.23 Overseas correspondents

Summarising an article from a non-English-language newspaper

Level: Intermediate–Advanced

Preparation

For this activity, which is designed for a monolingual group learning English in their own country, you will need to bring to class different newspapers from your students' country. Alternatively, ask your students beforehand to bring their own copies to the lesson. As far as possible, you should try to make sure that no two newspapers are from the same day. You will need one newspaper for each pair of students. In addition, you will need a set of bilingual dictionaries.

In class

1 Begin the lesson by explaining to your students that overseas national newspapers frequently use international news agencies (e.g. Reuters) or local correspondents abroad as sources for a number of their stories – it is simply too expensive to have journalists in every country in the world.

2 Pair students and give each pair one of the newspapers brought to class. Explain that each pair are overseas correspondents who are on the lookout for a story which would be of interest to an international (English-language) newspaper. Tell them that they should look through their newspaper to find a suitable story, which should not be too long, as it will only be used as a filler.

3 When each pair has found a story, ask them to report back briefly to the class, explaining which story they have chosen and the reasons why they think it would be of international interest.

4 Now explain that each pair should summarise their article in the form of a short News in Brief article in English, with a maximum word limit of fifty words (or other suitable word limit). At the end of their article, they should add the line 'From our local correspondents' and they should add their names.

5 When they have finished, ask each pair to display their article around the classroom, and invite everyone to read each other's work.

6 Finally, collect in all the articles your students have written to correct their work.

2.24 Favourite phrases

Using phrases from an article as a basis for creative writing

Level: Intermediate–Advanced

Preparation

Choose an article which tells a human-interest story and which you think will interest your students. Add a gloss (a translation or an explanation) to deal with any problem vocabulary or language and make one copy of the article for each student in the class.

In class

1 Give each student a copy of the article you have chosen and ask them to read it carefully for detailed understanding.
2 When your students are ready, discuss the content and the general theme of the article with the class.
3 Allow some minutes for this discussion phase and then ask your students to look through the article again. Explain that each student should choose one or two sentences or phrases from the article which for them are the most evocative, the most powerful or the most moving. What they choose should be something which they strongly relate to on a personal level.
4 When all your students have done this, ask each student in turn to write their sentences or phrases on the board, and briefly explain the reasons for their choice. Students who have chosen duplicate phrases should not write them on the board but they should still explain why they chose them.
5 Now pair students and explain that each pair should use as many of the sentences and phrases on the board as they can to write a piece of prose or a poem, using the headline of the article as the title for their piece of writing.
6 When your students have completed this writing stage, ask them to display their work around the classroom, or exchange it with other pairs to read. If you wish, invite students to read their work aloud to the class.

Comment

Rather than getting students simply to 'borrow' language full of factual information from an article, this activity encourages students to react to a story on a more affective level. The resulting piece of writing is a collection of personal reactions to a story, rather than a bland, dispassionate retelling of it.

Acknowledgement

I learned the first part of this activity from Mario Rinvolucri.

Cross-references

For suitable lead-in activities, see 1.3 and 1.4. A quick oral version of 10.4 can serve as a suitable lead-in activity. If the article you choose has an accompanying photograph and caption, 3.1 and 3.2 can serve as suitable lead-ins.

2.25 Change the news

Rewriting negative articles to make them positive

Level: Intermediate–Advanced

Preparation

Cut out a number of short newspaper articles containing rather depressing, unhappy news stories. These are not usually difficult to find. Paste each article onto a separate sheet of paper, leaving space below for your students to write, and add a gloss (a translation or an explanation) to deal with any problem vocabulary or language.

In class

1 To introduce the activity, write one of the articles on the board and suggest to your students the idea that it would be a pleasant change to open a newspaper and find happy stories – articles about success and not failure, kindness rather than cruelty.

2 Begin by brainstorming all the positive vocabulary your students can think of and write this on the board grouped into nouns, verbs, adjectives and adverbs. Then work with the whole class to rewrite the article (including the headline) to make it into a happy, positive story by making whatever changes, additions or deletions are necessary. The list of words on the board will be a useful point of reference during this rewriting stage. In places, you may need to make only minimal changes, e.g. *sadly* → *happily, Ten people were injured* ...

→ *No one was injured* ... However, other more substantial changes may be necessary, and you may need to rewrite complete sentences or sections of the article.

3 When you have finished rewriting this article, pair students and give each pair one of the articles you have selected. Explain to your students that, as before, they should rewrite their article to make it into a positive news story. Tell them that they should write this below the original article.

4 When they have finished, ask your students to display their 'happy' articles on walls or desktops and ask everyone to read each other's work.

5 Finally, working with the whole class, ask them to decide which article they think has now been transformed into the most positive news story.

2.26 Common denominators

Finding common points shared by pairs of articles

Level: Pre-Intermediate–Intermediate

Preparation

Compile a page of short articles of about the same length, using the first ones you find rather than attempting to be selective in any way. Arrange them clearly in pairs on a sheet of paper and number each pair for ease of reference. Add a gloss (a translation or an explanation) to deal with any problem vocabulary or language and make one copy of this sheet for each pair of students in the class.

In class

1 Pre-teach any key vocabulary in the articles, then pair students and give each pair a copy of the articles sheet.

2 Explain to your students that although the articles in each pair appear quite different on the surface, there may be some common points between them, e.g. both stories happened on the same day, both involve two people, neither story has been resolved, and so on. If you wish, demonstrate the activity using one of the pairs of articles.

3 Now tell your students that they should read each pair of articles and make a list of as many similarities or common factors as they

can find. They should do this for all the pairs of articles on the sheet.

4 When your students have finished, check their findings with the whole class. Beginning with the first pair of articles, ask your students to call out any common points and write their suggestions on the board.

5 Continue this procedure for the other pairs of articles.

Cross-references

The same materials can be used in 2.8, 2.16, 2.17 and 2.28. These activities can also serve as suitable lead-ins or follow-ups. For a suitable lead-in activity, see 4.1. A quick oral version of 10.4 can serve as a suitable lead-in activity.

2.27 Potted biographies

Identifying 'potted biographies' in newspaper articles

Level: Pre-Intermediate–Intermediate

Preparation

Bring to class four or five examples of articles which each contain a *potted biography* (see Box 10 for sample texts). This is a sentence opening usually found in the first or second paragraph of an article which contains information about the person in the article, e.g. *Supermarket checkout girl, Sylvia Bianconi ...*, *Unemployed steel-factory worker, Mike Horne ...*, *Ex-barmaid, Barbara Sutton ...* This is a space-saving device used by journalists. It avoids the need for longer, complex sentence constructions containing relative clauses (see note below). In addition, you will also need a selection of tabloid and broadsheet newspapers (see note in 1.1), which you should separate into individual pages.

In class

1 To introduce the idea of potted biographies, read aloud the opening line only of each of the articles you have selected and ask your students to say what one feature all the articles have in common. If they are going off on the wrong track, write the first five or six words of two of the articles on the board to help them.

2 When your students have spotted that all the articles begin with a potted biography, discuss with the class why journalists use this convention and what information the reader learns about the person in the article.
3 Pair students and give each pair several sheets from both a tabloid and a broadsheet newspaper. Tell them that they have ten minutes to find as many potted biographies as they can. They should write any examples they find (including the name of the person mentioned in the article) as well as the name of the newspaper in which they were found.
4 Begin the activity. At the end of the time limit, ask your students to read out their potted biographies and the names of the source newspapers. Write their findings on the board in the form of a grid. The results should show quite clearly that potted biographies are a feature used mainly by tabloid newspapers.
5 Go through the list on the board and ask your students to say what they learn about the people in the articles from their potted biographies.
6 Finally, ask your students to say how the potted biographies could be expressed in other words, e.g. Little Buddha *screenplay writer Bernado Bertolucci* ... could be rewritten as *Bernado Bertolucci, who wrote the screenplay for the film* Little Buddha ... This will give students useful practice in the use of non-defining relative clauses.

Extension 1

Tell your students to refer back to articles they found which did not contain potted biographies. Ask them to create potted biographies using information contained within the article.

Extension 2

Ask your students to create potted biographies for themselves, for other students in the class, or for prominent people they all know (including yourself and other members of staff).

Variation

Delete the potted biographies from several articles and ask your students to read the articles and create suitable potted biographies based on what they learn about the characters. These can later be compared with the originals.

Note

The use of potted biographies both in headlines and in the opening words of an article, as described by Keith Waterhouse (1993, pp. 206–210), is a practice that is commonly found in tabloid newspapers and is a way of 'cramming the most information into the shortest space'.

As Waterhouse further comments (p. 209), 'A curious side product of the name-tag industry is the growing tendency, particularly in headlines, to identify persons in the news either by what makes them newsworthy, as in *coma boy, death-fall teacher, desert-horror hubby, sex-ban star, tax-tangle comic, love-tangle rock star, stab dad, sex-storm barmaid, kidnap Briton, plunge mum*; or, more obscurely, by some event or object associated with their newsworthiness – *holiday girl, rhino trek man, bridge man, crossbow girl, rugby boot boy.*'

A particular difficulty caused by this convention is that it may not be until quite far into the article that the biographical information becomes clear to the reader, and, even then, the link may be extremely tenuous.

Box 10 **Sample texts**

1

Beastly tastes of furry Frank

BEARDED Health Secretary Frank Dobson looks like TV naturalist David Bellamy and apparently shares the same interests. The other day Health Minister Alan Milburn brought his two young children into the department. Frank promptly cleared his desk and announced: "Right, you two. Let's go to the zoo."

from the *Sunday People*

2

Gary's battle for fitter kids

SOCCER star Gary Lineker is backing a new campaign to get children fitter.

It comes as researchers reveal the alarming extent to which youngsters are hooked on TV.

Early findings from a study of 4,500 children aged eight to 16 suggest most spend only three hours a week playing sport or in outdoor activities.

But they watch TV for 16 hours a week.

The research by top sports scientists for London's Science Museum will carry on during the year.

from the *Mirror*

3

Johnson's Cup K.O.

SOUTH African Test full-back Gavin Johnson is out of Saracens' Tetley Bitter Cup fourth round tie at Blackheath on Sunday.

He has strained knee ligaments and is replaced by England Under-21 international David Thompson.

New Zealand wing Brendon Daniel, who has a calf strain, is also sidelined, so Matt Singer deputises.

from the *Mirror*

4

Oasis pay the price

ROCK yobs Oasis flew into New Zealand yesterday with a reported £20,000 price on their heads.

Hotel bosses in Auckland are said to have ordered the band to deposit the cash as a good-behaviour bond.

The demand came after the band was said to have daubed graffiti on the walls of a hotel in Sydney. And at a hotel in Brisbane, staff had to step in after a foul-mouthed row in the bar.

from the *Express*

5

Kung Fu kick saves a man

KUNG FU expert Eamon Timmons kicked down a front door and saved a man trapped in a blazing house.

Eamon, 36, of South Elmsall, West Yorks, said: "I connected just right and the door flew off its hinges."

from the *Mirror*

6

Julie is hit by sound of silence

SOUND Of Music singing legend Julie Andrews may never sing in public again after losing her voice.

Brit Julie, 62, underwent surgery after being struck down by laryngitis last summer.

But doctors say it will be "at least" two years before the Mary Poppins star regains her voice – if ever.

Her publicist Gene Schwan said: "It's a terrible heartache. She is in a great deal of emotional pain."

from the *Sun*

2.28 Fillers

Choosing a suitable article to fill a space in a newspaper

Level: Intermediate–Advanced

Preparation

Compile a sheet of short newspaper articles which cover a wide variety of subject-matter. All the articles you choose should be about the same length, and they must all contain 'soft' news. This can be defined as light news items which can be used at more or less any time, and can be colourful and witty, with journalistic commentary and opinion. This is in contrast to 'hard' news – the news of the day, which is based on factual detail and contains little description, journalistic comment or analysis. 'Soft' news items can often be used as fillers in newspapers.

Add a gloss (a translation or an explanation) to deal with vocabulary or language problems and make one copy of this sheet for each student in the class.

In class

1 Give each student a copy of the articles sheet and allow them a few moments to look through it.
2 Explain that a national newspaper has a space on an inside page for the next day's edition, and needs one short article to fill the space – about the length of each of the articles on their sheet.
3 Tell your students that they should read the articles and decide which one they would use to fill this space and why. They should also decide why they would not use the other articles.
4 When your students have made their choice, form groups of three or four students. Explain that they are the editorial team of the newspaper and that they must now have a meeting to decide which one article from the sheet they should finally use to fill the space on the page.
5 During the meeting, each student should argue the case for using the article they have chosen, as well as explaining why they think the other articles would be less suitable.
6 Tell your editorial teams that if they cannot reach a unanimous agreement, then a majority vote will be acceptable.
7 Tell your students that they have only ten minutes (or other suitable time limit) to reach a decision, and begin the activity.
8 Stop your students at the end of the agreed time limit and ask one

member of each editorial team to explain to the class which article they have chosen and why. Allow this to develop into a discussion, with everyone commenting on the other teams' decisions.

Cross-references

The same materials can be used in 2.8, 2.16, 2.17 and 2.26. These activities can also serve as suitable lead-ins or follow-ups. For a suitable lead-in activity, see 4.1. A quick oral version of 10.4 can serve as a suitable lead-in activity.

2.29 Spot the differences

Finding differences between two versions of the same story

Level: Post-Intermediate–Advanced

Preparation

From two different newspapers, one tabloid and one broadsheet (see note in 1.1), choose one story which both newspapers cover. Make copies of one version for half the students in your class and copies of the second version for the rest of the class, adding a gloss (a translation or an explanation) where necessary to deal with vocabulary or language problems.

In class

1 Pair students and give each student in each pair one of the different versions of the story you have chosen. Tell your students not to show these to each other.
2 Explain that each pair has the same story, but covered by two different newspapers. Their task is to discover any factual differences between the two versions.
3 Tell them that each student in turn should mention something stated in his/her article, and his/her partner should check his/her own article to see if this information is given, is not given, or is different. Tell your students to make a note of any differences they find.
4 When your students are ready, hold a feedback session with the whole class to discover which differences, if any, they have found and to discuss the possible reasons for these differences. This is also an opportunity to discuss generally each newspaper's treatment of the story.

Variation

If you can obtain several copies of the same day's newspapers, compare how a number of newspapers deal with the same story and look for discrepancies between all the different versions.

Cross-references

For suitable follow-up activities, see 2.15 and 2.24.

3 Photographs

3.1 Jumbled captions

Reconstructing newspaper photograph captions

Level: Post-Elementary–Advanced

Preparation

Select a wide variety of interesting newspaper photographs, each with a one-sentence caption which clearly summarises the content of the photograph. For a class of twenty, you will need about fifteen such photographs.

Paste each photograph (without its caption) onto a separate sheet of paper, and number each sheet for ease of reference. In addition, copy each caption onto a separate sheet of paper, but with the words in a jumbled order. Make sure that you begin the first word with a capital letter, and also add a full stop to the final word – typically omitted in photograph captions. Number these caption sheets with the same numbers as the photograph sheets they correspond to. Keep the original captions safe, as these will later serve as your answer key.

In class

1 To demonstrate the activity, show your students one of the photographs and ask them to tell you, in as much detail as they can, exactly what they can see in the photograph and what is happening.
2 Now write the accompanying caption in a jumbled order on the board, explain what it is and ask your students to try to reconstruct the original sentence. Begin by asking them to identify the first and last words of the sentence (using the capital letter and full stop). Emphasise the importance of using the content of the photograph to help them.
3 When your students have done this, pair students and give each pair one of the photographs with its accompanying caption sheet. Tell them that, as in the demonstration, they should try to reconstruct the sentence. Ask them to write their sentence on a sheet of paper.

4 Tell them that as soon as they have done this, they should call you over to check their answer. If it is correct, they can try again with another photograph and caption. Tell your students not to write on the jumbled caption sheets, so that you can use them again with other classes.
5 Begin the activity. Move from pair to pair to deal with vocabulary and language problems as they arise. It is important not to let your students get stuck and begin to feel frustrated, so, where necessary, give enough help to allow them to move forward.
6 Stop the activity when all the pairs have worked on at least two different photographs and captions. If you wish, focus attention on any particularly interesting constructions in the captions.

Variation

The photographs you choose can be specifically related to the theme of your lesson. This is an interesting way of introducing a particular topic.

Comments

This activity works well with mixed-ability classes. By including captions of varying lengths and linguistic complexity, you can select materials to cater to a range of levels in the class.

Cross-references

The task of reconstructing a photograph caption (but using the board) can serve as a suitable lead-in to many of the activities in Chapter 2 if the article you use has an accompanying photograph and caption.

3.2 **Predicting photographs**

Predicting the content of newspaper photographs

Level: Post-Elementary–Advanced

Preparation

MAIN ACTIVITY

Select an article which you think will interest your students. The article must be accompanied by a photograph with a caption. The more predictable the photograph (i.e. the stronger the link between the photograph, its caption and the headline), the easier the activity will be. The more tenuous these links are, however, the more challenging the activity becomes.

EXTENSION

As this is a preparatory activity for working with a newspaper article, you should also choose a suitable activity from Chapter 2 to exploit the article you have selected.

In class

1 Write the headline of the article you have chosen on the board and explain any key vocabulary. If you wish, you can ask your students to speculate on the content of the article from their understanding of the headline.
2 Tell your students that there is a photograph which accompanies this article and that, keeping the headline in mind, they should try to imagine what the content of the photograph might be. At this stage, your students may offer wildly different suggestions, but you should accept all their ideas and question them to elicit details about the photographs they see in their minds.
3 When your students have run out of ideas, write the caption which accompanied the photograph on the board, explaining what it is and also explaining any key vocabulary.
4 Now ask your students again to imagine the content of the photograph and call out their ideas. Giving your students the caption will inevitably eliminate many of their original ideas and will help them focus their thoughts on a limited number of possibilities. You should now question your students in depth to elicit very specific details about the content of the photograph they imagine.
5 Finally, show your students the photograph and ask for their reactions: Does it surprise them? Can they see the connection between the photograph and the headline? Do they think the caption explains the content of the photograph well? Do they like the photograph? Would they have chosen a different picture? If so, can they describe it?

Cross-references

The idea of predicting the content of a photograph can serve as a suitable lead-in to many activities in Chapter 2 if the article you use has an accompanying photograph and caption.

3.3 Famous faces

Writing profiles of famous people

Level: Elementary–Intermediate

Preparation

MAIN ACTIVITY

Cut out lots of newspaper photographs (or drawings/caricatures) of well-known people your students are certain to know (e.g. pop stars, actors and actresses, politicians). Remove any accompanying captions and paste each photograph onto a separate sheet of paper, leaving plenty of space for writing. You will need at least as many photographs as you have students in the class.

EXTENSION

Keep the articles which accompanied the photographs to distribute for this part of the activity.

In class

1 Show your students all the photographs you have selected and make sure they can identify and name each person. Reject any that your students do not know – these can be used in future lessons with different classes.
2 Choose one of the photographs and elicit as much information as you can about the person. This may include a physical description, personal details and biographical and career information. If necessary, prompt your students with questions. This stage will fuel your students' minds with ideas for the next part of the activity.
3 Spread out the photographs and ask each student to choose a person that interests them. Tell them to display their photographs on walls or desktops.
4 Explain that each student should begin with their own photograph, write one or two things they know about the person on the sheet, and then move to another student's photograph sheet and do the same. They should continue working this way until they have written something about all the people. Tell them to read what other students have written to make sure that they do not repeat any information.
5 Begin the activity. Be ready to supply any vocabulary or language your students need.

6 When everyone has run out of ideas, tell each student to collect the photograph sheet they first chose.
7 Now tell your students that they should read all the information on their sheet and use it to help them write a short profile of the person.
8 When your students have finished writing their profiles, display their work around the classroom and ask everyone to read each other's work. If you wish, you can collect in your students' profiles to mark and comment on.

Extension

At the writing stage, give your students the articles which accompanied their photographs, and tell them that they can incorporate in their profiles any extra information they find in their articles.

3.4 Appearances

Matching people to newspaper stories

Level: Pre-Intermediate–Post-Intermediate

Preparation

Select between five and ten short articles, each of which concerns one person. The stories should all be about women or they should all be about men, and the people should be unknown to your students. Each article must have an accompanying portrait of the individual person involved in the story. Separate the pictures from the texts, remove any accompanying captions, paste the texts onto a sheet of paper and number these for ease of reference. Add a gloss (a translation or an explanation) to deal with any problem vocabulary or language and make one copy of this sheet for each student in the class.

Paste each (original) photograph onto a separate sheet of paper and letter these from A onwards. Display these sheets around the classroom on walls or desktops. You can protect these photographs by inserting them in plastic covers.

In class

1 Ask your students to look at all the photographs on display. Explain that all these people were involved in different newspaper stories.
2 Ask your students to study picture A closely for a few moments and

then ask them to try to guess anything they can about the person from his/her appearance – age, nationality, status, character, occupation, and so on. Ask your students to also try to imagine what involvement this person had in the newspaper story. Tell your students to call out their ideas, but do not confirm or reject any of their suggestions at this stage.

3 Now give each student a copy of the articles sheet and explain that these are the newspaper stories about the people in the photographs. Tell them that they should read these carefully and try to match each one to the correct photograph, using their own intuition and any clues in the text which might help them. They should write the letter of the photograph sheet next to the article they think it matches.

4 When your students are ready, tell them to compare their answers with a partner and explain and justify their decisions.

5 Allow a few minutes for this exchange and then, with the whole class, invite individual students to call out their answers and explain the reasons for their decisions.

6 Finally, tell your students the correct matching pairs of people and articles and ask for their reactions when they learn the correct answers.

Comment

In this activity, some basic information can usually be gleaned from the text. It is then the task of the reader to translate this information into their own personal image, which in turn they try to match to the faces before them. We cannot help but be influenced by our most basic stereotypical expectations and preconceptions of the world, however subconscious this process may be. If the person mentioned in the text is forty years old, we naturally look for someone who matches our mental representation of a forty-year-old. If the person is a bank robber or a mugger, we will look for someone who, in our opinion, has the look of a criminal.

Cross-references

A quick oral version of 10.4 can serve as a suitable follow-up activity.

3.5 **Thoughts**

Writing the thoughts of people in photographs

Level: Pre-Intermediate–Post-Intermediate

Preparation

MAIN ACTIVITY

Cut out a number of dramatic photographs of people with unusual or interesting expressions on their faces, or who are in strange positions or situations. The sports pages of newspapers are often a good source for such (action) photographs. Remove any accompanying captions and paste each photograph onto a separate sheet of paper, leaving plenty of space for your students to write. You will need about as many photographs as you have students in the class.

EXTENSION

Keep the accompanying articles and make a note of which photograph each article corresponds to.

In class

1 To demonstrate the activity, show your students one of the photographs and ask them to imagine what the person in the photograph might be thinking at that moment. Your students will usually come up with some amusing suggestions, and you should write all their ideas on the board.

2 Display all the other photograph sheets around the room and explain to your students that they should study the people in the photographs carefully – how they are standing, what they are doing and, in particular, the expressions on their faces. They should then write what they imagine the person in each photograph might be thinking at that moment. When they have decided, they should write this on the sheet. They should do this for all the photographs, making sure that they do not repeat any other student's ideas.

3 When all the sheets have several contributions, stop this writing stage and ask your students to read each other's ideas.

4 Finally, with the whole class, discuss and comment on the most imaginative and amusing thoughts they wrote.

Extension

Display all the articles next to their corresponding photographs, and ask your students to read them. Ask your students to comment on whether they think the photographs are appropriate for the articles they accompany, and whether the thoughts they wrote are appropriate within the context of the stories.

3.6 Vocabulary review connections

Matching new vocabulary to newspaper photographs

Level: Elementary–Intermediate

Preparation

Select ten to fifteen completely different newspaper photographs which cover a variety of subject-matter. The photographs you choose can be quite bland and ordinary in their content, or they could be intriguing and more open to interpretation. Remove any accompanying captions and paste each photograph onto a separate sheet of paper.

In class

1 Ask your students to look through their coursebooks or notebooks and find about ten new vocabulary items (i.e. single words, expressions, idioms) which they have recently met. Ask them to write each one on a separate slip of paper with their name.
2 Spread out the photographs around the room, on the floor or on desktops, and ask your students to walk around and look at them all.
3 When they have seen all the photographs, tell them that they should now try to find a connection between their vocabulary items and the photographs. This can be for whatever reason they choose. They should place each vocabulary slip next to the photograph they connect it with. If they wish, they can match more than one vocabulary item to a photograph.
4 When your students have used up all their vocabulary slips, put the students into pairs and tell them to walk around with their partner and explain to each other the connections they made between their vocabulary items and the photographs they matched them with.
5 Finally, with the whole class, invite students to explain any particularly interesting connections they made themselves or heard from their partner.

Extension

Ask each pair to choose one of the photographs and write a short story, a poem or piece of prose using as many of the matched vocabulary items as they can. The finished work can then be displayed for your students to read, or you can ask pairs to read their work aloud to the class.

Cross-references

The same materials can also be used in 3.10, 3.11, 3.12, 3.13 and 3.14.

3.7 Photo stories

Illustrating a newspaper article with photographs and visual materials

Level: Intermediate–Post-Intermediate

Preparation

Cut out a number of short newspaper articles dealing with topics which you think will interest your students. For a class of twenty, you will need twenty articles so that you can offer each pair of students a choice.

In addition, bring to class sheets of A3 paper, pairs of scissors, glue and a supply of newspapers and magazines containing lots of photographs and visual material.

In class

1 Pair students, spread out all the articles you have chosen and tell each pair to choose one which interests or appeals to them.
2 Allow your students a few minutes to read through their articles. Deal with any vocabulary or language problems at this stage. Explain to your students that they are going to make their articles into photo stories.
3 To do this, each pair should read their article carefully, divide it into small sections, and then look through the newspapers for photographs or visual material to illustrate these sections. They should try to use a minimum of three pictures (or parts of pictures), but there is no upper limit. Their photo story must follow the original order of the story.
4 When they find a suitable picture, they should paste it onto a large

sheet of paper and, below it, write the section of the article it illustrates. If they cannot find a suitable picture for a section of their story, then that section can be text only.

5 When pairs have finished their photo stories, ask them to display them around the classroom and ask all your students to walk around and read each other's work.

6 Finally, comment on and discuss with your students any particularly interesting photo stories they have produced.

3.8 Famous for a day

Writing stories to accompany photographs

Level: Intermediate–Advanced

Preparation

MAIN ACTIVITY

Cut out a large selection of short newspaper articles each of which has a photograph of the person the story is about. You should choose people who you are sure your students will not know – ideally, ordinary members of the public. You will need at least as many such articles as you have students in the class. Remove any accompanying captions and paste each photograph with the article headline only on a separate sheet of paper, leaving room below for your students to write.

EXTENSION

Keep the accompanying articles and make a note of which photograph each article corresponds to.

In class

1 Spread out all the photograph plus headline sheets and ask your students to look at them and then choose one which interests them.

2 When they have made their choice, explain to your students that they have each chosen a picture of someone quite ordinary who appeared in the newspaper. Tell your students that they should each study their photograph and headline and prepare the details of the story the person was involved in.

3 Allow your students a few minutes for this. When they have prepared their stories, pair students and ask them to exchange photographs

and tell their stories to each other. Tell them that they should each make notes of their partner's story. They should also ask each other questions to make sure that they get the story in real detail.

4 When they have finished exchanging stories, tell your students that they should now write their partner's story in the form of a short newspaper article on the sheet. You may wish to set a time and word limit for this. Your students should work alone to write their articles, but tell them that they can consult their partner if they need to clarify any details.

5 At the end of this writing stage, display all the stories along walls or on desktops and ask your students to read each other's work.

6 Finally, comment on and discuss with the class any particularly interesting articles your students wrote.

Extension

Give your students the articles which accompanied their photographs to compare with their own stories. These can also be displayed next to your students' work for everyone to read.

3.9 Stories

Story-telling with mixed newspaper items

Level: Intermediate–Advanced

Preparation

Cut out a very large selection of newspaper items, including photographs, headline words or phrases, crosswords, weather forecasts, football results, advertisements, and so on. You will need at least three times as many different items as you have students in the class, and this activity is an ideal way to use up any leftover scraps of newspapers.

In class

1 Spread out all the newspaper items and tell your students to each choose three.

2 Form groups of three students and explain that each group should make up a story using all the nine items which the three members of the group have selected. They can use these in any order they wish, and the story itself can be about any subject they choose.

3 Tell your students not to write their stories – they should prepare them orally.

4 When all the groups have prepared their stories, put two groups together and tell them that they should take it in turns to tell the other group their story. Each member of the group should take over the role of story-teller as each of their items appears in the story, and they should 'illustrate' their story by showing the listeners each item as they use it in the story.

5 If you have time, you can repeat this final stage several times by putting different groups together. Alternatively, invite groups to tell their illustrated stories to the whole class.

Extension

In class or for homework, ask your students to write their story, illustrating each section with the corresponding newspaper item. Each item can be stuck onto a sheet of paper, and that section of the story can be written below. The complete stories can then be displayed around the classroom for everyone to read.

3.10 Headline connections

Matching headlines to photographs and inventing stories

Level: Intermediate–Advanced

Preparation

From newspapers and magazines, cut out a wide selection of photographs, choosing creative and dramatic ones which require interpretation, rather than static portraits of people or scenes. For a class of twenty, you will need at least as many photographs. Remove any accompanying captions and paste each photograph onto a separate sheet of paper to make it more durable. In addition, bring to class a supply of newspapers and several pairs of scissors.

In class

1 Spread out all the photographs and ask your students each to choose one which interests them.

2 When they have made their choice, ask them to explain to a neighbour why they chose their photograph, what it represents for them, and what kind of story they think accompanied their photograph.

3 Allow a few minutes for this exchange and then tell your students that their task is to look through the newspapers and find a suitable *headline* (not story) to accompany their picture. Tell them that when they have each found a suitable headline, they should cut it out.

4 Begin the activity. Circulate to deal with any vocabulary problems as they arise.

5 When your students have found suitable headlines, ask them to find a partner. Explain that, in turn, they should show their partner their chosen picture and accompanying headline and explain the link between them. They should then briefly tell each other the story behind the photograph and the headline.

6 After this first exchange, ask your students to find a new partner and repeat this procedure of explaining the link between headline and photograph, and telling stories to each other. This stage can be repeated several times until your students have worked with three or four partners.

7 Finally, with the whole class, ask students to say whose stories they enjoyed and found particularly interesting or imaginative.

Comment

The success of this activity rests on your choosing photographs for which it would be extremely difficult to imagine a newspaper headline. The right choice of (bizarre) photographs will force your students to use their imaginations to create connections rather than looking for obvious ones. Once they have achieved this, the story-telling task should come easily.

Cross-references

The same materials can also be used in 3.6, 3.11, 3.12, 3.13 and 3.14.

3.11 Moving pictures

Producing a poster to evoke the atmosphere of a photograph

Level: Intermediate–Advanced

Preparation

Select a number of powerful, moving newspaper photographs (without their captions) which cover a variety of subject-matter, and which are open to some degree of interpretation. You will need a large selection to offer your students a real choice. In addition, you should also bring to class a supply of newspapers, as well as glue, several pairs of scissors and sheets of A3 paper.

In class

1 Spread out the pictures you have chosen, form groups of three students and ask each group to agree on and select one photograph that interests them all.
2 Tell each group to spend a few minutes discussing their photograph, in terms of the atmosphere, feelings and emotions which their picture evokes.
3 Explain that each group should look through the newspapers and cut out headline words and phrases which they think capture the atmosphere, feelings and emotions in their photograph. Put scissors and newspapers at everyone's disposal and begin the activity.
4 When all the groups have collated a good supply of material, tell them that they should now produce a poster. This should show their photograph and ten to fifteen of the headline words or phrases they have collected. All the members of each group should pool their material, then agree on which items to use. They should make their poster as visually powerful and eye-catching as possible.
5 When groups have finished their posters, ask them to display their work around the classroom. Ask all your students to walk around to look at each other's work and to ask members of other groups to explain their posters.
6 Finally, with all your students, discuss each of the posters and the impact they make on the reader.

Variation

Instead of asking groups to display their posters, ask each group to present their poster to the class, talking about their photograph, and explaining their choice of headline words and phrases.

Cross-references

The same materials can also be used in 3.6, 3.10, 3.12, 3.13 and 3.14.

3.12 Picture this story

Finding suitable photographs to accompany newspaper articles

Level: Intermediate–Advanced

Preparation

Select a variety of short newspaper articles without accompanying photographs which you think will interest your students. You will need one article for each student in the class. Paste each article onto a separate sheet of paper and add a gloss (a translation or an explanation) to deal with vocabulary or language problems where necessary. In addition, cut out a number of newspaper photographs (without their captions) covering a wide variety of subject-matter. For a class of twenty, you will need sixty or more photographs to offer your students a real choice.

In class

1 Give each student one of the articles you have selected, but allow them to exchange with another student if their article really does not interest them.
2 Tell your students to read their articles carefully and then list five to ten keywords which would help them summarise the article.
3 When they have done this, take back all the articles.
4 Now pair students and ask them to tell their partners their stories with the help of their list of keywords. As they are doing this, spread out all the photographs you have selected.
5 When your students have exchanged stories, tell them that they should each look through the photographs and find two that they feel could accompany their partner's article – perhaps illustrating the theme of the article, picking up on a small detail of the story, or capturing the general atmosphere.
6 When they have each made their choice, ask them to show the photographs to their partner and explain their reasons for choosing them. For each article, they should then decide together which photograph of the two originally selected would best accompany it.
7 When your students are ready, give back the original articles to their owners. Tell them to display the article with the photograph they have chosen on walls or desktops.
8 Ask all your students to read each other's articles and look at the accompanying photographs to find the link between them and judge their suitability.

9 Finally, with the whole class, ask your students to comment on the suitability of the different combinations of articles and photographs.

Variation

Instead of displaying the original articles next to the photographs, ask your students to display their lists of keywords with the photographs. This will give your students the opportunity of trying to reconstruct each other's articles themselves, and then finding the link with the accompanying photographs.

Cross-references

The same materials can also be used in 3.6, 3.10, 3.11, 3.13 and 3.14.

3.13 Putting the picture in the story

Incorporating a newspaper photograph into an unrelated article

Level: Intermediate–Advanced

Preparation

Choose an article which you think will be of interest to your students and paste it down the left-hand side of a sheet of paper, leaving plenty of room on the right for your students to write. Make one copy of this sheet for each pair of students in the class. In addition, cut out a large selection of unusual, interesting and dramatic newspaper photographs. These should be totally unrelated to the article you have chosen, and you should remove any accompanying captions. For a class of twenty, you will need the same number of photographs to offer each pair of students a choice.

In class

1 Pair students, spread out all the photographs and tell each pair to choose one photograph which catches their eye.
2 When they have made their choice, give each pair a copy of the article and ask them to read it through. Deal with any vocabulary or language problems at this stage.
3 Explain that the photograph each pair has chosen relates to an element missing from the article, and that they have to introduce this

element into the story as naturally as they can so that it merges into the story-line. This might involve adding only a few words (in the appropriate place), or perhaps inserting a completely new paragraph. It might also involve making other changes in the article. They should not, however, delete or change any existing information in the original article – they can only add *new* information. Tell them that they should write in the space on the right of the article, indicating (with a line or an arrow) where their new text fits in.

4 When they have finished, ask pairs to display their articles on walls or desktops with their photographs, and ask everyone to read each other's work. Discuss with your students how well each pair has managed to fit their picture into the original article, and invite your students to suggest other ways pairs could have managed this.

Variation 1

Instead of using the same article, give each pair a different article. This will produce interesting results, and will reduce photocopying.

Variation 2

In a similar vein, give students a newspaper article but with the headline from a completely different article, and ask them to incorporate this into the story-line.

Comment

At first sight, this seems a difficult task, and students may be concerned that it will be impossible for them to fit their photograph into the story; they may even ask to change their photograph. However, I have yet to meet a student who does not succeed in the task – usually with great ingenuity.

Cross-references

The same materials can also be used in 3.6, 3.10, 3.11, 3.12 and 3.14.

3.14 **Student-generated worksheets**

Preparing discussion worksheets based on newspaper photographs

Level: Pre-Intermediate–Advanced

Preparation

Cut out a large variety of interesting newspaper or magazine photo-graphs (without their captions) which show people in quite ordinary situations (see sample photo below) as well as in situations which are open to more speculation or interpretation. For a class of twenty, you will need the same number of photographs to offer each pair of students a choice.

In class

1 To demonstrate the activity, choose one photograph and pass it around the class so that each student has the opportunity to see it clearly. Write the following headings across the board: Useful Language, Interpretation, Dialogues, Situations, Discussion Topics.

2 Ask your students to call out vocabulary and expressions they would need to describe the photograph and that would be useful in the situation shown in the photograph. If you are teaching a monolingual group, let your students call out words in their own language if they do not know the English terms, and provide suitable translations. Elicit other useful vocabulary and expressions through careful questioning and write all your students' ideas under the heading 'Useful Language'. For the sample photograph below, you might include the following: *to have your hair cut, to wash, to rinse, to dry, a/to perm, to blow-dry, to put in highlights.*

3 Now ask your students who the people are and what they are doing in this situation. Encourage your students to try to answer these questions and then write the questions (i.e. *Who are they? What are they doing here?*) on the board under the heading 'Interpretation'. Ask your students to suggest other questions which would help them interpret the situation, and write their suggestions under this same heading.

4 Under the heading 'Dialogues', write *A dialogue between one of the women and the hairdresser about how she wants her hair cut* and *A dialogue between the woman and a friend: the hairdresser has cut the woman's hair badly.* Now ask your students to suggest other possible dialogues that could take place in this situation, or as a result of this situation. Again, write their ideas on the board.

5 Under 'Situations' write: *Ring up your hairdresser to make an appointment* and *Thank your hairdresser for cutting your hair so well.* Now ask your students to suggest other situations suggested by the photograph and again write their ideas on the board.

6 Finally, under 'Discussion Topics' write: *Women spend too much money on their hair* and *Hairdressers should charge less.* Again, ask your students to suggest other ideas related to the content of the photograph which could form the basis of a short discussion.

7 Now spread out all the photographs you have chosen, pair students and ask each pair to choose one photograph which interests them.

8 Tell your students that they should discuss their photograph using the headings on the board and prepare a worksheet (as you have done in your example on the board) for their photograph.

9 Begin the activity and deal with vocabulary and language problems as they arise. You can also encourage your students to use bilingual dictionaries to look up new words.

10 When each pair has finished, ask them to exchange their photograph and discussion sheet with another pair. Tell them that they should now talk about the photograph using the ideas on the discussion sheet.

Extension

At the end of the lesson, collect in all the photographs with accompanying discussion sheets and keep them for use in future lessons with this class or other classes. This will also be an opportunity to check the language your students have produced.

Cross-references

The same materials can also be used in 3.6, 3.10, 3.11, 3.12 and 3.13.

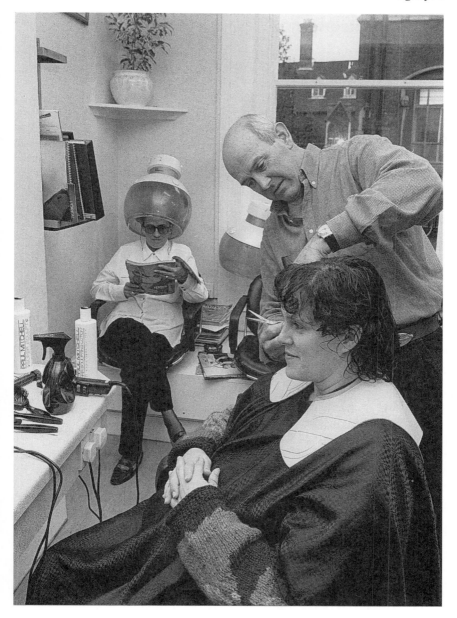

4 Advertisements

4.1 Quick turn

Fast reading to answer questions based on advertisements

Level: Elementary–Intermediate

Preparation

Fill a sheet with newspaper advertisements (see Box 11 for sample ads) which deal with either a variety of subject-matter or one particular theme such as holidays or job vacancies. Number each advertisement for ease of reference and make one copy of this sheet for each student in the class. In addition, prepare fifteen to twenty questions (with an answer key for your own reference) based on the advertisements. You may wish to refer to Appendix 3 for an explanation of abbreviations used in small ads.

In class

1 Give each student a copy of the advertisements sheet face down, explain what it contains, but tell them not to turn it over yet.
2 Tell your students that you are going to ask them questions based on these advertisements. Explain that you will read out a question, they should then turn their sheets over, look for the answer as quickly as possible, and write down the answer the moment they have found it. You will allow them thirty seconds (or however long you feel is a suitable length of time) to find the answer – at the end of this time limit, you will tell them to turn their sheets back over.
3 Begin the activity and ask your students the first question. Allow them exactly the amount of time you have stated to find the answer and, at the end of this time limit, ask them to indicate with a show of hands how many have found the answer.
4 Ask your students to call out the answer(s) they found. Confirm the correct answer and indicate where this was to be found on the sheet by giving the advertisement number.
5 Continue this procedure for the remainder of your questions, perhaps

reducing the time limit as your students become increasingly familiar with the material.

Extension

For a future lesson, compile two different sheets of advertisements, pair students and give each pair copies of the two advertisements sheets. Tell each student to make up ten or fifteen questions (plus an answer key) based on his/her advertisements to ask his/her partner. Pairs should then follow the basic lesson procedure above.

Variation

This activity works particularly well with newspaper small ads (see note in 4.2) because they are short, self-contained and full of detailed information. However, almost any other newspaper item (e.g. horoscopes, letters, articles, football results) can be used.

Comment

Fast-reading activities too often fail to achieve their aims, simply because the material is on view for too long and students pore over it trying to understand every word. This activity overcomes these problems by limiting access to the text.

Cross-references

The general procedure used here can serve as a lead-in to 2.16, 2.26, 2.28, 4.2, 4.4, 4.9, 4.10, 4.12, 4.13, 4.17, 4.19, 5.2 and 7.1. A quick oral version of 10.4 can also serve as a suitable follow-up activity.

Box 11 Sample ads

1

DRAWFLIGHT LTD
Property Management
LANDLORDS
Are you considering letting your property?
We have a large number of qualified tenants waiting for properties **NOW**
Phone us or drop in for details of our service
Let us take the weight from your shoulders

01424 424030
190 Queens Road
Hastings

2

Property For Sale

TOWN CENTRE
Small one bedroom garden flat with own entrance. Modern pine fitted kitchen, oven/hob, tiled bathroom, double glazed. Outbuilding with washer/dryer, newly decorated.
£16,500 ono
(01424) 432453

3

Stables Theatre
and Art Gallery THE BOURNE · HASTINGS
BOX OFFICE 423221   *Open 10.30am to 1pm daily*

Friday 7, Saturday 8 *and* **Tuesday 11 to Saturday 15 November, 7.30pm**

HABEAS CORPUS
by **ALAN BENNETT**
★ A STABLES THEATRE GUILD PRODUCTION ★

THIS PLAY IS NOT SUITABLE FOR YOUNG CHILDREN
TICKETS £5.50, £5.00 (Members and under-18s £3.50, £3.00)
(50p off all tickets at Friday 7 November performance)

IN THE ART GALLERY Commencing Saturday 8 November ★IDEAL FOR PRESENTS★
THE CHRISTMAS SHOW PAINTINGS, PRINTS, CERAMICS BY LOCAL ARTISTS

4

HASTINGS TOWN FOOTBALL CLUB
F.A. Trophy 2nd Qualifying Round
Saturday 8th November
TONBRIDGE
Kick Off 3.00pm *Follow the Town and Follow the Town* **AWAY**
SUPPORTERS COACH RUNNING
For details contact Tony Cosens 01424 444635
Dr Martens Premier League
Saturday 15th November
GLOUCESTER CITY
Kick Off 3.00pm **HOME**
The Pilot Field · Elphinstone Road
Hastings (01424) 444635

5

MISSING STOLEN
VERY SUBSTANTIAL REWARD OFFERED
for any information leading to recovery of silver/grey Bengal cat (male). Last seen Gensing Rd/North Street area, St Leonards on Wed 22nd Oct, 9pm wearing blue collar + I.D tag He is very distinctive and looks like a baby snow leopard (Spots/stripes).
IF YOU KNOW ANYTHING CALL IN STRICTEST CONFIDENCE, 24 HRS.
721120 An/Phone
NO POLICE NO COMEBACKS

6

CLEMENTS
CURTAINS
MADE TO MEASURE IN OUR OWN WORKROOM, WE ALSO HAVE A MEASURING & FITTING SERVICE FOR TRACKS, POLES & BLINDS
Tel: Hastings 423570
55-57 London Road St Leonards
also at 19 High Street, Battle
01424 774072

7

WASHING MACHINE ON THE BLINK?

CALL
Headway Domestic Appliances
18-19 George Street, Hastings
Repairs & Servicing to most makes of:
• Washing Machines • Tumble Dryers • Fridges
• Freezers • Electric Cookers • Dishwashers
ALL WORK GUARANTEED
LARGE RANGE OF SPARES IN STOCK

TEL: (01424) 438810

9

AIRPORT CARS

The No.1 Airport Service *(Travel agents approved)*
• First Class Service • Quality Vehicles
• 24 hour Service • Reliable Friendly Drivers • OAP/Disabled Assistance
• All Airports/Destinations • Executive Cars/Minibus
• Low fares • No Hidden Extras

Tel/Fax: (01424) 731366

Bargains

BEC, SUPER scooter, 3 wheel, electric wheelchair. New batteries, and charger £650 excellent condition Bexhill 211611.

BED spread fitted double size pale gold with cushion ex condition as new £16.00 dresses two size 14 good quality clean £8.00 01424 846586

BELLING magicoal electric fire, complete wood surround and hearth, length 60ins, height 28ins, £50.00 ono. 01424 446197.

BICYCLE boys orange mountain bike kalananda apollo 18: frame 26: wheel 10 gears very good condition £60.00 phone 851676

BICYCLE mans old fashioned heavy frame £10.00. Bexhill 731838.

10
Property To Let

ABOVE average large furnished bed sitting room, St Leonards. Clean quiet house. Own kitchen area and shower. Door entry phone. Single person only. Deposit and employer's reference required.£42.00 per week. 01424 434808

BEXHILL Cooden Drive purpose built two bedroom furnished flat. Garage. £350 pcm 01424 220060.

BEXHILL three bedroom detached furnished house, garden, garage £550 pcm 01424 220060.

13
Lost & Found

REWARD available for information leading to the recovery of a ladies gold watch. Sentimental value. Lost sometime since December 1996. Telephone Shiela, daytime 458810, evening 716221

11
Could you spare a few hours a week to listen to those in crisis?

The Samaritans
Hastings & Rother Branch
are currently looking for

VOLUNTEERS
For February Preparation Classes
Please phone 01424 436666
for an application form
Please support the Samaritans — Regd Charity 233437

12
SILVERDALE C. P. SCHOOL
PERTH ROAD
ST LEONARDS-ON-SEA
TEL: 01424 426423
CLASSROOM TEACHER (.8)
required from 1/1/98-31/8/98
A temporary teacher is required to teach Year 5/6 class for two terms. Visits to the school are welcomed.
Please contact the Headteacher for an application form and further details. Closing date for applications: Monday 17th November.

from the *Hastings and St Leonards Observer*

4.2 Classifying ads

Classifying small ads

Level: Elementary–Pre-Intermediate

Preparation

Compile a sheet of small ads (see note below) taken from different classifications you commonly find in this section of the newspaper. You will need between one and three advertisements from each of the classifications you choose (see Box 13 for sample ads). Make one copy of this sheet for each group of three students in the class, and make up a set for each group by cutting this sheet into individual advertisements. Store each set in an envelope for safe-keeping.

In addition, make a list of the titles of the classifications from which you have chosen your advertisements (see Box 12 for sample classification titles).

You may wish to refer to Appendix 3 for an explanation of abbreviations used in small ads.

In class

1 Write the small ads classification titles on the board and explain any your students do not understand.
2 Choose one of the small ads, pre-teach any key vocabulary and then read the ad aloud. Ask your students under which classification in the small ads they would expect to find this advertisement.
3 When they have found the answer, put your students into groups of three and give each group one of the sets of small ads.
4 Explain to your students that these are more small ads from various classifications. Their task is to sort them into groups and to choose a suitable classification for each group from the titles on the board. Tell your students that this is a team competition: the group to classify the highest number of advertisements correctly in ten minutes (or other suitable time limit) will be the winners.
5 Begin the activity. While your students are working, go from group to group to help with problem vocabulary as it arises. In addition, you can also encourage your students to use dictionaries.
6 Stop the activity at the end of the time limit and check your students' answers. Read aloud each small ad in turn and ask your students to call out its classification. Award one point for each correct answer

and ask each group to keep their own scores. Deal with any incorrect classifications as they arise.

7 Finally, ask all the groups to add up their scores to find the winning team.

Note

The *classified ads*, or *small ads*, as this section of a newspaper is commonly known, is where you find advertisements usually placed by individuals. The advertisements in this section are grouped into different classifications (e.g. Pets, Gardening, For Sale) and in some local papers, there can easily be thirty or more different classifications.

Cross-references

The same materials can be used in 4.3. This can serve as a suitable lead-in to 4.3. For a suitable lead-in activity, see 4.1. For a suitable follow-up activity, see 4.4.

Box 12 **Sample classification titles**	
Aquatics	Entertainers
Articles Wanted	Furniture
Baby Equipment	Health & Beauty
Bicycles	Miscellaneous for Sale
Cars	Musical
Child Care	Pets
Computers	Situations Vacant
Domestic Appliances	To Let
Electrical Services	TV & Hi-Fi

Box 13 **Sample ads**

1 **SOLID OAK** framed three-piece suite, £145. Pine dining suite, new £145. Ring 648556.

2 **NEARLY NEW** carrycot, pushchair and raincover, cost £500 vgc, £150. Telephone 427565 eves.

3 **LAND ROVER SERIES 3**, truck cab, 33,000 miles, V-reg, needs some attention. £700. Telephone 426094.

4 **SKIN CLEAR** as seen on television, the most advanced skin treatment for acne scarring, anti-ageing, pigmentation and stretch marks. Free demonstration now available at Hair and Beauty Care. Telephone 868922.

5 **AQUARIUM ACCESSORIES**, internal power filter, heaterstat, still boxed £60. No offers. Ring 715557.

6 **QUALIFIED RETIRED** electrician for all your small electrical requirements. Telephone 431024.

7 **SOUTHDOWN** playgroup at Southdown Athletic Club, Green Common, Ages 3–5 years 9.30 am–12 pm. Give your child an early start in life. Limited spaces available. Ring 213127 or call in.

8 **TROPICAL FISH** aquarium, 24 gallon, lamp, heater, light, pump, foliage. Two months old. Buyer must collect. Cost £574. Offers around £300. Ring 733447.

9 **TABLE FOOTBALL** game, as new £12, old calor gas heater £15. Call 773588.

10 **TRICITY TIARA** electric cooker, very good condition, £75. Toshiba microwave £35. Will deliver. Ring 438137.

11 **BEAUTIFUL SHORT** drawing-room grand piano, John Broadwood London. Walnut. 1980–1990. Lovely piece of furniture. Recently tuned. £1100 ovno. Telephone 321111.

12 **FLUTE**, excellent condition £200. Telephone 851519.

13 **STORAGE HEATERS** secondhand. All sizes, can deliver. Ring 401214.

14 **EXCEL HEALTH** and Beauty products now available locally. Phone Stevie 441253.

15 **MOUNTAIN BIKE**. 21 speed, 21" frame. Excellent condition. Absolute bargain. Only £175. Telephone 892842.

16 **HAIR STYLIST.** If you are an experienced full-/part-time stylist and would like to earn more money than you are now, work in a central position, pleasant atmosphere with great clients ring David 224116.

17 **AMSTRAD SYSTEM** unit PC1640DD. Boxed, keyboard, monitor, manuals, mouse, lots of games and programs, £70. Phone 212313.

18 **KRAZY KARAOKE** and Disco plus Disco Quiz Nights available. By professional. Cheap Rates for Pubs and Hotels. Excellent rates. Call John Woodman NOW on 445085.

19 **TECHNICS WORLD DJ** Championship mixer. The best money can buy. Too many features to list, cost £349 offers. Ring 177129.

20 **BLACK MALE** collie cross, six months old, £50. Phone after 4pm. 445218.

21 **MOUNTAIN BIKES,** 2 x girls, age 4–7 years, 1 x boys, £35 ono, including stabilisers if required. Ring 717273.

22 **HOTPOINT AUTOMATIC** top loader, excellent condition £95. Zanussi Spin dryer £20. Telephone 769106.

23 **MR STEADY–** Playing 'Stones', 'Beatles', 'T-Rex', 'Clapton', 'Doors', 'Dylan', 'Hendrix' and 'Animals' and others. Bookings phone Sue 796874.

24 **BICYCLE BARGAINS.** BMX!! Mountain!! Scooters!! Kids Xmas Club!! Andrews Cycle Market. For details telephone 444013.

25 **BEAUTIFUL STUDIO** flat. Nice house, nice position, close to shops, sea view, carpets. Quiet single lady. £45pw. Ring 444470.

26 **BOOKS WANTED,** hardbacks and paperbacks, collections large and small. Telephone 423413.

27 **COOK, EXPERIENCED** in good home cooking required at pleasant Rest Home, Mon to Fri, 9.30 am –1.30 pm. Telephone 215335.

28 **BORDER COLLIE** puppies, registered (Grand Sire) supreme trials champion. Ring 890316.

29 **THREE PIECE** suite, £1400 new, excellent condition, £375 ono. Telephone 465382.

30 **FLAT TO LET,** 2 beds, lnge, din rm, sea views, entryphone, gch, £360 pcm. Telephone 447322.

31 **HAIR & BEAUTY** Mobile. Experienced and qualified. Phone Jade 252310. Weddings a speciality. All areas.

32 **BUGGY, PLAYPEN,** stairgate £10. Travel cot £18. Doorbouncer £6. Ring 430481.

33 **JAGUAR SERIES 1** XJ6 2.8, Tax exempt, 75,000 miles, lots spent, bargain £650. No offers. Ring 289934.

34 **MODERN REMOTE** control portable TV, vgc only £60. Phone 723611.

35 **BABY CLOTHES** all in excellent condition, from new-born, to one, 20p to £2 per item or £25 the lot. Ring 465195.

36 **BABY CHINCHILLAS** from £25. Experienced advice. New cages. Telephone 462453.

37 **CARPENTRY TOOLS** wanted, planes, chisels, etc. etc. Also power tools. Ring 773462.

38 **SWIMMING POOL** pump and filter seen working £300. Some chemicals, 24 x 14 summer cover, vacuum tube and brush £85. Ring 428203.

39 **BOSCH MICROWAVE** large, good working order, tested, brown, £50. Ring 444025.

40 **COFFEE TABLE,** oak, £22. Ring 343424.

41 **COT** £25. Change table £10. Pushchair, £25. Steam steriliser, £5. Baby clothes 0–3 years. Ring 213360.

42 **REG. CHILDMINDER** has vacancy full/part-time. Woodend area. Call 711220.

43 **CASIO CPS-720** electronic keyboard, VGC, £250 ono. Telephone 445387.

44 **RAY SPARKLE,** Magician, Punch and Judy, Balloon animals, White Rabbit. Close up magic for dinners and promotions. Details ring 509822.

45 **MAZDA 323,** 1984 A-reg, Red, tax, stereo, rear belts, VGC, £395. Call 893600.

46 **MEGA CD** & Megadrive, 20 games, 2 light guns, 2 control pads, lots of magazines and books. All boxed, excellent condition. £150 ono. Telephone 712835.

47 **GAS COOKER.** Excellent condition, white and brown, eye-level grill, large oven £90 ono. Tel 730454.

48 **COMPUTER TUITION.** Learn Windows 95, Microsoft Office, Internet, trouble-shooting, etc. Telephone 4685074.

49 **FLAT SHARE** Sea views, £40 ono per week. No smokers. Ring 444995.

50 **MR FUMBLES** Children's Magic Show, suitable for all Occasions. Telephone 721477.

51 **CLEANER REQUIRED,** early morning or early evening. 2hrs per day. Ring 751555.

52 **WANTED OLD** record player, must be in good condition. Ring 724763.

4.3 Role-play ads

Role-playing advertisers and potential buyers or customers

Level: Post-Elementary–Advanced

Preparation

Compile a sheet of advertisements from different sections of the small ads (see note in 4.2, and see Box 14 for sample ads). Add a gloss (a translation or an explanation) below each advertisement to deal with key vocabulary and make two photocopies of this sheet. Cut out all the ads from both photocopied sheets and make pairs (sets) of identical ads. You will need one different set of advertisements for each pair of students in the class.

You may also wish to refer to Appendix 3 for an explanation of abbreviations used in small ads.

In class

1 Pair students and give each pair one of the sets of advertisements. Allow your students a few moments to read these and then explain that each pair is going to have a telephone conversation based on their advertisement – one student will play the role of the person who placed the advertisement and his/her partner will play the role of the person answering the advertisement. They should choose which role they want to play.

2 When your students are ready, tell them to begin their conversations.

3 Stop the conversations as the buzz begins to die down. Then tell each pair to exchange their advertisement set with another pair.

4 Explain that each pair now has a different advertisement. Tell them

119

that, as before, they have a few moments to read them, and that they should begin a new conversation when they are ready.
5 Repeat this procedure of pairs exchanging advertisements and holding new conversations for as long as their interest and energy seem to be holding.
6 Finally, invite pairs to perform one of the conversations in front of the class.

Variation

Instead of using a mixture of advertisements, use a set of advertisements which focus on one particular area, e.g. a set of job advertisements or a set of Houses for Sale advertisements. This will give your students practice in a more narrowly defined area of language and should help you predict the kind of language they will need for the task.

Cross-references

The same materials can be used in 4.2. This can serve as a suitable follow-up to 4.4. For a suitable lead-in activity, see 4.1 and 4.2. The materials used in 4.2 can also be used in this activity.

Box 14 **Sample ads**

1 **FRIENDLY REGISTERED** childminder has vacancy Wednesday–Friday, full- or part-time. Tel 442907.

2 **PAINTING & DECORATING** undertaken. First-class tradesman with 20 years' experience, and refs provided. Please telephone 896821.

3 **SEAFRONT FLAT** 1 bedroom, good condition. £60pw. Telephone 349658.

4 **DOOR ENTRY** phone systems repaired and installed. Call 852440.

5 **SLIM WITH** Sue, every Wednesday 7 pm. High Beach Community Centre, Old Dover Road. Private weighing available. Pop along or phone 252310.

6 **RSPCA NEEDS** good loving homes for rescued dogs. Telephone 813795. 9.00 am–5 pm.

7 **SMALL VAN**, also transit, with driver for hire, anywhere. Telephone 716643.

8 **ABSOLUTELY FOR** the best deal on Mobiles. Telephone 721111.

9 **COLOUR TV** £55. Delivered. Ring 447364.

---

10 **HANDYMAN FOR** all your small jobs, electrics, plumbing, carpentry, painting, decorating and DIY. Telephone 712200.

11 **HOPE SCHOOL** of Motoring. Pass your test first time. Experienced, qualified instructor. Free assessment lesson. For details telephone 439657.

12 **EVENING CLEANERS** required. Town centre offices. Monday to Friday. Telephone 465311.

13 **SECURITY OFFICER** for weekends and two weeks' cover over Christmas. Local work. For interview tel. 733146.

14 **SPORTS HALL** for hire at weekends. Ideal for football parties, for adults or children (plus bouncy castle if required for 8-year-olds or under). For more details telephone 751555.

15 **CHILDREN'S PARTY** Theatre Company. Organised children's entertainment. All occasions. Includes costumes, games, disco, stories, face painting, quizzes, activities and party bags. Telephone 200710.

16 **JILLY'S SWIMMING** School for beginners and improvers in local training pool. Telephone 713453 for details.

17 **METAL FILING** cabinet, 6 drawers, £15. Telephone 220698.

18 **PART-TIME** sales-assistant req for town centre carpet shop, hrs 10 till 5, days by negotiation. Telephone 719505.

4.4 Small ads abbreviations

Understanding abbreviations in small ads

Level: Pre-Intermediate–Intermediate

Preparation

Compile a sheet of advertisements from the accommodation sections (e.g. To Let, Houses For Sale, Property) of the small ads (see note in 4.2), making sure that these advertisements contain lots of abbreviations. Make one copy of this sheet for each student in the class. You may wish to refer to Appendix 3 for an explanation of abbreviations used in small ads.

In class

1 On the board, write the following abbreviations: *pw, gdn, bed*. Explain to your students that these are three abbreviations commonly used in advertisements in the accommodation sections of newspaper small ads.

2 Tell your students that each example shows a different way such abbreviations are created. Before you explain them, ask your students to guess what the abbreviations mean. Then explain the three systems:

> *pw* = **per week** The first letter of each word is used in the abbreviation.

> *gdn* = **garden** Here, consonants only are used, and always in the order they appear in the word. This is a good general rule, but there are variations: if the final letter of the word is 'e', this may be retained (e.g. *sngle* = single), especially if the abbreviated word could be confused with another word, e.g. *lnge* = lounge. Without the final 'e', this could be confused with the word 'long'. Also, not all the consonants may be used (e.g. garage is usually abbreviated to *gge* and the letter 'r' is omitted). If the meaning is plural, a final 's' will usually be added to the abbreviation (e.g. *rms* = rooms).

> *bed* = **bedroom(s)** The first few letters of the abbreviated word are given, but only enough to make it absolutely clear what the intended word is. The last letter of such abbreviations will invariably be a consonant. If the meaning is plural, a final 's' will usually be added to the abbreviation. If a number precedes the abbreviation (e.g. *3 bed*), then the 's' to indicate plurality can safely be omitted.

3 Now give each student a copy of the advertisements sheet. Ask them to look through these advertisements and make a list of all the different abbreviations they can find. When they have done this, they should try to work out the meanings of the abbreviations using the three general rules you have outlined. Begin the activity. Circulate to deal with any problems concerning vocabulary (but not abbreviations) as they arise.

4 Finally, check the answers with the whole group. Ask your students to call out the abbreviations they have found, with their meanings, and write these on the board. Guide your students towards the meaning of any abbreviations they are still having problems with.

Extension 1

Ask your students to write an advertisement for their own houses or flats, using as many of the abbreviations as possible. They can then exchange these with other students, who should try to write the advertisements in full.

Extension 2

In future lessons, repeat the activity but with advertisements from other sections of the small ads (e.g. Jobs, Holidays, For Sale, Entertainment, Meeting Place).

Cross-references

This can serve as a suitable follow-up to 4.2. For a suitable lead-in activity, see 4.1. For suitable follow-up activities, see 4.3 and 4.5.

4.5 For sale

Writing For Sale advertisements

Level: Post-Elementary–Intermediate

Preparation

Make one copy of the advertiser's form below (see Box 15) for each student in the class. This is the form which readers complete when they wish to place an advertisement in the For Sale section of the classified advertisements (see note in 4.2).

In addition, cut out a selection of For Sale small ads so that each student has several examples (see Boxes 13 and 14 above for sample ads). You may also wish to refer to Appendix 3 for an explanation of abbreviations used in small ads.

In class

1 Give each student several different small ads (see note in 4.2) and ask them to look through these and call out the type of information people include in small ads when they are selling something. Write their suggestions on the board. Depending on the particular items, this list could include age, colour, make/brand, condition, size,

guarantee and, of course, the price asked. You should aim for quite a long list of suggestions which would cover all different types of article.

2 Now ask your students to think for a moment about something which they (or members of their family) own but no longer need or want – however big or small – and which they would like to sell. When they are ready, ask them to turn to their neighbour and quickly describe the item and explain why they want to sell it. This will help fix it more clearly in their minds. You should remind your students to refer to the list on the board to help them describe the items they wish to sell.

3 Give each student a blank copy of the small ads form and tell them that they should complete the form, with a description of the article they want to sell.

4 Point out that there is a word limit on the form and that they must write their advertisement in exactly this number of words – no more and no fewer. Advise them to prepare a rough copy of their advertisement before they complete the form with their final version.

5 When they have finished writing, collect all their forms and display them on the board. Ask all your students to read through them to see if there is anything they would like to buy. Protracted haggling over prices should be left until after the lesson!

Variation 1

If any of your students really cannot think of anything they wish to sell, perhaps they can think of something they would like to buy. If this is the case (and you may even want to offer this as an option to the whole class), their advertisements can be placed in a Wanted section on the board.

Variation 2

This activity can be adapted for use with some newspaper articles, e.g. a criminal on the run from the police might be included in the Wanted section, or a stolen work of art (or something your students once lost) in the Lost section. Also, for humorous effect, your students might try to write a For Sale advertisement to 'sell' a member of their family, or even their English teacher!

Cross-references

This can serve as a suitable follow-up to 4.4.

124

Box 15 **Sample advertiser's form**

classified coupon
For use by private advertisers only
Please fill in details below

Your name..

Address..

....

Phone number..

PLEASE USE BLOCK CAPITALS. PRICE OF ITEM MUST BE INCLUDED

ADVERT DETAILS: one word per box

ADVERTISE YOUR ITEMS UNDER £200 IN VALUE

FREE

4.6 Shopping for a friend

Finding suitable presents for people

Level: Elementary–Intermediate

Preparation

Compile several sheets of newspaper advertisements (small ads as well
as larger advertisements for luxury items such as cars, video recorders
or computers; see note in 4.2) showing different items and/or services
for sale. For a class of twenty, you will need between ten and twelve
sheets, each one containing no more than five advertisements. Another

potential source of such material would be mail-order catalogues, which are sometimes included in weekend editions of some newspapers.

In class

1 Tell each student to write a list of three people (e.g. a friend, a relative, a neighbour) they would like to buy presents for, and the reasons why, e.g. Christmas, a birthday, a Thank You present, a special occasion, and so on.

2 Pair students and ask partners to exchange lists and tell each other about the people on their lists, particularly their hobbies and interests, what kind of things they like and are interested in, and how they spend their free time. Tell your students that they should make brief notes based on this information next to the name of each person on their partner's list.

3 When your students are ready, explain that they each want to buy a present for the three people on their list, and that their partner has offered to go shopping for them. Tell your students that money is no object – for this activity they are temporarily millionaires – and their partner is going shopping for them in the advertisements of a newspaper.

4 Display the sheets of advertisements around the room, spreading them well apart to ensure easy access. Tell your students that they should look through the ads and choose suitable presents for the three people on their partner's list. Emphasise to your students that the suitability of the presents they choose should be the most important consideration. You should also point out that the present could perhaps be a service such as a manicure or a horse-riding lesson, although this will depend on the advertisements you have chosen. When they find a suitable present, they should copy the details of the advertisement next to the name of the person.

5 When your students have finished their shopping trip, ask them to explain to their partner what presents they have chosen and the reasons why.

6 Finally, with the whole class, invite individual students to comment on the suitability of the presents their partner has chosen.

4.7 Vocabulary posters

Making vocabulary posters

Level: Elementary–Advanced

Preparation

To demonstrate this activity, you will need to cut out one or two large newspaper or magazine advertisements showing photographs or illustrations of one particular type of goods for sale, e.g. clothes.

In addition, think of other products or goods commonly found in large advertisements (see Box 16 for a list of advertisement coverage) and write each one as a title on a separate sheet of A3 paper – these will become the vocabulary posters. For this activity, you will also need a set of bilingual dictionaries and a supply of old newspapers and magazines, including ones from your students' own country.

In class

1 Explain to your students that one way of collecting new vocabulary is to use pictures which they can label. To demonstrate this, show your students the advertisements (e.g. clothes) you have found, display them on the board and ask your students to try to name the things shown there. As they do so, label the picture by drawing a line from each item and writing the name. Supply the English words for any items your students do not know.

2 Now designate different tables around the room as work stations by placing a different vocabulary poster sheet on each. At each table, you should also provide a bilingual dictionary, scissors, glue, pens and a supply of newspapers and magazines.

3 Put your students into group of three and ask each group to go to one of the work stations.

4 Tell your students that they should cut out any pictures from advertisements in the newspapers which relate to the vocabulary area on their sheet. They should make up a large vocabulary poster (as attractive and eye-catching as possible) by pasting the pictures onto the sheet and labelling them clearly with the English words.

5 Explain to your students that groups have only a few minutes to work on their vocabulary poster. They will then change work stations and continue work on a different vocabulary poster.

6 Begin the activity. While your students are working, go from group to group helping to find suitable advertisements and supplying new

vocabulary. You can also encourage your students to look up new words in the dictionary.

7 Stop all the groups after a few minutes and ask them to change work stations and begin work on a different vocabulary poster. Continue this procedure for as long as your students' interest and energy holds.

8 Finally, ask the groups to display around the room the posters they were last working on, and ask all your students to circulate and look at each other's work.

Extension

For homework, ask your students to look in local or national newspapers for more pictures from advertisements which they could add to their vocabulary posters. They should also look for advertisements for products which could be the start of new posters.

Comment

This can be an on-going activity – all the vocabulary posters can be brought out for your students to work on in future lessons.

If you teach regularly in the same classroom, you may be able to leave the posters up on the walls on permanent display. For future lessons, you can devise activities to help your students practise and learn the new vocabulary, and you can, of course, use the posters with other groups.

Box 16 Advertisement coverage

Food	Garden tools
Drinks	Cars
Electrical appliances	Computers
Tools	Make-up and toiletries
Clothes (different ages and sexes)	Mobile phones
Kitchen gadgets and appliances	Video equipment
Kitchen design	Hi-fi equipment
Bathroom design	Photographic equipment
Furniture	DIY (do-it-yourself)

4.8 The price is right

Guessing the cost of everyday products and services

Level: Post-Elementary–Intermediate

Preparation

Using newspapers from one country only (e.g. Britain), compile a sheet of advertisements covering a variety of goods and services for sale, and spanning a wide price range, e.g. a can of Coke, a driving lesson, a night in a two-star hotel, a chocolate bar, a loaf of bread, a VCR. Delete the prices of the items from the advertisements and make one copy of this sheet for each group of three or four students in the class. Keep a note of the actual cost of each item, as this will later serve as your answer key.

In addition, you will also need a marker pen for each group and several sheets of paper.

In class

1 On the board, write the exchange rate for the English pound (or US dollar if you are using materials from American newspapers) and your students' own currency with a number of examples for quick and easy reference, e.g. the equivalents in your students' currency of 50p, £1, £5, £10, £50, and so on.

2 Put your students into groups of three or four, give each group a copy of the advertisements sheet and allow them a few moments to look through it. Tell your students that each group is in competition with the others to guess the real selling price in Britain of the items on their sheet.

3 Explain to your students that you will call out an item on their sheet and that, in their groups, they should discuss how much they think it would cost in Britain. They must agree in their group on one amount and they should write this amount clearly on a sheet of paper. When you ask for the groups' answers, they should hold this sheet up for you to see. Writing their answer on the sheet will commit a group to one answer and prevent them from changing it when they hear the other groups' answers.

4 Give each group a marker pen and several sheets of paper. Begin the 'sale' with the first item. Give help with vocabulary and language problems as they arise.

5 When each group has decided on a price, invite all the groups to hold

up their sheets at the same time, showing the amount each has agreed on. When you have all their answers, tell your students the actual selling price in Britain, and then announce which group has the closest amount to the real price. If you have a spare copy of the advertisements sheet, it is a nice touch if you cut this into individual advertisements and give them to the successful group in each case.

6 Continue this procedure for the remaining items on the sheet.

7 At the end of the activity, discuss the prices of the items with your students – whether they would be cheaper, the same price, or more expensive in their own country, what general impression they get about prices in Britain, whether it seems a relatively cheap or expensive country, or whether prices seem generally about the same as in your students' own country.

Extension

In a future lesson, repeat the activity using newspapers from another country (e.g. the USA) in order to discover the cost of items in another part of the world.

4.9 Salaries

Matching salaries with jobs

Level: Pre-Intermediate–Advanced

Preparation

Compile a sheet of several different job advertisements which mention the wages or salary offered for each job (see Box 17 for sample ads). Number each one for ease of reference, and deal with problem vocabulary or language by adding a gloss (a translation or an explanation) where necessary. Delete the pay from each advertisement and make one copy of this sheet for each student in the class. You should make a note of the pay offered for each job, as this will later serve as your answer key.

In class

1 Give each student a copy of the jobs sheet and ask your students to read the first advertisement. When they are ready, ask them to decide what they think would be appropriate remuneration (i.e. monthly

salary, weekly wage or hourly pay, depending on the particular advertisement) for this job. Write all their suggestions on the board. There may be a lot of strong disagreement within the class, but make sure that you take note of everyone's ideas.

2 Tell your students the correct answer and then discuss with them whether they think this payment is fair or not, and the reasons why.

3 Now explain to your students that they should read the other job advertisements and decide what payment would be fair or reasonable for each. Tell them that they should make a note of their answers. Make it clear for each advertisement whether the pay your students should award is per year, per month, per week or per hour.

4 When your students are ready, ask them to compare their answers with a partner and talk about any differences they have.

5 At the end of this discussion phase, bring the class together and, dealing with the jobs one by one, ask your students to call out the payment they gave to each job. It will help your students if you can convert these into local currency, although this will not be necessary if you have taken advertisements from a local English-language newspaper.

6 Finally, tell your students the correct answers, and ask them to compare these with their own estimates. Encourage class discussion, and if you have used advertisements from newspapers from an English-speaking country, you can ask your students to say whether they would expect any differences in payment for the same jobs in their own country.

Variation

If you are teaching a class studying a specialist subject, it may be particularly interesting to them if you use advertisements relating to jobs your students may have now, or will apply for in their future careers.

Cross-references

For a suitable lead-in activity, see 4.1. For suitable follow-up activities, see 4.17 and 4.18.

Box 17 Sample ads

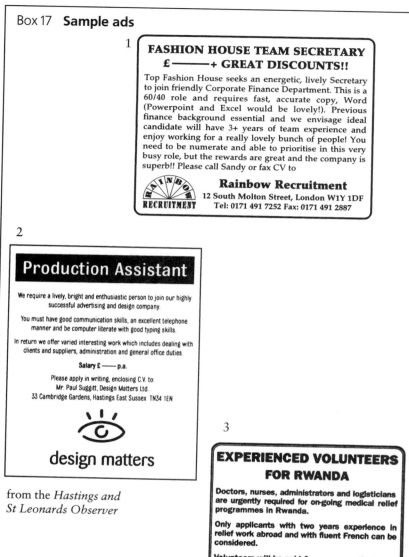

1

FASHION HOUSE TEAM SECRETARY
£ ——— + GREAT DISCOUNTS!!

Top Fashion House seeks an energetic, lively Secretary to join friendly Corporate Finance Department. This is a 60/40 role and requires fast, accurate copy, Word (Powerpoint and Excel would be lovely!). Previous finance background essential and we envisage ideal candidate will have 3+ years of team experience and enjoy working for a really lovely bunch of people! You need to be numerate and able to prioritise in this very busy role, but the rewards are great and the company is superb!! Please call Sandy or fax CV to

Rainbow Recruitment
12 South Molton Street, London W1Y 1DF
Tel: 0171 491 7252 Fax: 0171 491 2887

2

Production Assistant

We require a lively, bright and enthusiastic person to join our highly successful advertising and design company.

You must have good communication skills, an excellent telephone manner and be computer literate with good typing skills.

In return we offer varied interesting work which includes dealing with clients and suppliers, administration and general office duties.

Salary £ ——— p.a.

Please apply in writing, enclosing C.V. to:
Mr. Paul Suggitt, Design Matters Ltd.
33 Cambridge Gardens, Hastings East Sussex TN34 1EN

design matters

from the *Hastings and St Leonards Observer*

3

EXPERIENCED VOLUNTEERS FOR RWANDA

Doctors, nurses, administrators and logisticians are urgently required for on-going medical relief programmes in Rwanda.

Only applicants with two years experience in relief work abroad and with fluent French can be considered.

Volunteers will be paid £ —— per month plus all expenses.

For further information, please write to:

Annie Macklow-Smith
MERLIN

14 David Mews
LONDON W1M 1HW
Fax: 0171 487 4042

merlin
Medical Emergency Relief International

4

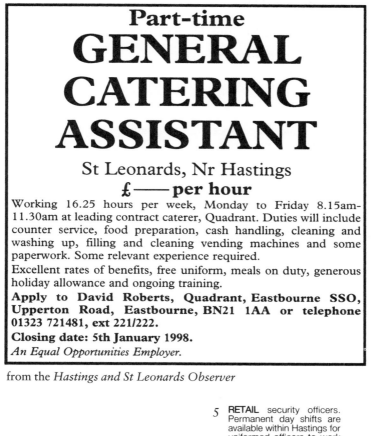

Part-time
GENERAL CATERING ASSISTANT

St Leonards, Nr Hastings
£——per hour

Working 16.25 hours per week, Monday to Friday 8.15am-11.30am at leading contract caterer, Quadrant. Duties will include counter service, food preparation, cash handling, cleaning and washing up, filling and cleaning vending machines and some paperwork. Some relevant experience required.

Excellent rates of benefits, free uniform, meals on duty, generous holiday allowance and ongoing training.

Apply to David Roberts, Quadrant, Eastbourne SSO, Upperton Road, Eastbourne, BN21 1AA or telephone 01323 721481, ext 221/222.

Closing date: 5th January 1998.

An Equal Opportunities Employer.

from the *Hastings and St Leonards Observer*

from the *Hastings and St Leonards Observer*

5   RETAIL security officers. Permanent day shifts are available within Hastings for uniformed officers to work an average 56 hours per week. The rate of pay is starting at £——per hour, with a package that includes profit related pay, 6 monthly loyalty bonus, free life assurance and paid annual holidays. Full training and uniform is supplied and promotional prospects are excellent in a fast developing Company that specialises in the provision of high calibre officers to the retail industry. Phone now on 0181 707 0503 to arrange an interview.

(Answers: 1 £19,000 per annum; 2 £11,000 per annum; 3 £450 per month; 4 £3.87 per hour; 5 £4.50 per hour.)

4.10 Looking for a partner

Finding partners in the Meeting Place section of the classified ads

Level: Pre-Intermediate–Intermediate

Preparation

From the Meeting Place section of a newspaper, cut out an equal number of ads from men and women looking for partners (see Box 18 for sample ads). Paste them onto a sheet of paper in two groups – all the male advertisers together and all the female advertisers together. Number the male advertisers and letter the female advertisers for ease of reference. You will need one copy of this sheet for each student in the class. You may wish to refer to Appendix 3 for an explanation of abbreviations used in small ads.

In class

1 Give each student a copy of the Meeting Place sheet and explain that these advertisements are all from people looking for partners.
2 Explain any key vocabulary, then tell your students that they should read the advertisements carefully and try to find any suitable matching partners among the people on the sheet.
3 When they are ready, ask your students to work with a partner to compare and discuss their pairings.
4 Finally, with the whole class, invite students to call out what pairs they have made and to explain the reasons why.

Extension 1

Now that your students have been introduced to this type of advertisement, an enjoyable follow-up activity would be to ask them to write small ads either for themselves or for a partner. These can then be pooled and suitable partners found. The true identity of the advertisers can be revealed at the end. It would almost certainly appeal to the impish nature of some students if you allowed (or even encouraged) them to write personal ads for members of the teaching staff, including yourself.

Extension 2

At the end of the activity, lead a discussion on whether your students agree with or disapprove of this way of meeting people, why people

134

choose to advertise for a partner, the advantages and disadvantages of meeting a partner this way, and whether they would ever consider trying to meet people this way.

Comments

If you prepare your own material, you should carefully vet advertisements to avoid any content your students might find unacceptable. In addition, you should avoid selecting male and female advertisers which seem to produce obvious pairs. Doing so will limit the interest and the challenge, and will restrict the open-ended nature of the activity.

Cross-references

For a suitable lead-in activity, see 4.1.

Box 18 **Sample ads**

Male advertisers

1 MALE, aged 25, WLTM female, n/s, 20–30 for friendship, possible romance. I like pubs, clubs, staying in, as well as going out. I live in the Windsor area and I get on well with kids.

2 IF you are not separated or emotionally unstable but are a widow over 55 & looking for partner with view to long-term & meaningful relationship, then this 67 year old widower could be the one for you.

3 HI, I'm Andy, 32yo and divorced. A happy-go-lucky person looking for a lady between 25 and 40. Single parents welcome as I love children and a home life.

4 MALE, 50s, caring & sincere, with a GSOH, seeks an affectionate lady for friendship, possible romance.

5 I am an energetic man of 63, but don't look it. I have a good head of hair, I like country and western music and historical places, walking, a pint now and again. I'm still working part-time, but I don't drive. I have a GSOH.

6 FRIENDLY male, 35, 5'9", dark hair, brown eyes, WLTM young lady of similar appearance for fun nights out & evenings in.

7 I'M a widower, 60+, GSOH, like pubs & clubs, intelligent conversation, sound, honest, outgoing, love life & meeting people.

8 SINGLE male, 46, n/s, genuine, sincere, loving and caring who enjoys music and socialising. Looking for like-minded friendship. Maybe relationship.

9 MALE, 24, 6'3", educ, house & car owner, has GSOH, gentle & caring. Looking for female 18–30, single mums are welcome.

10 MALE, 37, 5'11", medium build, loyal, genuine, honest and reliable WLTM female up to 30, who is affectionate and easy going.

Female advertisers

A FEMALE, 26, prof, fairly slim, WLTM a slim male, 26–33, for friendship and possible romance.

B ACTIVE lady, living in Maidstone area, early 60s WLTM females or males for friendship and to share interests, mostly travel.

C ARE you the romantic, friendly, articulate male with varied interests and a GSOH that this woman is looking for? If so and you're 40ish–50ish but feeling 30ish then we will have a lot in common.

D LADY, 48, fairly slim, seeks a kind, generous, warm-hearted man, about same age, for friendship and outings.

E HELLO, my name is Liz. I am 19 yrs old and live in the Cambridge area. I am seeking a male 20–25. I enjoy pubs and clubs and I like nights in or out and I like children. I am 5'5" with blonde hair.

F ATTRACTIVE single lady, 32, redhead, slim, seeks prof male 30–40, GSOH, genuine friendships/relationships, likes theatre, music and walking.

G LADY in her late 40s requires gentleman 45–50 for long-term r/ship. Must have a GSOH, like dancing and all sorts of social life.

H FEMALE, 48, 5'9", fair hair, blue eyes, medium build, no ties, GSOH. I'm looking for TDH male, no ties, GSOH, between 40 & 52.

I CULTURED lady, 40s, 5'7", non-smoker. Looking for tall, attractive, well-educated male of similar age to enjoy life with.

J UNATTACHED lady, 32, 5'8", attractive, with young son, seeks slim, local man, 30 something, to hold hands, maybe join hands, have a laugh & a fresh start.

4.11 Choosing holidays

Discovering holiday preferences and choosing holidays

Level: Pre-Intermediate–Post-Intermediate

Preparation

Cut out between fifteen and twenty different summer-holiday advertisements covering the widest possible variety of holidays. Paste each one onto a separate sheet of paper and number each sheet for ease of reference.

In addition, make one copy of the holiday preferences questionnaire (see Box 19 for sample questionnaire) for each student in the class.

In class

1 To introduce the activity, tell your students in as much detail as you can about the summer holiday you most enjoyed. When you have finished your story, pair students and ask them to exchange their own stories about a summer holiday they particularly enjoyed.

2 Give each student a copy of the holiday preferences questionnaire and read through this with the class to deal with any vocabulary or language problems.

3 Tell your students that they should interview their partner and make a note of their partner's answers on the sheet. Point out that more than one answer is possible in each section.

4 Begin the interviews. While your students are working, display the holiday advertisement sheets around the classroom.

5 When they have finished their interviews, bring the class together and point out that around the room are a number of summer-holiday advertisements. Tell them that they should look at all the holiday advertisements and, using the information their partner has given them, find suitable holidays (a first and second choice) for their partner. They should also choose suitable holidays for themselves. Tell them that they should write the appropriate holiday numbers in the spaces provided at the end of the questionnaire.

6 When your students have made their choices, tell them to compare their results with their partner. They should explain which holidays they have chosen for each other and for themselves, and the reasons why they chose these particular holidays.

7 Finally, bring the class together and ask your students if any pairs made exactly the same choice of holidays.

Extension

In a future lesson, repeat the activity but use winter holidays in order to cover different areas of vocabulary.

Variation

Rather than give your students a ready-made questionnaire, give them a selection of holiday advertisements to study and then ask them to work in groups to devise their own questionnaire.

Box 19 **Sample questionnaire: holiday preferences**

The questionnaire below will help you find out about your partner's tastes in holidays. Interview your partner and make a note of his/her answers.

On holiday, do you like the weather to be:
(a) very hot?
(b) pleasantly warm?
(c) cool?

Do you like to spend your holidays:
(a) in a holiday camp?
(b) by the sea?
(c) in the mountains?
(d) in the country or on the river?
(e) in a large city?
(f) in a popular tourist spot?
(g) in an exotic or out-of-the-way place?
(h) touring around and staying in different places?

Is your idea of an enjoyable holiday:
(a) relaxing on the beach or by the pool?
(b) sightseeing and shopping?
(c) going on excursions to local places of interest?
(d) doing sport or something adventurous or active?

On holiday, do you like to stay:
(a) in a hotel which has good facilities?
(b) in a bed and breakfast?
(c) in a youth hostel?
(d) in self-catering accommodation?
(e) in a tent?
(f) in a caravan?

On holiday, do you like:
(a) sampling the local food and drink?
(b) eating in your hotel or the place where you are staying?
(c) cooking for yourself?
(d) eating out in expensive restaurants?
(e) eating the same sort of food as at home?

Do you generally choose holidays which:
(a) cost a lot of money?
(b) are affordable – not too expensive?
(c) are low-budget?

Do you dislike travelling:
(a) by plane?
(b) by car or coach?
(c) by train?
(d) by boat on the sea?
(e) by boat on a river?

Do you have any other particular likes, dislikes or preferences concerning holidays?

....

....

....

....

....

Your partner's holiday:
1st choice: Holiday no. _____   2nd choice: Holiday no. _____

Your own holiday:
1st choice: Holiday no. _____   2nd choice: Holiday no. _____

© Cambridge University Press 1999

4.12 Searching for a house

Finding houses 'lost' in the small ads

Level: Post-Elementary–Pre-Intermediate

Preparation

Compile a sheet of advertisements for houses and flats from the accommodation sections of the classified ads (see note in 4.2). Number each advertisement for ease of reference and add a gloss (a translation or an explanation) to deal with problem vocabulary or language where necessary. Make one copy of this sheet for each student in the class. You may wish to refer to Appendix 3 for an explanation of abbreviations used in small ads.

In class

1 Give each student a copy of the advertisements sheet and ask them to look through this and call out the type of information mentioned in such advertisements.
2 Write your students' suggestions on the board in the form of note-like questions, e.g. *Number of bedrooms? Central heating? Garden at back? Garage? Cellar?*, and so on.
3 Work on this language to elicit the full question forms, then practise this language with your students so that they can form the questions correctly and comfortably, e.g. *How many bedrooms are there / has it got? Is it centrally heated / Has it got central heating? Has it got a back garden? Is there a garage?*
4 Pair students and explain that one student in each pair should choose one of the advertisements but not tell their partner which one. Their partner has to find the advertisement they have chosen by asking questions (as above) until they locate their partner's house (or flat) on the sheet. Their aim is to find the correct advertisement as quickly as they can.
5 Begin the activity. When your students have finished playing this first round, tell them to change roles.
6 If your students' interest is holding, they can play several rounds, each time trying to find their partner's advertisement as quickly as they can.

Cross-references

The same materials can be used in 4.13. For a suitable lead-in activity, see 4.1.

4.13 House-hunting

Finding matching descriptions of houses and flats

Level: Pre-Intermediate–Intermediate

Preparation

Compile a sheet of small ads (see note in 4.2) from the accommodation sections of the classified ads. You should use advertisements with the most detailed descriptions you can find. Add a gloss (a translation or an explanation) to deal with problem vocabulary or language where necessary, and make one copy of this sheet for each student in the class. You may wish to refer to Appendix 3 for an explanation of abbreviations used in small ads.

In class

1 Begin the lesson by telling your students about your ideal house or flat, describing it in as much detail as you can.
2 Now pair students and ask them to describe their own dream house or flat to their partner, again in as much detail as possible. Tell your students that they should make brief notes of their partner's description, as this will help them in the next stage of the activity.
3 When all the pairs have finished, give each student a copy of the housing advertisements sheet. Tell them that they should read these and try to find the closest possible match to their partner's ideal house/flat that they can.
4 When all your students have found what they think is the closest possible match to their partner's description, ask them to show the advertisement to their partner and explain why they chose it for them. Their partner should decide to what extent they agree with this choice, and explain any differences they can find between the house advertised and the one where they would really like to live.

Cross-references

The same materials can be used in 4.12. For a suitable lead-in activity, see 4.1.

4.14 Reducing ads

Reducing information-dense advertisements to small ads

Level: Intermediate–Advanced

Preparation

Select a number of information-packed advertisements from news-papers, magazines and colour supplements, covering a wide range of products and/or services. You will need one advertisement for each pair of students in the class.

In addition, make copies of the form (see Box 15 above for sample form) used by readers when sending in small ads (see note in 4.2) to a local newspaper. You will need one copy of this form for each pair of students in the class.

In class

1 Pair students and give each pair one of the advertisements and a copy of the reader's advertising form.
2 Tell your students that their task is to reduce their large advertisement to the size of a small ad, and to write their advertisement on the form, which has a maximum word limit. Explain that they must retain all the important information contained in the advertisement, and cut out any unnecessary detail.
3 Begin the activity. Circulate to deal with vocabulary and language problems as they arise. You can also encourage your students to use dictionaries to look up new vocabulary.
4 When they have finished, put two pairs together to discuss each other's work. They should decide whether their small ads are, indeed, accurate summaries of the originals, and if all the relevant infor-mation has been included. If necessary, allow some time for reformu-lation and rewriting after this discussion stage.
5 Finally, ask your students to display their original ads next to their rewritten ads around the classroom and invite everyone to read each other's work. Use this opportunity to comment on any particularly well-written small ads your students have produced.

Variation

An interesting variation is to use glossy advertisements of the type which often advertise luxury goods such as cars, perfume, cigarettes and so on. These often present an image to the reader but give very little factual information about the product itself, relying very heavily on the visual impact of the advertisement. Using this type of advertisement, you can again ask your students to write a small ad with a word limit of, say, twenty-five words. This, however, now becomes a text-expansion exercise, and also calls on your students to use their knowledge and their imaginations to write the advertisement.

Comment

For this activity, you can also use advertisements written in your students' own language. This then becomes not only a text-reduction exercise, but also a small-scale translation exercise.

Cross-references

This can serve as a suitable follow-up to 4.15.

4.15 Ad adjectives

Matching adjectives to advertisements

Level: Intermediate–Post-Intermediate

Preparation

Cut out ten or more large advertisements from newspapers or magazines, each one with a bold heading or slogan containing an adjective. Blank out the adjective from each advertisement, paste each advertisement onto a separate sheet of paper and number each sheet for ease of reference. If necessary, add a gloss (a translation or explanation) to deal with any problem vocabulary or language, and display the sheets around the classroom on walls or desktops. For your own reference, you should also make a note of the adjectives you have deleted and the advertisements they relate to.

In class

1 Refer your students to the advertisements displayed around the room and explain that you have deleted one word – an adjective – from each advertisement. Tell your students that they should read the advertisements carefully and try to think of one or more suitable

adjectives to fill each empty space. They should make a note of their answers, indicating the advertisement number and the adjective(s) they have chosen to fill the gap.

2 Begin the activity. When your students are ready, ask them to compare their answers with a partner.

3 Finally, check the answers with the whole class and discuss the acceptability of alternative answers they have thought of. Depending on the advertisements you use, an answer may be wrong in the sense that it does not collocate with, for example, a particular noun in an advertisement. In this case, try to elicit from your students what collocations would be possible with their adjectives. This is a good opportunity to extend your students' vocabulary by dealing with each adjective and the words(s) with which it collocates.

Variation

Write the adjectives you have deleted from the advertisements on the board in a jumbled order and tell your students to match each one with a suitable advertisement to fill the empty space.

Cross-references

For a suitable follow-up activity, see 4.14.

4.16 Advertising phrases

Writing poems or chants using advertising phrases

Level: Pre-Intermediate–Advanced

Preparation

Bring to class a number of newspapers which you have looked through to make sure they contain large advertisements. Magazines and weekend supplements are also a particularly good source of material for this activity.

In class

1 On the board, write several of the following phrases, explain any problem vocabulary and ask your students to say where they think these phrases come from:

Reserve immediately!
Unbeatable prices!
Send no money now!
Just compare our prices!
Don't miss this opportunity!
Unbelievable prices!
Please allow 28 days for delivery.

2 This is a good opportunity to point out to your students the use of imperative forms in advertisements and the use of powerful and persuasive language (e.g. *incredible, unbeatable, unbelievable, immediately*).

3 Hand out copies of the newspapers and magazines. Ask your students to look through them and quickly try to find one or two other examples of advertising expressions and phrases. Some of these may include examples of advertising 'hype' – advertisers' language which is exaggerated and high-powered and is used to make something sound attractive or exciting in order to persuade us to buy. Write the examples your students offer on the board.

4 Pair students and explain that each pair should go through the newspapers and magazines more carefully to collect as many other advertisers' expressions and phrases as they can. When they have a good collection, they should try to use a selection of them (including the ones on the board) to make a poem or a chant with the title *Poetry in promotion* (see Box 20 for example poem). Explain to your students that they should order the phrases they find in the best way they can, without making any changes to them. However, they are allowed to use the same phrase several times if they wish.

5 When they are ready, put two pairs together and ask them to read each other's work.

6 Finally, invite students to read their work aloud to the class, and perhaps ask the class to vote for the one they most liked.

Extension

Once your students have collected a good number of advertising expressions and phrases, ask them to divide these into two groups: those which deal with fact (e.g. *Allow 28 days for delivery*), and those which deal with opinion (e.g. *Unbeatable prices!*).

Comment

Phrases such as those listed above abound in advertisements, and in just a few minutes, and in just a few pages, I found twenty-five such phrases.

Cross-references

For a version of this activity using mixed newspaper items, see 10.14.

Box 20 **Example poem**

Poetry in promotion

Please reserve immediately
Faster, safer delivery
Don't miss this opportunity
Call us now
Call us now

Satisfaction guaranteed
Send no money now
Personal callers welcome
Send no money now

At least £45 off the rrp
Allow 28 days for delivery
Just compare our prices
Just compare our prices

4.17 Favourite jobs

Ranking jobs from most popular to least popular

Level: Pre-Intermediate–Post-Intermediate

Preparation

Compile a sheet of job advertisements covering a wide variety of jobs. Add a gloss (a translation or an explanation) to deal with problem vocabulary or language where necessary. Make one copy of this sheet for each student in the class.

In class

1 Begin the lesson by discussing the topic of jobs with your students. Use prompt-questions to elicit their opinions on a number of points: *Which jobs do you think are interesting/boring/difficult/easy/ dangerous/well-paid/badly paid? Which jobs do you think you would*

be capable of doing well? Which jobs would you least like to do? Which jobs would you be interested in doing?

2 When the discussion is beginning to die down, give each student a copy of the job advertisements sheet and allow them a few moments to read this quickly.

3 Explain to your students that they should consider all of these jobs carefully, and then rank them from the job they would most like to do to the one they would least like to do. They should write their results as a list, beginning with the name of the job they would most like to do at the top.

4 When your students are ready, form small groups of three or four students and ask them to compare their ranking orders. Tell them that they should try to explain the reasons for ranking the jobs in this way.

5 Finally, with the whole class, try to find out the three most popular jobs on the list. Call out each job in turn and ask for a show of hands if the job was in first, second or third place on a student's list. If so, award the job one point. When you have called out the last job on the sheet, add up all the points to discover your students' top three choices. This can lead into a discussion about why these particular jobs are so popular.

Extension

In class or for homework, ask your students to write a letter of application for the job which they decided they would most like to do.

Variation

If you are working with a group of students involved in a particular area of speciality (e.g. business, medicine, law), use a selection of jobs related to their field of work or study.

Cross-references

The same materials can be used in 4.18. This can serve as a suitable follow-up to 4.9. For a suitable lead-in activity, see 4.1. For a suitable follow-up activity, see 4.18. A quick oral version of 10.4 can also serve as a suitable lead-in or follow-up activity.

4.18 Job interviews

Conducting job interviews

Level: Intermediate–Advanced

Preparation

Cut out a wide variety of job advertisements and make one copy of each advertisement. You can use a different advertisement for each student in the class, or choose a smaller selection of jobs and make several copies of each.

In class

1 With the class, brainstorm questions which are typically asked in job interviews and make two keyword lists on the board under two headings – Interviewer's Questions and Candidate's Questions. Typical ideas might include the following: personal details, previous work experience, previous positions held, career history, qualifications, motivation for applying for the job, salary, working-hours, holidays, benefits, duties and responsibilities, company background, and so on.

2 When your students have exhausted their ideas, display the job advertisements and tell each student to choose one job which interests them or appeals to them.

3 When all your students have made their choice, put them into groups of three, and explain that two students in each group will play the roles of interviewers. They should prepare questions to interview the third student (the candidate) for the job s/he has chosen. The candidate should also prepare questions, as well as background personal/career information. Tell the candidates that they can invent any information which is relevant and will help their job application.

4 Tell them that each interview should last five minutes only, and then another student from the group will play the role of candidate for the job they have chosen.

5 Give the interviewers in each group a copy of the candidate's job advertisement. Allow a few minutes' preparation time before they begin the first interviews.

6 Stop groups at the end of five minutes and ask them to prepare for the second interview. Continue this procedure until all three students in each group have played the roles of both interviewer and candidate.

7 At the end of the interviews, bring the class together and ask your

students to say which candidates they felt performed well and if they would have considered them for the job. In addition, you can ask your students which questions they found difficult to answer, and discuss possible answers to these with the class.

Extension

For homework or during class-time, ask your students to write letters of application for the jobs they have chosen. Another possibility is to ask interviewers to write letters of acceptance or rejection to the candidates.

Cross-references

The same materials can be used in 4.17. This can serve as a suitable follow-up to 4.9 and 4.17.

4.19 Job descriptions

Matching job descriptions to job titles

Level: Intermediate–Advanced

Preparation

Compile a sheet of job advertisements and delete the job titles (e.g. Marketing Manager) and any subsequent use of them (e.g. *As Marketing Manager you will be responsible* ...) in the job descriptions. Number each advertisement for ease of reference and add a gloss (a translation or an explanation) to deal with problem vocabulary or language where necessary. Make one copy of this sheet for each student in the class. For your own reference, make up an answer key showing the job titles which match the job advertisements.

In class

1 To demonstrate the activity, write all the job titles on the board in a jumbled order, pre-teach any key vocabulary from the first job advertisement and read this advertisement aloud to the class. Ask them to try to match it to the correct job title from the list on the board. When they have done this, discuss with your students how they did this and what language in the advertisement helped them to match it correctly.

2 Now give each student in the class a copy of the job advertisements

sheet and explain that you have removed all the titles of the jobs – these are on the board in a jumbled order.

3 Tell your students that they should read the job descriptions and match them to the appropriate job titles on the board.

4 When your students have finished, form small groups of three or four students and ask them to compare their answers. Tell them that they should explain and justify their reasons for matching each advertisement to a particular job title.

5 Finally, check the answers with the whole class and deal with any job advertisements and job titles your students were unable to match.

Variation

Instead of supplying the job titles on the board, ask your students to deduce them from the job descriptions. In this case, you should allow your students to use bilingual dictionaries if they know what a particular job is, but need to look up the English term.

Comment

Many jobs today are so specialised that their titles can be very confusing and quite baffling to the uninformed. This activity is particularly useful for students who are working in a specific field (e.g. engineering, marketing, sales, management) and who, perhaps for their future careers, will need to be clear about job descriptions and job titles.

Cross-references

For a suitable lead-in activity, see 4.1. A quick oral version of 10.4 can also serve as a suitable lead-in or follow-up activity.

4.20 Charity appeals

Completing unfinished sentences based on charity appeals

Level: Intermediate–Post-Intermediate

Preparation

Compile a sheet of four charity appeals. Each one should show a photograph of one person and should represent a different cause, e.g. the blind, handicapped people, the homeless, starving children, and so on (see Box 21 for sample appeals). Below each appeal, add a gloss (a translation or an explanation) to deal with problem vocabulary or language where necessary. Make one copy of this sheet for each group of four students in the class, and cut each sheet into separate appeals to make a set.

In addition, you will also need to make one copy of the unfinished sentences sheet (see Box 22 for sample sheet) for each student in the class.

In class

1 Begin a discussion with your class on the subject of charities, using prompt-questions: *Which charities exist in your country? How do they raise money? Have you ever donated money to a charity? Do you support a particular charity? Do charity shops exist in your country?* Use this discussion phase to introduce some basic vocabulary related to the topic.

2 Put your students into groups of four and give each group a set of the charity appeals. Tell your students that, within their group, they should each choose one which concerns or interests them.

3 When your students have made their choice, ask each group to find a space in the room and display their four appeals some distance apart – this will make access to them easier at a later stage. Give each group member one of the unfinished sentences sheets to display alongside their charity appeal and tell them to write their name on this sheet.

4 Tell your students that they should first think carefully about the situation of the person depicted in their own appeal and complete one of the unfinished sentences. They should then move on to an appeal chosen by another member of their group, read it and, thinking again about the person shown there, complete one of the unfinished sentences. They should continue this procedure of going from one appeal to another and completing the unfinished sentences. Make it clear that they should keep returning to all four sheets to complete more unfinished sentences, but stress that they should not repeat anything that another student has already written.

5 At the end of this writing stage, ask each student to reclaim their own charity appeal and unfinished sentences sheet, and ask them to read what everyone has written.

6 Now form four groups, each one comprising all the students who chose the same appeal. Ask them to discuss all the unfinished sentences they have, and then select which three they think would best accompany their charity appeal.

7 Finally, working with the whole class, ask a representative from each of the four groups in turn to say which cause their charity appeal was for, and which three sentences their group chose to accompany it and the reasons why.

Box 21 Sample appeals

IF YOU DON'T RESPOND NEITHER CAN HE

Liam is brain damaged, but he is not a lost cause, beyond help.

Every year Brainwave's Centre for Rehabilitation helps hundreds of children like Liam to take the first big step towards being able to perform basic functions that you take for granted, like walking and talking.

It's a long, hard slog, for the children and their parents.

For you it's a little easier. Please fill in the coupon and send what you can afford to support our work.

I would like to help a braindamaged child and enclose my cheque for £............... payable to Brainwave, Marsh Lane, Huntworth Gate, Bridgewater, Somerset TA6 6LQ. Or phone 01278 429089 with credit card donations.

Name ....

Address ....

.... Postcode ....

DT15/12

BRAINWAVE
HELP US TO GIVE THEM A FUTURE
A Registered Charity No. 285781

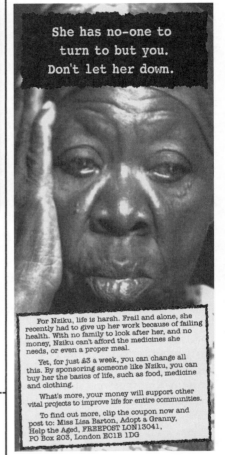

She has no-one to turn to but you. Don't let her down.

For Nziku, life is harsh. Frail and alone, she recently had to give up her work because of failing health. With no family to look after her, and no money, Nziku can't afford the medicines she needs, or even a proper meal.

Yet, for just £3 a week, you can change all this. By sponsoring someone like Nziku, you can buy her the basics of life, such as food, medicine and clothing.

What's more, your money will support other vital projects to improve life for entire communities.

To find out more, clip the coupon now and post to: Miss Lisa Barton, Adopt a Granny, Help the Aged, FREEPOST LON13041, PO Box 203, London EC1B 1DG

Yes, I'm interested in sponsoring an elderly person. Please tell me what I can do.

Mr / Mrs / Miss / Ms

Address

Postcode   Tel.No.

97 20 - AFX 2201

Send to : Miss Lisa Barton, Adopt a Granny, Help the Aged, FREEPOST LON13041, PO Box 203, London EC1B 1DG

Help the Aged

☎ Or phone 0171 250 4481

Adopt a Granny
Registered Charity No. 272786

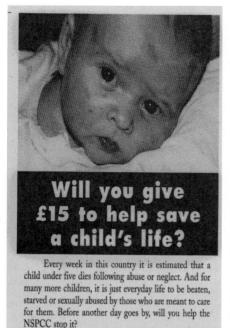

Will you give £15 to help save a child's life?

Every week in this country it is estimated that a child under five dies following abuse or neglect. And for many more children, it is just everyday life to be beaten, starved or sexually abused by those who are meant to care for them. Before another day goes by, will you help the NSPCC stop it?

Just return this coupon with a donation of £15. To a child at risk, your £15 could mean the difference between life and death.

Here is my gift to help protect an abused child

☐ £15   Other amount £ [＿＿＿＿＿]

I enclose a cheque/postal order made payable to NSPCC Registered Charity, or please debit my MasterCard/Visa/American Express/Diners Club/CAF Charity Card.

(delete as applicable)   Please send your donation to:
Card Account No.   NSPCC, FREEPOST WC1613, London EC2B 2NS.

[| | | | | | | | | | | | | | | | | | |]

                                                                    981502

Expiry date [| | |]

NAME: Mr/Mrs/Ms/Miss＿＿＿＿＿＿＿

ADDRESS＿＿＿＿＿＿＿＿＿＿＿＿＿

＿＿＿＿＿ POSTCODE＿＿＿＿＿

The NSPCC protects children in England, Wales and N. Ireland.
Photo posed by model.
The NSPCC can sometimes raise extra funds by occasionally allowing other charities to write to you. If you would prefer *not* to receive this correspondence, please tick this box. ☐

NSPCC

Charity Registration No. 216401.

THE NUMBER OF HOMELESS families in the UK has almost doubled in the last fifteen years. Shelter thinks much more decisive action is needed.

Providing decent housing for homeless people makes economic sense in the long term. The savings on health care costs alone would make it financially worthwhile. And what price do you put on ruined lives? The children, for instance, who may never know a real home...

It's not about politics, it's about getting homeless people decent homes, and off the streets. But to tackle Britain's housing crisis effectively we have to keep in touch with public opinion.

Please spend just two minutes of your time completing this survey, and return it as soon as you can.

If you can also make a donation of £15 (or whatever you can afford) we would be very grateful. Please let us have your answers within 14 days.

Thank you.

Box 22 **Sample unfinished sentences**

This is a person . . .

who wants ....

who needs ....

who can't ....

who hasn't ....

who is ....

who will never ....

who must ....

who should ....

who doesn't ....

who used to ....

who isn't ....

who could ....

who won't ....

who shouldn't ....

who ....

who ....

5 Horoscopes

Although reading horoscopes is undoubtedly popular with many people, teachers should be aware of, and sensitive to, the fact that horoscopes and their connection with astrology might be offensive to members of some religious communities.

Before attempting any of the activities in this chapter, teachers are advised to discuss this point with their students to avoid causing any embarrassment or offence.

5.1 Horoscope dictation

Dictating horoscopes without using the original words of the text

Level: Pre-Intermediate–Post-Intermediate

Preparation

Cut out the day's horoscope and cut this into individual star signs. You will need one copy of each student's star sign so find out what they are before the lesson in order to reduce photocopying.

In class

1 Dictate the sentence *You are going to dictate your neighbour's horoscope* word by word to your students without actually saying the words themselves, but by giving the explanations and definitions of the words as suggested in the list below. After giving your explanation of a word, tell your students that they should start calling out possible words until they find the exact word you are dictating.

> Not *I* but ... (to elicit *you*)
> Part of the verb *be* in the Simple Present (to elicit *are*)
> The opposite of *coming* (to elicit *going*)
> Part of the infinitive (to elicit *to*)
> It's what you do when you speak or read aloud and another person writes exactly the words you say (to elicit *dictate*)

157

Not *my* but ... (to elicit *your*)
The person who lives next door to you (to elicit *neighbour*)
Make the last word possessive (to elicit *neighbour's*)
What you can read in a newspaper to find out what will happen to you that day (to elicit *horoscope*)

Each time your students guess a word correctly, acknowledge it clearly and tell all your students to write it.

2 When you have finished dictating the sentence, pair students with different star signs and give one of the students (Student A) in each pair a copy of their partner's (Student B) horoscope. Ask them not to show this to their partner.

3 Explain to the As that this is the horoscope for the day for the Bs. For the Bs to discover what it says and what will happen to them today, the As have to 'dictate' the horoscope in exactly the same way as you did with the example sentence. The Bs should try to guess each word being dictated to discover their horoscope.

4 Tell your students that they should dictate as much as they can in ten minutes before they change roles.

5 Begin the activity and, at the end of the time limit, ask the As to let their partner read the rest of the horoscope if they did not manage to finish dictating it.

6 Now give the Bs their partner's horoscope and tell pairs to reverse roles.

7 At the end of this second dictation stage, ask each pair to discuss how true they think their horoscopes for today are.

8 Finally, find out which words your students had difficulty in communicating and invite other students to suggest how they could have done this.

Comment

This activity can, of course, be used with any short text. However, by using the day's horoscopes, you capitalise on your students' natural curiosity and their motivation to discover as much of their horoscopes as they can in the time allowed.

Cross-references

The same materials can be used in 5.3. For a suitable follow-up activity, see 5.6.

5.2 Matching star signs

Matching star signs to newspaper horoscopes

Level: Pre-Intermediate–Post-Intermediate

Preparation

Compile a sheet with the previous day's horoscope cut into individual star signs and rearranged in a jumbled order. Number each sign for ease of reference and delete the names of the star signs, as well as any reference to ruling planets if they are mentioned. Add a gloss (a translation or explanation) to deal with problem vocabulary or language where necessary, and make one copy of this sheet for each student in the class. You should keep a copy of the original horoscope, as this will later serve as an answer sheet.

In class

1 Ask your students to call out points which are typically mentioned in newspaper horoscopes (e.g. family, friends, work, health, relationships, plans, money), and write their suggestions on the board.
2 Pair students and ask them to tell each other about their previous day, using the ideas on the board as a checklist. This will help fix the day's events in their minds ready for the next stage of the activity.
3 Give each student a copy of the jumbled horoscope sheet. Tell them that this is the horoscope from the previous day and that you have deleted the names of all the star signs.
4 Explain that they should read all the predictions carefully and then, with the events of the previous day in mind, decide which one they feel most closely corresponds to what actually happened to them that day. Tell them that they should write the name of their star sign next to this prediction.
5 Begin the activity. When your students are ready, ask them to work with their partner again to explain their choices to each other.
6 Allow a few minutes for this exchange and then, with the whole class, tell your students which star signs the numbered horoscopes actually correspond to. Ask if anyone succeeded in identifying their star sign and invite comments about the accuracy or inaccuracy of the predictions. This is a good opportunity to discuss with your students the reliability of predictions based on astrology in general.

Cross-references

The same materials can be used in 5.3. For a suitable lead-in activity, see 4.1. A quick oral version of 10.4 can also serve as a suitable lead-in activity. For a suitable follow-up activity, see 5.6.

5.3 Make my day

Combining versions of horoscopes

Level: Pre-Intermediate–Post-Intermediate

Preparation

Cut out the horoscope from several different newspapers and cut them into individual star signs. For this activity, it is not necessary to use the horoscopes of the day. Paste all the different versions of one sign (e.g. all the versions of Pisces) onto one sheet of paper, and make up similar sheets for all the other signs. For each student, you will need one copy of their sheet of horoscope versions, so find out your students' star signs before the lesson in order to reduce unnecessary photocopying.

In class

1 Pair students with different star signs, and give each student his/her partner's combined horoscope sheet.
2 Explain that each student is going to write a new horoscope for his/her partner. This will be a composite horoscope taking information from all the different versions, but the rewritten version will be completely positive – there will be nothing negative at all. In other words, it will be the ideal horoscope.
3 Tell your students that they can do this by retaining positive points, rewriting negative points and making neutral points positive.
4 Begin the activity. Circulate to deal with problems concerning vocabulary or language as they arise.
5 When your students have finished this writing stage, ask them to exchange their rewritten horoscopes with their partner to decide if they are happy with the new version. If they are not, they should negotiate with their partner to make changes to it.
6 Finally, ask your students to display their new horoscopes on walls or on desktops next to the original versions. Ask everyone to walk around and read each other's new, improved horoscopes.

For a suitable follow-up activity, see 5.6. The materials used in 5.1, 5.2, 5.4 and 5.5 can be used in this activity.

5.4 Pinpoint predictions

Comparing horoscopes to find the most accurate astrologer

Level: Pre-Intermediate–Post-Intermediate

Preparation

Cut out the horoscopes from two or three of the previous day's newspapers and cut them into their individual star signs. Paste all the different versions of one star sign onto a separate sheet of paper and, below each version, write the name of the newspaper it was taken from. Prepare the materials for each of the other star signs in the same way. Each student will need their own sheet of different horoscope versions, so find out your students' star signs before the lesson in order to reduce unnecessary photocopying.

In class

1 Give each student a copy of their own star sign sheet and explain that these are several different astrologers' predictions for the previous day.
2 Tell the class that they are going to do a survey to find which newspaper astrologer is the most accurate.
3 Explain that they should read the different predictions carefully and, bearing in mind the actual events of their previous day, give each one a score between 1 (the least accurate) and 5 (the most accurate).
4 Begin the activity. Circulate to deal with problems concerning vocabulary or language as they arise.
5 When your students are ready, draw a grid on the board to record their findings. Along the top, write the star signs included in the survey. Down the side, write the names of the newspapers the horoscopes were taken from.
6 Ask each student in turn to call out his/her star sign and the scores for each newspaper astrologer, and write these in the appropriate spaces on the grid.
7 When all the scores have been recorded, add them up and write the

totals. The newspaper astrologer with the highest number of marks will be the winner.

8 Finally, invite students to tell the class about predictions that had been very accurate, and also where astrologers had got it completely wrong.

Cross-references

The same materials can be used in 5.3. For a suitable follow-up activity, see 5.6.

5.5 Miming horoscopes

Dictating and miming horoscopes

Level: Pre-Intermediate–Intermediate

Preparation

Cut out the day's horoscope from a newspaper and underline between eight and ten words in each star sign – a mixture of nouns, verbs and adjectives. Add a gloss (a translation or an explanation) to deal with problem vocabulary or language as necessary. You will need to prepare the star sign of each student in the class in this way, so find out their star signs before the lesson in order to reduce unnecessary preparation and photocopying.

In class

1 Pair students with different star signs and give each student a copy of his/her partner's horoscope. Tell them that they should not show these to each other.

2 Explain that one student in each pair should dictate their partner's horoscope, and their partner should write it. However, the student dictating is not allowed to say the words which are underlined – each time they reach an underlined word, they must stop and mime it.

3 If this is the first time your students have done a miming activity in class, demonstrate gestures which they can use to help them with their mimes (see Box 5 in Chapter 1 for miming techniques).

4 Tell your students that if the students who are writing clearly understand the mime (perhaps they can give the word in their own language) but do not know the English word, then their partners can tell them the word.

5 When the first student in each pair has finished dictating their partner's horoscope, they should compare the dictated version with the original and check the spelling. They should then change roles.

6 At the end of the activity, ask your students to call out any words they found difficult to mime and invite other members of the class to suggest and demonstrate how these words could be mimed.

Variation 1

An enjoyable but noisy variation of this activity is to tell students to stand in two parallel lines about three metres apart, with partners facing each other. All the students in one line dictate and mime their partner's horoscope as described above, but with the added difficulty of being heard above the voices of all the other students. This is a good way of giving students practice in filtering out sound and dealing with background noise and distractions which can make listening difficult.

Variation 2

Pair students, pin up the horoscope of one member of each pair on the wall at one end of the classroom and tell the owner to sit at the other end of the room. Their partner has to read the horoscope and run back to them to dictate and mime as much as they can remember. They continue this procedure until they have dictated all the horoscope.

This is a fun and frantic way of using dictation and it can be used as a lesson warmer. It is also a useful way of giving students practice in holding chunks of language in their short-term memory.

Comment

A number of other interesting ideas for mutual dictation can be found in *Dictation*, P. Davis and M. Rinvolucri, Cambridge University Press (1988).

Cross-references

The same materials can be used in 5.3. For a suitable follow-up activity, see 5.6.

5.6 Learning by association

Learning vocabulary through personal association

Level: Intermediate–Advanced

Preparation

Make a copy of the sample questions (see Box 23) for each student in the class. No other preparation is necessary for this activity, which is intended to be used as a follow-up to other activities in this chapter.

In class

1 Ask your students to read the horoscope predictions for their star signs to find one or two idioms, expressions or phrasal verbs they think would be useful for them to learn, e.g. *to put all your eggs in one basket, to drive yourself too hard, to fall out with someone, to make up with someone.*

2 When your students have decided which language items they want to learn, help them understand these items by explaining them, translating them or letting your students use dictionaries to look up their meaning.

3 To explain the aim of the activity, tell your students that one way of remembering new (difficult) vocabulary is by making strong personal associations and connections with it.

4 To demonstrate the activity, ask for a volunteer to come to the front of the class and to sit opposite you. Ask this student to tell you one vocabulary item s/he wishes to learn (e.g. *to make up with someone*), and make sure that s/he understands its meaning.

5 Ask your student to think of one particular occasion when s/he made up with someone, and to fix this event clearly in his/her mind.

6 When your student is ready, ask a suitable first question based on the sample questions below (e.g. *When did you last make up with someone?*), and let your student answer (e.g. *I last made up with someone about two weeks ago.*). It is important that you include in your question the vocabulary item your student has chosen to learn, and that you encourage him/her to use it in the answer. Repeatedly hearing the new vocabulary item, and using it while focusing on its connection with a specific personal event, are key aspects of this vocabulary-learning technique.

7 Continue asking several other appropriate questions, following the

direction given by your student's answers. The sample questions in Box 23 are given only as suggestions. They will not usually be suitable in the order given, and not all of them will be suitable for all vocabulary items.

8 When you have finished your demonstration, pair students and give each student a copy of the sample questions list. Tell your students that, in their pairs, they should take it in turns to play the roles of interviewer and interviewee to help each other learn one of their vocabulary items. Remind them that they should try to follow the natural flow of the conversation and ask appropriate questions, using the vocabulary item as much as possible.

9 When they have each worked on one of their chosen expressions, ask them to write it in their vocabulary notebooks. However, rather than simply writing a translation or explanation, they should write a short note about the strongest associations they made with their vocabulary item.

10 Finally, point out to your students that this is a technique they can use on their own to learn new vocabulary.

Comment

Although other texts can also be used for this activity, newspaper horoscopes are a particularly rich source of idioms, proverbs, phrasal verbs, colloquial expressions and collocations.

Cross-references

This can serve as a suitable follow-up to any of the other activities in this chapter.

Box 23 **Sample questions**

When did you last ... (e.g. make up with someone)?

How old were you?

Were you alone? Who else did it involve? Who was the other person?

What time of year was it? What time of day was it?

What was the weather like?

Can you remember the physical environment? Where were you?

Do you remember the colours around you (e.g. of the room)?

Do you remember any particular smells around you?

Was it the first time you had ever...?

What were you doing at the time?

How were you feeling? Do you remember your emotions before, during or after? What about your physical or mental state? Were you tired, happy, nervous, excited?

Why did it happen?

How long did it go on for?

What was the outcome?

What did you learn from it?

© Cambridge University Press 1999

6 Problem Page letters

6.1 The hole problem

Discovering the content of a Problem Page letter

Level: Pre-Intermediate–Intermediate
Special equipment: overhead projector (OHP)

Preparation

Choose a short Problem Page letter about a subject appropriate for your students. Make an OHP transparency of the letter, enlarging it if necessary to ensure that it can be seen easily from the back of the class (see Box 24 for sample letter). With a sharp pencil, punch a small hole through the centre of a large sheet of paper, and use tape to secure the sheet onto the glass of the OHP, with the hole in the middle. The hole should be large enough to allow up to three or four letters to be seen through it.

In class

1 Tell your students that they are going to see a newspaper Problem Page letter. Explain that you will move the letter (i.e. the transparency) over the hole, and they should call out any words they can read or guess from what they can see.
2 Move to all different parts of the text and, periodically, check what your students have understood by asking them to piece together the story-line. Any points they have missed or misunderstood can be dealt with by focusing on those particular sections of the letter. Explain any vocabulary or language problems as they arise.
3 When your students have grasped the main points of the letter, reveal it and let them read it quickly. Turn off the OHP and ask the class to retell the story in as much detail as they can.
4 Finally, use suitable prompt-questions to discuss the problem with the class. For example, for the sample letter in Box 24, I ask the following questions:

What options are open to the letter-writer?
What advice would you give her?
Why is the showbiz personality acting this way?
How could he have handled the situation better?
How would *you* have handled the situation if you had been the letter-writer / the showbiz personality?
What do you think will happen next?

Variation

If you do not have access to an OHP, it is possible to do this activity by writing keywords from the letter on the board. In this case, write between ten and fifteen keywords on the board, in the same order as in the letter, but with spaces between them to insert further words later. Ask your students to try to reconstruct the story using these keywords.

Next, insert another selection of five to ten keywords (in the correct position) and, again, ask your students to try to reconstruct the story.

Continue this procedure of inserting more keywords (in their correct position) until your students have successfully reconstructed the story-line of the letter.

Finally, ask the class to retell the story, and then read them the original letter for them to compare with their own version.

Extensions

These extensions are based on the variation above. Ask your students to take turns at retelling the story in pairs, using the keywords on the board. As they are doing so, slowly erase words from the board. Continue erasing words slowly until there are no words left and your students have committed the story-line to memory.

This can then lead into a writing activity in which students have to write the Problem Page letter (or a reply to it), or a Problem Page letter from the showbiz personality (see 6.7 *The other side of the story*).

Alternatively, the letter can form the basis for a role-play, where pairs of students play the parts of the letter-writer and the jilted lover, who meet to discuss the problem (see 6.5 *Problem Page role-plays*).

Acknowledgement

I first learned this technique for using the OHP from Herbert Puchta at Pilgrims, in 1990, when he demonstrated it using a picture story.

Cross-references

The same materials can be used in 6.4, 6.5 and 6.7. For suitable follow-up activities, see 2.6, 6.4, 6.5 and 6.7.

Box 24 Sample letter

Dear Nina

I CAN'T tell you the name of the man I've fallen in love with because he's a well-known showbiz celebrity and it would embarrass him.

I met him at a party, and we spoke for hours. In fact, we spent the whole evening together. He was wonderful to be with, and was so friendly and interesting.

We began seeing each other, but he was often away working, so we couldn't really spend a lot of time together. But he rang me almost every day, and once he said he loved me. He isn't married and I am desperately in love with him.

But a few weeks ago, he suddenly stopped calling. I rang him to ask why, but he just made excuses about being very busy.

He hasn't called for three weeks now. I've left messages on his answerphone and written, but he hasn't replied.

I really do love him and want him back. I long to see him and hear his voice. What did I do wrong? Please, please help me.

6.2 Why don't you ... ? Yes, but ...

Giving and rejecting advice

Level: Pre-Intermediate–Intermediate

Preparation

Cut out three suitable Problem Page letters dealing with three entirely different issues (see Box 25 for sample letters). Remove the columnist's replies and paste the three letters onto one sheet of paper. Make one copy of this sheet for each group of three students in the class, and cut each sheet into a set of three individual letters.

In class

1 Put your students into groups of three and give each group a set of the three Problem Page letters. Tell them that they should read all

three letters quickly and that each student should choose one of the letters. Deal with any vocabulary or language problems when your students have made their choice.

2 Explain that one student in each group should read aloud their letter or explain the problem to their partners. When they have understood the problem, they should try to make helpful suggestions and give advice using the opening phrase *Why don't you . . .?*

3 The letter-readers, however, should try to counter all the help and advice they are given by thinking up reasons for rejecting it. They should preface their objections with the opening phrase *Yes, but . . .*

4 Explain that the aim of the letter-readers is to try to find any excuse they can think of to reject the advice and suggestions they are given. The aim of the advice-givers is to continue giving advice until the letter-reader cannot think of any excuse or reason to turn it down.

5 After the first round, repeat this procedure until all the members of each group have taken turns as letter-readers and advice-givers.

6 Finally, with the whole class, invite students to tell the class the most amusing, the most imaginative and the most unlikely reasons they heard/used for turning down advice.

Comment

We often like to think that we can solve other people's problems and are only too pleased to offer our help and advice to find a solution to what can seem like an insurmountable problem. Indeed, it invariably is, for as Eric Berne explains (see below), the thesis of this game is for us to try to think of a solution which the other person cannot find fault with. It is this challenge which gives impetus to the activity.

Acknowledgement

This activity is named after one of the 'games' in human relationships documented by Eric Berne (1964). It is the oldest subject of game analysis and one of the best understood.

Cross-references

The same materials can be used in most of the other activities in this chapter. For a suitable follow-up activity, see 6.4.

Box 25 **Sample Problem Page letters**

Pre-Intermediate–Intermediate

Dear Nina

AS PART of my university course I have to spend a year away in Spain. I'm really excited about it, but I'm afraid that it will end my relationship with my boyfriend.

We're both 21 and everything is wonderful between us at the moment.

My boyfriend says we should enjoy our time together now and worry about me going when it happens.

Am I silly to worry about the future? I wonder if we should stop our relationship now and save any heartache when I leave.

Dear Nina

A FEW months ago I found out that my brother's wife was having an affair with a married man from her office.

I know her marriage isn't perfect, and my brother can be difficult, but I love him, and don't want to see him hurt. I told her she had to end the relationship, and she promised it would stop.

But she's still seeing him. I found out by accident that she even went away with this man for a weekend to Paris recently. What should I do to end this situation before someone gets hurt?

Dear Nina

I LOVE dancing, but my husband refuses to take me to clubs or discos. We are only in our early thirties, but he says we are too old to go dancing.

He is a loving husband and we have two wonderful children. But he never takes me out anywhere, and when I suggest a night out together he just makes excuses.

We have a happy marriage, and I love my husband dearly. But I'm finding life boring, and I need to have some fun before I really am too old. What's wrong with him?

Dear Nina

A FEW weeks after my husband and I got married, we had to move to Italy because of his job. That was nearly a year ago. He loves it here, and wants to stay, but I'm miserable.

We live in a tiny village, and I feel lonely and isolated. We haven't really made any friends here, and I just spend my day waiting for him to come home from the office. When he does, he's so tired, he just has dinner and falls asleep.

I love my husband, but I miss my family and friends so much, there are days I just want to pack my bags and leave. Do you think things will get better?

Intermediate

Dear Nina

I SPEND every weekend alone, except for my sister and her husband. I live in the same house as them and their baby.

The other day was my birthday, and I told everybody at work that my boyfriend took me out to a really expensive restaurant and bought me flowers and perfume.

But it was all lies. I haven't even got a boyfriend, and I spent my birthday alone at home, baby-sitting for my sister.

The truth is that I'm unattractive, and men aren't interested in me.

I went to see my doctor because I was feeling so miserable, but he just told me I should stop feeling sorry for myself.

I'm writing to you as a last resort, so please don't tell me off for all this self-pity but try to help me.

Dear Nina

MY DAD and my two brothers are making my life a misery, and I don't know what to do. They treat me like a slave, and they expect me to do all the cooking, washing and cleaning just because I'm a girl. I've talked to them about this, but it makes no difference.

I'm sixteen years old, and still at school, but I've got no time to study, and I'm afraid I'll fail my exams. My Mum's been ill for the last few months, and she can't do much, but it isn't fair that I should do everything around the house.

My boyfriend's parents say I can go and live with them, but I don't want to leave my Mum. I feel trapped. What should I do?

Dear Nina

MY BOYFRIEND and I are planning to get married soon. We've both been married before, but we're hoping that things will be better the second time around.

There's just one problem. His daughter is refusing to share her bedroom with my daughter after we move into his house, which is much bigger than mine.

I can't understand why she's being so difficult. We've both tried talking to her, but she won't change her mind. This is causing a lot of problems and arguments between all of us, and my daughter is terribly upset by her attitude.

Do you think my boyfriend and I should do what we want and hope for the best?

Post-Intermediate–Advanced

Dear Nina

A FEW weeks ago, I gave my girlfriend the PIN number for my bank account so she could draw some money out. She needed it to do some shopping, and I couldn't see any harm in it.

But the other day, I got a letter from the bank saying that I was more than £500 overdrawn.

You can imagine what else has happened. A couple of days before I got the letter, my girlfriend finished with me.

I've tried asking her for the money, but she just says it's my problem now, not hers.

I still love her and want her back, but it will wreck my chances if I push her for the money.

You don't need to tell me how stupid I am, but what can I do now?

Dear Nina

WHEN I was about 18, I noticed that I was going a bit thin on top.

Now I'm 21, it's getting worse and worse, and I'm beginning to panic that I'll be bald soon.

Every time I comb my hair, lots of it comes out, and I had a blazing row with my girlfriend the other day because she said something about how thin my hair is.

Even my friends have started to tease me about going bald, and I don't even like going out now, because I think people are laughing at me. I'm really scared. I'm too young to go bald.

Dear Nina

THERE SEEMS to be all kinds of help and support for single mums – but what about single dads? Nobody ever seems to give us a second thought. Our problems just seem to get swept under the carpet.

I am 45 years old and I have two young sons to look after and bring up on my own. My wife died a few years ago. I would love to have some kind of social life and have the chance to look for a new partner, but it's impossible with the hours I work.

I am a chef in a local restaurant, which means I have to work every evening and at weekends. Sometimes the kids come with me, but usually I have to leave them with my mother.

How are working single dads like me supposed to find a partner?

6.3 Unfinished business

Reacting to Problem Page letters

Level: Pre-Intermediate–Post-Intermediate

Preparation

Compile a sheet of suitable Problem Page letters (without the columnist's replies) dealing with a wide variety of issues. Number each letter for ease of reference (see Box 25 above for sample letters). Deal with any vocabulary or language problems by adding a gloss (a translation or an explanation) where necessary. Make one copy of the Problem Page letters sheet as well as the unfinished sentences sheet (see Box 26 for sample sheet) for each student in the class.

In class

1 To introduce the activity, choose one of the Problem Page letters, read it aloud to your students and check that they understand it. Ask your students for their reactions to the letter, using questions based on the ideas in the unfinished sentences sheet, e.g. *Do you think this problem is easy to solve? Do you feel any sympathy for the letter-writer? Do you think this problem is unusual?* Discuss your students' reactions and encourage your students to explain and justify them.

2 Now give each student copies of both the unfinished sentences sheet and the Problem Page letters sheet. Deal with any problem vocabulary or language in the unfinished sentences at this stage of the activity.

3 Tell your students that they should read the letters carefully and decide which one is most appropriate to each unfinished sentence. They should write the number of the letter next to the sentence, i.e. next to the sentence which most closely reflects their feelings about the letter. Tell them that they should try to complete all the unfinished sentences.

4 When your students are ready, ask them to work in pairs or small groups to compare their answers.

5 Finally, with the whole class, check your students' answers by reading out each unfinished sentence in turn and asking your students to call out the numbers of the Problem Page letters they completed them with. This can lead into a lively and interesting discussion.

Cross-references

The same materials can be used in most of the other activities in this chapter. A quick oral version of 10.4 can serve as a suitable lead-in activity. For a suitable follow-up, see 6.4.

Box 26 **Unfinished sentences**

Try to complete each unfinished sentence below with the number of the appropriate Problem Page letter.

The problem I'm least likely to have is in letter number . . .

The problem I'm most likely to have is in letter number . . .

The problem I'd least want to have is in letter number . . .

The easiest problem to solve is in letter number . . .

The most difficult problem to solve is in letter number . . .

The most understandable problem is in letter number . . .

The most unusual problem is in letter number . . .

The most ridiculous problem is in letter number . . .

I know someone who has / has had the same problem as in letter number . . .

I've also had the same problem as in letter number . . .

I feel most sympathy for the person in letter number . . .

I feel least sympathy for the person in letter number . . .

The person I'd most like to help is the one in letter number . . .

© Cambridge University Press 1999

6.4 Debating the issue

Debating the choices facing the writer of a Problem Page letter

Level: Intermediate–Advanced

Preparation

Select a Problem Page letter in which the letter-writer is clearly faced with a choice or a decision which s/he must make (see Box 25 above for sample letters). You should ensure that the letter you choose concerns an issue suitable for the particular class you are teaching. It is wise to bring to class two or three other suitable Problem Page letters in case your first letter fails to achieve your purpose.

In class

1 Pre-teach any difficult vocabulary or language in the Problem Page letter, then read it aloud to your students, more than once if necessary, checking that they understand it fully. Ask them to say which alternative courses of action are open to the letter-writer and write their ideas on the board. Now ask your students, with a show of hands, to vote for the choice they think the letter-writer should make.

2 If a majority votes for the same option, repeat the above procedure with a different Problem Page letter. Ideally, what you want is for the class to be roughly equally divided in their opinion and for there to be enough support for each alternative in order to hold a debate.

3 When you have achieved this, split the class into the two opposing groups and allow them a few minutes to prepare their arguments to support their points of view.

4 When they are ready, tell the class that they have exactly ten minutes to debate the issue. You should act as chairperson to keep the debate in order and to make sure that both sides have equal opportunities to express their opinions.

5 At the end of the time limit, bring the debate to a close by asking all your students, again with a show of hands, to vote for the decision they think the letter-writer should take.

Extension

For homework, ask your students to write a short letter to the Problem Page letter-writer, saying which course of action the class think s/he should take and explaining why.

Cross-references

The same materials can be used in most of the other activities in this chapter. This can serve as a suitable follow-up to most of the other activities in this chapter.

6.5 Problem Page role-plays

Role-playing the people concerned in Problem Page letters

Level: Intermediate–Advanced

Preparation

Select a suitable Problem Page letter which involves conflict between two people (see Box 25 above for sample letters). Remove the columnist's reply, and make one photocopy of the letter for each pair of students in the class.

In class

1 Pair students, give each pair a copy of the Problem Page letter and allow them a few minutes to read and digest the information. Deal with any vocabulary or language problems at this stage and, when they have understood the situation, take back the letters.
2 Put two pairs of students together to make groups of four, and tell each group to place two chairs facing each other. One student from each pair should sit in these places – their partners should place chairs behind them and occupy these positions.
3 Explain that in each group, one pair should together play the role of the letter-writer and the other pair should play the role of the other person mentioned in the letter. Tell them that this is a face-to-face meeting between the two parties to discuss and try to resolve the issues raised in the letter.
4 Each side should argue its case – but only the students occupying the front chairs are allowed to speak. If either of these students feels they need help, they can reach behind and tag (touch lightly) their partner, and they should immediately change places. Alternatively, if the student sitting behind feels that they could argue the case more convincingly, they can reach forward and tag their partner. Again, they should immediately change positions.
5 Tell each pair to decide which role they wish to play, and begin the activity.

6 At the end of the activity, ask which groups managed to resolve the problem and to explain briefly the outcome of their discussion.

Variation 1

Rather than using Problem Page letters which involve only two people, use letters which involve third and even fourth parties.

Variation 2

Set up the activity as before but give a different letter to each group. This can make the reporting-back stage more interesting for the rest of the class, and you may even wish to invite pairs to perform their role-plays to the class.

Variation 3

Give letters to only half the groups in your class and ask the other groups to act as observers, perhaps stopping the conversation at certain points to comment on what they have observed, and to suggest other possible paths of discussion and negotiation.

Cross-references

The same materials can be used in most of the other activities in this chapter. This can serve as a follow-up to 6.1. A quick oral version of 10.4 can serve as a suitable lead-in activity. For suitable follow-up activities, see 6.4 and 6.7.

6.6 Right to reply

Collaborative writing of replies to Problem Page letters

Level: Intermediate–Post-Intermediate

Preparation

Select between four and eight Problem Page letters covering a variety of issues which would be appropriate for your class of students. Remove the columnist's replies and paste each letter onto a separate sheet of paper, leaving plenty of space below for your students to write. Deal with any problem vocabulary or language in the letters by adding a gloss (a translation or an explanation) where necessary. Each group of (four to eight) students in your class will need one set of letters – one different letter for each student in a group. Keep the columnist's replies for the final stage of the activity.

In class

1 Form groups of between four and eight students, tell each group to sit in a circle and give each group a set of the Problem Page letters – one different letter for each student in the group.
2 Explain that each student should read his/her letter and then pass it to the person on his/her right. This student should read the letter and, on the sheet, write a comment, a reaction, a suggestion or a piece of advice to the letter-writer. When they have done this, they should again pass the letter to the person on their right. Each time a student receives a new letter, s/he should write something different and not repeat anything other students have already written.
3 Continue this procedure until each letter has done a full circle and finally arrives back with its 'owner'. Each student should then have a number of ideas to draw on as a basis for writing a reply to his/her letter.
4 Tell your students that they should now read all the comments, reactions, suggestions and advice on their sheet, and compose a reply to the letter-writer. They can use what other students have written to help them, and they should, of course, include their own ideas.
5 When they have finished, tell your students to display their replies with the original Problem Page letters around the classroom. Next to these, you should display the replies which the columnist actually wrote in response to the letters. Now ask everyone to read each other's work as well as the columnist's replies, looking for similarities and differences between them.

Extension

Having the columnist's replies as well as your students' replies can naturally lead into a discussion to decide where the writers agreed or disagreed, and which writer gave the most helpful or realistic advice in each case. It may also be that for each Problem Page letter, there are useful points made both by your students and by the columnist. If this is the case, ask each student to take back their Problem Page letter, the columnist's reply and their own reply, and, for homework, reformulate their reply to incorporate any useful ideas made by the columnist.

Comment

The larger the groups of students you form, the more reading will be involved and the longer the activity will take. To speed up the activity, form smaller groups and allow the Problem Page letters to circulate two or even three times. As students become more familiar with the content of each of the letters, the less time they will need for reading, and the more time they will have for thinking about and writing their ideas.

Cross-references

The same materials can be used in most of the other activities in this chapter. For a suitable follow-up activity, see 6.4.

6.7 The other side of the story

Replying to a Problem Page letter on behalf of the person criticised in the letter

Level: Intermediate–Advanced

Preparation

Select a Problem Page letter which deals with conflict between the letter-writer and another person (see Box 25 above for sample letters). Remove the columnist's reply and make one copy of the letter for each pair of students in the class. You will also need a second Problem Page letter involving conflict to introduce the activity.

In class

1 Pre-teach any problem vocabulary or language from the second Problem Page letter, then read it aloud to your students. Ask them to say how the person written about would feel if s/he read this letter in a newspaper. How would that person respond? What might s/he say in his/her defence? What is his/her side of the story? Bring out the point that Problem Page letters invariably give only one point of view – the 'wrongdoer' never has a chance to give his/her version.
2 Pair students, give each pair a copy of the Problem Page letter you have chosen and ask them to read through it carefully. Deal with any vocabulary or language problems at this stage.
3 Explain that each pair should write a letter of response to the columnist, on behalf of the person complained about, giving their side of the story.
4 When they have finished, ask pairs to exchange their letters with other pairs to read and compare each other's responses.

5 Ask your students to decide who, in this conflict, their sympathies now lie with, and why. This can give rise to some heated discussion.

Extension

Now that both sides of the story have been given, a columnist would be in a much better position to give advice to both parties concerned. This naturally lends itself to your students writing one reply in the role of the columnist to both letter-writers.

To do this, tell each pair to give the letter they have written to another pair. Taking this and the original Problem Page letter into account, students should write one response to both letter-writers. In class, let pairs read each other's work to decide if they give sound advice and a fair and unbiased reply to both parties.

Comment

A Problem Page letter is rarely objective; indeed, it usually paints rather a black picture of the other person(s) involved in the problem. Whether this is fair or not, we are not in a position to judge, as we only ever hear one side of the story. This activity gives a voice to the other party and puts us, the reader, in a better position to decide who, if anyone, is 'in the right'.

Cross-references

The same materials can be used in most of the other activities in this chapter. This can serve as a follow-up to 6.1 and 6.5. A quick oral version of 10.4 can serve as a suitable lead-in activity. For a suitable follow-up activity, see 6.4.

6.8 Dear Teacher...

Writing Problem Page letters to the teacher about language difficulties

Level: Pre-Intermediate–Advanced

Preparation

Give your students advance notice that they should bring their course-books, course notes and corrected homework assignments to this lesson. In addition, you will need to bring to class a selection of

Problem Page letters to familiarise your students with this genre of text (see Box 25 above for sample letters).

In class

1 Form groups of three or four students and give each group a selection of Problem Page letters. Ask your students to study these carefully, noticing in particular any similarity in the structure and organisation of the letters and in the language the writers use when saying how they feel, explaining the problem or situation and asking the columnist for help or advice. Deal with any key vocabulary or language problems as they arise, but emphasise to your students from the outset that they should not try to understand every word.

2 Allow a few minutes for this familiarisation stage, then bring the class together to discuss their findings. On the board, write any key language which your students have found to be repeated in the letters (e.g. *I'm desperate / I'm so unhappy / What should I do? / I ..., but ... / Do you think I should ... ?*). In addition, ask your students if they have found a common organisation in the letters, e.g. the writers say how they feel about the problem, then explain the problem or situation, then ask for help.

3 Now that your students are more familiar with Problem Page letters, they will be ready for the next stage of the activity. Ask them to look back over all the work they have covered recently – by looking through their coursebook, their own notes, homework assignments and copies of handouts or exercises you have given them.

4 Tell your students that, as they do this, they should make a note of any language points which they do not fully understand and which are still causing them difficulty.

5 When all your students have several ideas, explain that you would like them each to write you a Problem Page letter, but one asking for the help they need with their language problems. Emphasise that it is important that they should be as precise and specific as they can in explaining where their difficulties lie and what help they need. Allow them to refer to the Problem Page letters and the expressions you have written on the board to 'borrow' any language they need.

6 When they have finished, collect in all their letters.

Extensions

At this point, there are several possible ways of proceeding:

1 Answer each letter individually, offering whatever help or advice is needed.

2 Display all the letters and ask your students to read each other's letters and choose one where they feel they may be able to offer help. This might be by writing a reply or by speaking to the letter-writer personally. You should make sure that every student gets a reply to their letter, and this may mean that you will have to write some replies yourself if their letters are not taken up by other students.

3 For the next lesson, compile a Problems Page sheet of your students' letters, make a copy for each student in your class and ask them to read this and write a reply to the letter-writer(s) they feel they can help. Again, every student should get a reply to their letter, and this may mean that you will have to write some replies yourself if their letters are not answered by other students.

4 With your students' permission, give the letters to students from a higher-level group who are able and willing to offer help and advice.

Comments

(a) With lower-level students who share the same first language, you should consider allowing them to write their letters in their own language. This will depend on your own knowledge of your students' language, and may be impracticable with a multinational group.

(b) In extensions 2, 3 and 4, you may wish to (discreetly) monitor the help which is given. It may emerge that the person offering help also has problems with the very language point they are trying to clarify for another student.

(c) This activity can be repeated at different stages throughout the course, and may even be something you wish to do on a regular basis. It is important, however, to reassure your students that they should not be afraid to admit that they are experiencing difficulties with certain language points. It is a chance for them to receive help on an individual basis and is, therefore, ideal for mixed-ability groups.

Cross-references

The same materials can be used in most of the other activities in this chapter.

7 TV guides

Teachers with access to the Internet should be able to download newspaper television programme guides for major television channels. For a list of newspaper web sites, refer to Appendix 2.

7.1 A great day's viewing

Compiling a TV programme guide according to personal tastes

Level: Pre-Intermediate–Intermediate

Preparation

From an English-language newspaper, select a detailed TV programme guide showing the day's programmes for between two and four of the major channels (see Box 27 for sample programme guide). Deal with any vocabulary or language problems by adding a gloss (a translation or an explanation), and make one copy of this sheet for each student in the class.

In class

1 Begin the lesson by discussing with your students the type of television programmes they do / do not like watching, and whether they think the choice of programmes shown in their country caters to a wide enough range of viewers.
2 Give each student a copy of the TV programme guide, and ask your students to look through this quickly.
3 Tell your students that they should go through the programme guide carefully, and each select what they consider to be the most interesting and entertaining programmes. They should then use these to compile their own eight- to ten-hour TV guide for a new TV channel – one which for them would offer a great day's viewing and contain the programmes they would most like to watch.
4 Make it clear that they can select any programme from any of the

channels, but that their own TV guide should list them in descending order of preference. Tell them that they should copy out the titles of the programmes and any accompanying 'blurb' (a description or explanation) onto a sheet of paper, and they should also choose a suitable name for their new TV channel.

5 When they have finished, put your students into pairs or small groups and ask them to compare their TV guides. Tell them that they should explain their choice of programmes as well as their viewing order.

Cross-references

This can serve as a suitable follow-up for 7.2. The same materials can be used in 7.2. A quick oral version of 10.4 can serve as a suitable lead-in activity. For a suitable lead-in activity, see 4.1.

Box 27 **Sample programme guide**

BBC 1

6.30 MATCH OF THE DAY 7.45
Christopher Crocodile **7.50**
Teletubbies **8.30** Breakfast
with Frost **9.30** Lent in the
Park **10.15** See Hear **10.45**
Touched by an Angel **11.30**
CountryFile **12.00** On the
Record **1.00** EastEnders
**2.20 FILM: Gunfight at the
OK Corral** (1957) Western
with Burt Lancaster
**4.20 THE PINK PANTHER
SHOW 4.40** Tom and Jerry
4.50 The Clothes Show **5.15**
Antiques Roadshow **6.00**
News **6.20** Regional News
6.25 Songs of Praise **7.00**
Last of the Summer Wine
**7.30 AUNTIE'S NEW
BLOOMERS** Another batch
of celebrity cock-ups
8.00 BALLYKISSANGEL The
village is fiercely divided
over Quigley's latest plans
for Ballykay
8.50 NEWS; WEATHER
9.05 PLAYING THE FIELD Six-
part drama following a group
of Yorkshire women united by
friendship and their passion
for playing football
9.55 MATCH OF THE DAY FA
Cup sixth round highlights
10.35 OMNIBUS Profile of
American violin teacher
Roberta Guaspari-Tzavoras
11.30 HEART OF THE MATTER
12.10 THE SKY AT NIGHT
12.30 FILM: Zeppelin (1971)
Michael York tries to steal
airship plans during the
Great War
2.10 - 6.00 BBC NEWS 24
WALES **10.35** International
Scrum V **11.20** Omnibus **12.15**
Heart of the Matter **12.55** The
Sky at Night **1.15** Film: Zeppelin
3.00 - 6.00 Joins BBC News 24

BBC 2

6.10 OPEN UNIVERSITY 7.25
The Child in Mind **8.15** Suenos
- World Spanish **8.30** Rupert
8.35 Toonatics **9.10** The Little
Vampire **9.35** Peter Pan and
the Pirates **10.00** Grange Hill
10.25 The Wild House **10.55** No
Sweat **11.15** UK OK **11.45**
Robot Wars **12.15** Lee and
Herring's This Morning with
Richard Not Judy
1.00 AROUND WESTMINSTER
1.30 Sunday Grandstand **1.35**
Rallying **2.05** Basketball **2.45**
RallySprint **3.35** Figure Skating
4.45 Animal Zone **4.50** Watch
Out Monthly **5.20** Animal Zone
5.25 THE NATURAL WORLD A
film about wildlife which thrives
among the concrete and steel
skyscrapers of New York
**6.20 THE MONEY
PROGRAMME** Financial affairs
7.00 CRUFTS 98 Peter Purves
and Jessica Holm present the
remaining Toy, Utility and Gun
Dog competitions
**8.10 MAD COWS AND
ENGLISHMEN** Last of the
series breaks disturbing news
– especially for Europeans
smugly avoiding British beef
9.00 THE ENTERTAINMENT BIZ
Why are people prepared to
expose their deepest
problems on daytime talk
shows? In an attempt to find
out, the entertainment series
goes behind the scenes of two
of America's most popular –
the Ricki Lake and Jerry
Springer shows
9.50 A WOMAN CALLED SMITH
Essex girls Jean and Jean talk
about fun for women over 40
10.00 GETTING HURT First of
four dramas about people
driven by powerful emotions
stars Ciaran Hinds as a lawyer
whose affair with the wife of
the man he is defending
(played by Amanda Ooms)
leads to his destruction
11.45 FILM: Highway Patrolman
(1993) Bleak thriller from Repo
Man's Alex Cox
1.35 CLOSE 2.00 - 6.10 BBC
Learning Zone
WALES **1.00 - 1.30** Welsh Lobby

ITV

6.00 GMTV 8.00 Roadhog **9.25** Disney Club TV **10.15** Morning Worship **11.15** F1: Australian Grand Prix
1.20 NEWS 1.25 London Today **1.35** Up for the Cup Arsenal v Liverpool 1971
2.35 THE BIG MATCH: Arsenal v West Ham United FA Cup quarter-final action, followed by live coverage of the draw for the semi-finals
5.10 THE ROCK AND GOAL YEARS 5.40 Oddballs
6.10 LONDON TONIGHT
6.15 NEWS; WEATHER
6.30 MICHAEL BARRYMORE'S MY KIND OF MUSIC Another round of the musical quiz
7.30 CORONATION STREET Deirdre tries to cope with her worst nightmare – Jon has returned
8.00 TESS OF THE D'URBERVILLES Two-part adaptation of Thomas Hardy's tale of love and lust set in 19th-century England
10.00 THE CLIVE JAMES SHOW Guests include Oscar nominee Kate Winslet, actor and comedian Alan Davies and comedian Dave Allen
10.50 NEWS; WEATHER
11.05 F1: AUSTRALIAN GRAND PRIX 12.10 Theatreland **12.40** The Big Match Arsenal v West Ham **2.35** Not Fade Away **3.40** Judge Judy **4.20** ITV Nightscreen **5.30 - 6.00** Morning News

MERIDIAN as LWT except: 1.20 News **1.30** Meridian News **1.35** The Rock and Goal Years **2.05 - 2.35** Oddballs **5.10** Dogs with Dunbar **5.40** Rummage **6.10 - 6.15** Meridian News **10.50 - 11.05** News **12.10** Pier Pressure **12.40** The Big Match - FA Cup Replayed **2.35** Film: Dracula (1979) **4.30** ITV Nightscreen **5.00 - 5.30** Freescreen

> Due to a late kick-off in the football, the timings of other ITV afternoon programmes shown in People Magazine are also affected

CHANNEL 4

6.30 THE PINK PANTHER 6.55 Dig, Dug and Daisy **7.10** Trumpton **7.25** Sharky and George **7.55** Where on Earth Is Carmen Sandiego? **8.20** Pippi Longstocking **8.45** Rocko's Modern Life **9.20** Saved by the Bell - the New Class **9.45** Sister Sister **10.10** Happy Days **10.40** The Waltons **11.40** Hollyoaks
12.40 NBA 24/7 1.10 British Athletics **1.45** Football Italia **4.00** The Village
4.20 FILM: Blood Alley (1955) John Wayne in crude Red-baiting adventure
6.25 TIME TEAM REPEATS The best excavations of the last four series
7.30 HOWARD GOODALL'S CHOIR WORKS New series. The musical explorer travels the world in search of great choirs, starting in Bulgaria and Estonia
8.00 UNDRESSED - FASHION IN THE TWENTIETH CENTURY Series concludes by examining the relationship between sex and fashion
9.00 FATHER TED Long-awaited new run. It starts with Ted offending the Chinese community on Craggy Island
9.30 SLAP! - LOVE, LIES AND LIPSTICK New sitcom shuttles between the make-up floor of a Manchester department store and a nearby bank
10.00 FILM: Apocalypse Now (1979) Marlon Brando in chaotic war epic
12.50 FILM: The Walls (1989) Dark fable. With Ravi Vallathol
2.55 FILM: Beijing Bastards (1993) Drama from China
4.35 CRUCERO/CROSSROADS 5.05 Chinese Whispers **5.25** Off Limits **5.55 - 7.00** Sesame Street

from the *Sunday People*

7.2 Television programmes survey

Discovering what kind of programmes are shown in different countries

Level: Pre-Intermediate–Advanced

Preparation

Select a TV programme guide from an English-language newspaper (see Box 27 above for sample programme guide) and one from a newspaper from your students' own country. Deal with any vocabulary or language problems by adding a gloss (a translation or an explanation) where necessary. Make copies of both TV guides and cut them into individual TV channels. You will need enough copies for each student in the class to have one English-language channel and one channel from their own country.

In class

1 Brainstorm with the class all the different types of programme shown on television and write these on the board. This list could include the following:

Films	Music
Cartoons	Educational programmes
Weather reports	Sport
Documentaries	TV series (not comedy)
News	Soap operas
Current affairs	Children's programmes
Drama	Religious programmes
Comedy shows	Business
Talk shows	Politics
Situation comedies	Special interest (e.g. cookery, antiques,
Quiz shows	gardening)
Game shows	Other
Light entertainment	

2 Pair students and give each pair a copy of the day's programmes for one of the major English-language channels and one of the major channels from their own country. Explain that they are going to try to discover differences and similarities in the relative distribution of different kinds of programmes for the two countries.

3 Ask them to look at the programmes shown on both their channels and calculate how much time is given over to a particular type of

188

programme. They should note their findings (in hours/minutes) in the form of a grid (see Box 28 for sample grid) which you can write on the board for them to copy. They should calculate the total time for a particular programme type for each channel. In most cases, the title and any accompanying 'blurb' (i.e. a description or explanation) should help your students classify the different programmes, but tell your students to consult you if they are in doubt.

4 When your students have completed their grids, tell pairs with the same TV channels to check their results.

5 With the whole class, record their findings on the board. Extend the grid to include all the channels you are using in the survey. Ask each pair to call out the total amount of time allotted to each type of programme for their channels and write these in the appropriate spaces.

6 When the grid has been completed, add up the totals for each programme type for all the English channels and the non-English channels.

7 Discuss the results with your students and encourage them to interpret these results and draw conclusions about the distribution of different types of programme in each country.

Comment

If you are teaching a multinational group, ask students who have copies of newspapers from their countries to bring one in a day or two before the lesson. This will give you time to make copies of their newspaper TV programme guides.

Cross-references

The same materials can be used in 7.1. For a suitable follow-up activity, see 7.1.

Box 28 **Sample grid: television programmes survey**		
	Channel . . . . . . (Britain)	Channel . . . . . . (your country)
Films		
Cartoons		
Weather reports		
Documentaries		
News		
Current affairs		
Drama		
Comedy shows		
Talk shows		
Situation comedies		
Quiz shows		
Game shows		
Light entertainment		
Music		
Educational programmes		
Sport		
TV series (not comedy)		
Soap operas		
Children's programmes		
Religious programmes		
Business		
Politics		
Special interest (e.g. cookery, antiques, gardening)		
Other		

7.3 TV blurb

Writing the blurb for television programmes with ambiguous titles

Level: Pre-Intermediate–Post-Intermediate

Preparation

MAIN ACTIVITY

From a newspaper published in an English-speaking country (or from the Internet), compile a list of several ambiguous TV programme titles, i.e. where the content or subject-matter is unclear from the titles alone (see Box 29 for example programme titles). Avoid using any programmes which you think your students might know.

EXTENSION

If you have the accompanying 'blurbs' (i.e. descriptions or explanations) of the programmes you select, paste these onto a sheet of paper and make one copy of this sheet for each pair of students in the class.

In class

1 Write one or two examples of ambiguous TV programme titles on the board and ask your students to guess what the programmes are about. When they have run out of ideas, tell them the actual content of the programmes, explaining the link between the titles and the content.

2 Pair students, write the list of ambiguous TV programme titles on the board and tell each pair to copy it down. Explain that these are all genuine TV programme titles, but that the content of the programmes is unclear from the titles alone.

3 Tell your students that, in their pairs, they should discuss what the possible content of the programmes might be. When they have decided, they should write a one-sentence explanation (blurb) next to each title.

4 When your students are ready, put two pairs together. Ask them to compare their blurbs and explain their interpretations for each title.

5 With the whole class, read out each programme title in turn and ask your students to read aloud their blurbs. Discuss any particularly interesting ideas your students have come up with. If you wish, you can ask the class to vote on the most amusing, the most imaginative, or the most likely interpretations for each title.

6 Finally, if you know the content of the programmes relating to these

titles, tell your students. This can then lead into a discussion about the link between the programme titles and the accompanying blurbs: *Why this title? Is there a play on words? What is the connection between the title and the subject-matter? Do you like the title? Can you think of a better title?*

Variation

Ask each pair to exchange their blurbs (without programme titles) with another pair, who should try to match each one to an appropriate title from the list on the board.

Extension

Instead of telling your students the content of the programmes, give each pair of students a copy of the blurbs sheet and ask them to match these with the titles on the board.

Box 29 Example programme titles

1 *Only fools and horses*
2 *Goodnight sweetheart*
3 *Last of the summer wine*
4 *Porridge*
5 *One foot in the grave*

(These are all comedy programmes.)

7.4 Original titles

Finding the translated titles of English-language television programmes

Level: Pre-Intermediate–Advanced

Preparation

From an English-language newspaper, compile a sheet of English TV programme titles with accompanying 'blurbs' (i.e. descriptions or explanations). Choose a variety of programmes (e.g. quiz/game shows, TV series, films) which are being shown or have been shown recently in your students' country but make sure that the titles used in your students' country are not direct translations of the originals. Make one copy of this sheet for each group of three or four students in the class.

In class

1 Select one of the programmes from the programme titles sheet and write the original English title on the board. Ask your students if they know this TV programme, and if they have ever watched it. If they do not recognise it, read them the accompanying blurb. If they still do not know, give them a little more help by mentioning the names of one or two of the main characters, the place where the action takes place, or a brief scenario of the programme. If your students still cannot tell you, give them the name of the programme in their own language. They may be surprised by the way the original title has been translated, but avoid a lengthy discussion at this stage of the activity.

2 Put your students into groups of three or four and give each group a copy of the programmes sheet. Explain that this shows the original English titles for TV programmes which are well-known in their own country. Tell them that they should read the titles and accompanying blurb and try to think of the titles of the programmes in their own language.

3 When your students have done as many as they can, ask them to compare and share their answers with other groups.

4 With the whole class, check their answers by calling out the original English titles and asking your students to call out the titles in their own language.

5 Now write the following questions on the board:

What is the literal translation in your language of the original English title?
What is the translation in English of the title given to the programme as shown in your country?
Why do you think the original title was translated this way?
Which title do you prefer?

Ask your students to go back into their original groups to discuss these questions for several of the programmes.

6 Finally, choose one or two of the titles and hold an open discussion with the class, again using the focus questions.

Variation

If your students do not watch television regularly, write the titles in their own language on the board and ask them to try to match them with the original English-language titles.

7.5 Programme titles

Writing suitable titles for television programme blurbs

Level: Pre-Intermediate–Post-Intermediate

Preparation

From the TV programme guide of a newspaper, cut out a number of TV programmes, choosing those which have accompanying 'blurbs' (i.e. descriptions or explanations). The programmes you choose should not be immediately recognisable to your students as programmes they know. Remove the titles, paste (or copy) the blurbs onto a sheet of paper and number them for ease of reference. Deal with any problem vocabulary or language by adding a gloss (a translation or an explanation) where necessary, and make one copy of this sheet for each group of three students in the class. Keep the original titles for the final stage of the activity.

In class

1 To demonstrate the activity, write one of the TV programme blurbs on the board, and explain any new language. Ask your students to say what they think the programme is about, and ask them to suggest a suitable title for the programme.
2 Write your students' suggestions on the board and, when they have run out of ideas, ask the class to decide which title they think would be the most appropriate.
3 Now put your students into groups of three and give each group a sheet of TV programme blurbs.
4 Explain that these are TV programmes in need of suitable titles. Tell your students that they should read the blurbs carefully and discuss in their groups what title they think would be most suitable for each programme.
5 When all the groups are ready, work with the whole class to check their answers. Read out each blurb in turn and ask each group to

194

read aloud the title they have given it. Write all their suggestions on the board, and ask the class as a whole to vote for which title they think would be the most appropriate.

6 Finally, tell your students the original titles for the programmes and discuss with them how appropriate they think these titles are.

8 Cartoons and strip cartoons

8.1 Reading aloud in role

Reading strip cartoons aloud in role

Level: Elementary–Intermediate

Preparation

Compile a sheet with two or three strip cartoons. Each one should show two (or three) characters in conversation. Number each strip cartoon for ease of reference and make one copy of this sheet for each student in the class (see Box 30 for sample strip cartoons). Alternatively, to reduce photocopying, make an overhead-projector transparency of this sheet, large enough to be seen easily from the back of the class.

In class

1 Give each student a copy of the strip cartoons sheet and ask them to look at the first one. Deal with any vocabulary or language problems. With the class, discuss the setting, the situation, the relationship(s), the moods, the feelings and the thoughts of the characters, filling in likely background information about the characters as much as possible. You should also point out the use of typographical devices (e.g. bold or larger type) to show when a character is expressing strong emotions such as shock, anger or surprise.
2 Ask for volunteers to read the characters' parts. Coach them until they can perform the dialogue well, taking into account all the factors discussed in the previous stage. If you wish, you can repeat this with other students.
3 Choose another of the strip cartoons and discuss it in depth with the class (as in step 1). When your students are clear about the characters and the situation, put them into pairs (or groups of three) and give them a few minutes to prepare to read the dialogue aloud in role.
4 When they are ready, invite one pair to read their dialogue aloud to the class. Ask the class to offer help, advice and coaching as necessary

to help improve their performance. Repeat this reading-aloud stage with other pairs.

Cross-references

The same materials can be used in 8.2, 8.6, 8.7 and 8.8. For a more challenging version of this activity using the same materials, see 8.2. For a suitable lead-in activity, see 8.7. For suitable follow-up activities, see 8.6 and 8.8.

Box 30 **Sample strip cartoons**

from the *Daily Mail*

8.2 Acting out cartoons

Acting out strip cartoons

Level: Elementary–Intermediate

Preparation

See preparation guidelines for 8.1.

In class

1 Give each student a copy of the strip cartoons sheet and deal with any vocabulary or language problems.
2 Tell your students to look at the first strip cartoon. Read through it with the class and then discuss it in detail with your students – the situation, the setting, the mood, the characters, their feelings and their thoughts. Ask your students what they think led up to this situation and how they think it might continue, including the possible dialogue before the first picture and after the last picture.
3 Now ask for volunteers to act out the strip cartoon, and ask them to begin by getting into the same positions as the characters in the cartoon. You should take the role of director to coach your students through the scene, but encourage the rest of the class to help with this coaching role, giving help and advice with the way each character's lines should be spoken, their movements, gestures and facial expressions. When your volunteers feel ready, ask them to act out the scene in full.
4 Now form groups of four students and tell each group that they should choose one of the other strip cartoons and prepare it to act it out as the volunteers did in the demonstration. Tell them that within their groups, they should choose who will play the roles of actors or directors. Tell them that they can add dialogue which would be appropriate before and after the first and last pictures, but they must use the dialogue which appears in the strip cartoon.
5 Give groups enough time to prepare their performances thoroughly. While they are working, go from group to group reminding them that they should also adopt the posture, position and facial expressions of the characters.
6 When they are ready, ask groups to act out their strip cartoon to other groups or to the class. If you wish, invite comments from the audience about the performances they watch.

Comment

This activity is suitable with students who are comfortable with role-play and performing in front of their peers. It is also immense fun.

Cross-references

The same materials can be used in 8.1, 8.6, 8.7 and 8.8. For a less demanding version of this activity using the same materials, see 8.1. For a suitable lead-in activity, see 8.7. For suitable follow-up activities, see 8.6 and 8.8.

8.3 Matching captions

Finding matching cartoon pictures and captions

Level: Post-Elementary–Post-Intermediate

Preparation

Cut out a number of single cartoons covering either one particular theme or a variety of topics. You will need one cartoon with caption for each pair of students in the class. Separate the pictures from the captions, and paste the pictures onto small cards to make them easier to handle and more durable. Copy each caption onto a small individual card and deal with any vocabulary or language problems by adding a gloss (a translation or an explanation) where necessary. Store the pictures and the captions in two separate envelopes.

In class

1 Give half the students in your class the cartoon pictures and give the other half the cartoon captions. Tell them that they must not show these to each other.
2 Explain that each student has either a cartoon picture or caption and that the aim of the activity is for each student to find his/her matching picture or caption.
3 To do this, the students with pictures should describe their picture to the students with captions, who should read their caption aloud after they have heard a complete description of the picture. Tell your students that they should listen to all the descriptions before finally deciding who their partner is, as some pictures may be quite similar. This will certainly be the case if you use cartoons dealing with one particular theme.

4 When most students seem to have found their partners, stop the activity and check their matching pairs by asking each pair to display their cartoon picture and caption on the board for everyone to read. Explain any humour in the cartoons which your students have not understood.

Variation

For grouping students in threes or fours, use strip cartoons cut into separate pictures. Here, students have to find which other students hold pictures from the same strip cartoon story-line and also find their correct position in the story. If you use a mixture of different strip cartoons (e.g. Garfield, Andy Capp, Calvin and Hobbs), this will make the first part of this variation easier. For higher-level students, using several strip cartoons from the same series can make this variation extremely challenging.

Acknowledgement

My thanks to David Hill for pointing out his article (*Modern English Teacher* Vol. 10, No. 2, 1982) which includes a similar activity using newspaper cartoons. In his activity, each student is given a non-matching cartoon picture and caption, and tries to form a matching pair by exchanging either the picture or the caption with another student.

Cross-references

The same materials can be used in 8.7 and 8.8. For suitable follow-up activities, see 8.7 and 8.8.

8.4 Strip cartoon stories

Making sets of individual strip cartoon pictures and ordering them

Level: Pre-Intermediate–Intermediate

Preparation

Compile a sheet of five or more strip cartoons, each containing three or four pictures based on the same character(s) from different editions of the same newspaper. Make one copy of this sheet for each group of three students in the class. Cut the sheet of cartoon strips into individual pictures, jumble them up, and store each set of fifteen or more pictures in an envelope for safe-keeping. You should keep a copy of the original strip cartoons, as this will later serve as an answer key.

In class

1 Put your students into groups of three and give each group a set of the cut-up strip cartoons. Explain what each set consists of, and deal with any vocabulary or language problems at this stage.
2 Tell your students that the aim of the activity is to make complete cartoon strips, each one consisting of three or four pictures which, in the correct order, tell a story.
3 Begin the activity. While your students are working, go from group to group to give help where necessary, and to encourage them to speak in English.
4 As groups finish, ask them to check their answers with other groups in the class.
5 Finally, check through the answers with the class to confirm the correct order of pictures for each strip cartoon. Discuss with your students the linguistic and visual elements which helped them find sets of pictures and order them correctly. This is a good opportunity to explain any humour they were unable to understand.

Cross-references

The same materials can be used in 8.7 and 8.8. For suitable follow-up activities, see 8.6, 8.7 and 8.8.

8.5 Cartoon drills

Writing different endings to dialogue in strip cartoons

Level: Elementary–Intermediate

Preparation

Compile a sheet of several strip cartoons where the last speaker's utterance contains a structure or grammatical pattern your students need practice in. This is usually the punch line in strip cartoons (see Box 31 for example strip cartoons). With liquid paper, blank out the language you have decided to focus on. For example, if the last speaker's words are *Next time, I'm going to do it myself*, you should delete *do it myself* – in this case to give practice in *going to*. Number each cartoon for ease of reference and make one copy of this sheet for each pair of students in the class.

In class

1 Pair students and give each pair a copy of the strip cartoons sheet. Deal with any vocabulary or language problems at this stage of the activity.
2 Explain to your students that they should read each strip cartoon and complete the last utterance in as many ways as they can think of which would be appropriate within the context of the story.
3 When your students are ready, put two pairs together and ask them to compare their answers, eliminate any duplicate endings and produce one combined list of suggestions.
4 Finally, check your students' answers by asking pairs of students to read the strip cartoons aloud, adding their own endings. Write all their suggestions on the board and comment on the appropriateness and accuracy of their language.
5 Finally, tell your students the original endings to the dialogues.

Comment

This activity is a language drill in disguise, but because it is set within a meaningful context, it does to a certain extent overcome some of the inherent problems of decontextualised pattern practice drills.

Cross-references

The same materials can be used in 8.6, 8.7 and 8.8. For suitable follow-up activities, see 8.6, 8.7 and 8.8.

Box 31 **Example strip cartoons**

1

from the *Daily Mail*

2

© 1998 Paws, Inc

Complete cartoons

1

from the *Daily Mail*

2

© 1998 Paws, Inc

8.6 Strip cartoon narratives

Rewriting strip cartoons as short narratives

Level: Pre-Intermediate–Post-Intermediate

Preparation

Compile a sheet of several strip cartoons and make one copy of this sheet for each pair of students in the class. Alternatively, to reduce photocopying, make an overhead-projector transparency of the strip cartoons, large enough to be seen clearly from the back of the class.

In class

1 Pair students, give each pair a copy of the strip cartoons sheet and ask them to look at the first one. Deal with any vocabulary or language problems at this stage.
2 On the board, begin to write an appropriate opening sentence to tell the story of the strip cartoon, e.g. *It was a rainy Sunday afternoon, and Calvin was in his bedroom, lying on his bed, thinking* ... Do not finish the sentence. Instead, ask your students to suggest different ways to end it, and write their ideas on the board.
3 With the class, discuss all the alternatives they offer and, finally, agree together on the most suitable ending. Continue this procedure for the rest of the strip cartoon until you have a complete narrative. Any speaker's utterances should be included as reported speech in their narrative. It is also important to pay close attention to characters' facial expressions and body language, and include these in the narrative in an appropriate way, e.g. *with a bored look on his face, trying not to laugh,* and so on. The use of different typefaces (e.g. large, bold words) will also add important information about the person's feelings, e.g. *CALVIN!* would show that the speaker is shouting and is angry.
4 When you have completed the narrative, read through it with the class and make any improvements or embellishments to produce a polished version.
5 Now ask each pair to choose one of the other strip cartoons and, as before, rewrite it as narrative.
6 When they are ready, ask pairs who worked on the same strip cartoon to compare their narratives. If you wish, ask them to combine their ideas to produce one final version. These can then be displayed around the classroom for other pairs to read, or exchanged with pairs who worked on different strip cartoons.

7 Finally, discuss with the group whether they find the strip cartoon narratives as amusing as the strip cartoons they were based on. If not, why not? The point should come out clearly that the visual element is crucial to the humour in cartoons. You may be able to identify precisely those elements in the pictures which, in their original form as a strip cartoon, add to the humour, but which are lost in a narrative form.

Cross-references

The same materials can be used in 8.1, 8.2, 8.7 and 8.8. For a suitable lead-in activity, see 8.7. For a suitable follow-up activity, see 8.8. This activity can serve as a follow-up to 8.1, 8.2, 8.4 and 8.5.

8.7 What makes this English?

Identifying cultural references in cartoons

Level: Elementary–Advanced

Preparation

Using newspapers from one English-speaking country only (e.g. all British or all American), compile a sheet of single cartoons and/or strip cartoons (see Box 32 for sample cartoons), and number them for ease of reference. Make one copy of this sheet for each student in the class.

In class

1 Explain to your students that cartoons in one particular country often convey cultural information about that country. To demonstrate this, give each student a copy of the cartoons sheet and ask them to look at a particular cartoon – one in which you have already identified one or more features which are clearly culturally specific. Ask them to examine it closely and to decide if it could be a newspaper cartoon from their own country (aside from the fact that the cartoon is in English).
2 If their answer is 'No', it may be that aspects of the target-language culture feature in the cartoon. With the group, try to identify what these features are and which country the cartoon was published in.
3 With the class, try to compile a list of other possible cultural features which might be included in cartoons. This list might include (objects

in) interior or exterior scenes, people's physical appearance, dress and hairstyle, activities people are engaged in, particular ceremonies and special occasions, and so on. Write all their ideas on the board.

4 Form groups of three or four students. Ask them to look at the other cartoons on the sheet, and write a list of any culturally specific features they can find.

5 When all the groups are ready, bring the class together to discuss their findings. Deal with each cartoon in turn and ask your students to call out all the features they found which make the cartoon specific to the target-language culture.

Extension

For homework, ask your students to find single cartoons and strip cartoons from their own country's newspapers and write a list of any features they can find which make them specific to their own culture. Ask them to bring the cartoons to class and explain what culturally specific features they have found.

Variation

Depending on which newspapers you have easy access to and which national culture you wish to focus on, you might try this activity using local English-language newspapers, or newspapers from different English-speaking countries.

Cross-references

This can be used in combination with any of the other activities in this chapter. The same materials can be used in most of the other activities in this chapter.

Box 32 **Sample cartoons**

1

"When I said, 'Your sense of direction could drive a man to drink', it wasn't a request!"

from the *Sun*

2

'Now Daddy refuses to violate your human rights by smacking you ... but ...'

from the *Daily Mail*

3

THEY CLAIM YOU WHIPPED THEM ALL SOUNDLY AND SENT THEM TO BED.

4

from the *Daily Mail*

5

from the *Guardian*

8.8 Is this funny?

Evaluating the humour in cartoons

Level: Intermediate–Advanced

Preparation

Using newspapers from one English-speaking country only (e.g. all British or all Australian), compile a sheet of single cartoons (or strip cartoons), using the first ones you find rather than attempting to be selective. Number each cartoon for ease of reference and deal with any vocabulary of language problems by adding a gloss (a translation or an explanation) where necessary. Make one copy of this sheet for each group of three students in the class.

In class

1 Form groups of three students and ask your students to look at the first cartoon on the sheet. Ask your students to try to translate it. Write the translation they offer on the board, making sure that it is as accurate as possible.
2 Now ask your students to try to explain the humour in the cartoon and to decide if they think it is amusing or not. If they do not think it is amusing, ask them to explain why and to be as specific as possible. This may, of course, simply be a matter of the individual's sense of humour, so ask your students whether they think other people from their country might find it amusing. If they think not, it might be because the humour is too culturally specific and could not be appreciated by people from other cultural backgrounds.
3 Repeat this procedure with one or more of the other cartoons.
4 Now tell each group to discuss the other cartoons to answer the following questions, which you should write on the board:

> In which cartoons do you understand the humour?
> Do you think other people from your culture would also understand the humour?
> Do you personally find them amusing?
> Do you think other people from your culture would also find them amusing?
> In which cartoons don't you understand the humour? What do you think is the reason for this?

5 When your students are ready, work with the whole class to discuss

their findings. Dealing with each cartoon in turn, ask your students to answer the focus questions. If you can, you should try to explain any humour your students have failed to understand, as well as giving your own reactions to the cartoons.

Comment

This activity can be a step towards your students understanding the humour of the target-language community.

Cross-references

This can serve as a suitable follow-up to any of the other activities in this chapter.
The same materials can be used in most of the other activities in this chapter.

9 Weather forecasts

9.1 Predicting the weather

Predicting the forecast accompanying a weather map

Level: Elementary–Intermediate
Special equipment: overhead projector (OHP)

Preparation

MAIN ACTIVITY

Cut out a weather forecast which includes a map and make an enlarged
OHP transparency of it (see Box 33 for sample map and forecast).

EXTENSION

Write out the text of the weather forecast on a sheet of paper, but
include only the first letter of each word and spaces to represent the
missing letters in each word. Make one copy of this sheet for each pair
of students in the class.

In class

1 Show your students the weather map (masking the text of the
  forecast), explain any weather symbols they do not understand, and
  ask them to interpret the map as much as they can.
2 Tell your students that on the same transparency as the weather map
  is the accompanying text and that they should try to predict the exact
  wording of the forecast, using the map to help them.
3 Reveal the first word and ask your students to try to predict the next
  word, calling out their ideas. Show your students the first letter of the
  second word and then subsequent letters until they have guessed
  correctly. Continue this procedure for each word in the first line.
4 When you reach the end of the line, cover up the line and see how
  much your students can remember by helping each other to piece it
  together.

5 Continue this procedure for the other lines in the forecast, until you have elicited the whole text.

Variation

If you do not have access to an OHP, make photocopies of the weather map for your students and write the text on the board (word by word and letter by letter, as described above).

Extension

Put students into small groups and give each group a copy of the gapped text. Tell them to work together to rewrite the exact wording of the weather forecast. During this writing stage, allow your students to refer to the map.

When your students have done as much as they can, ask them to compare their texts with other groups. Finally, ask your students to check their versions against the original text.

Comment

You can repeat this activity at a later date, but with a weather forecast from a different time of the year. This will allow your students to practise different seasonal vocabulary.

Cross-references

This can serve as a suitable lead-in to 9.2 and 9.5. The same materials can be used for the introductory stages of both 9.2 and 9.5.

Box 33 **Sample forecast and map**

WEATHER

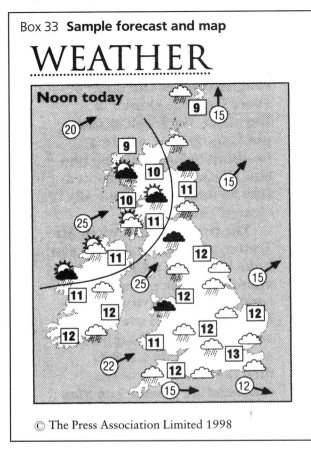

Rain over Northern Ireland and Scotland will be replaced by a mixture of sunshine and blustery showers for a time. The best of any sunshine will be in eastern Scotland with the heaviest showers in the west, and steadier rain will return to Northern Ireland before evening. England and Wales will be mostly cloudy with rain spreading to many areas, although the heaviest will be in the north. In the south-west it will be drizzly and the south-east will stay dry and quite bright for a while.

© The Press Association Limited 1998

9.2 Matching weather forecasts

Matching weather maps to weather forecasts

Level: Elementary–Intermediate
Special equipment: overhead projector (OHP)

Preparation

Cut out several weather forecasts which include maps and separate the maps from the texts. Paste half the maps and half the forecasts on one sheet, making sure they do not match, and label this sheet 'Student A'. Use the remaining maps and non-matching forecasts to compile another

214

sheet, and label this 'Student B'. Number all the items on one sheet and letter all the items on the second sheet for ease of reference. You will need one pair of these sheets for each pair of students in the class.

In addition, make an OHP transparency of an enlarged weather forecast with map (see Box 33 above for sample forecast and map). You will need this to familiarise your students with this type of text.

In class

1 With the whole class, elicit all the vocabulary and language they would expect to find in newspaper weather forecasts, and write their ideas on the board. Use this opportunity to teach new language related to weather and weather forecasts and to pre-teach any new vocabulary your students will see in the forecasts on the sheets.
2 Show your students the OHP transparency of the weather forecast and map and go through it with them, pointing out how the text is translated into the visual medium of the map. Focus also on the choice of language to be found in weather forecasts, particularly the use of the Simple Future tense as well as -*ing* forms.
3 Pair students and give one student in each pair a Student A sheet, and their partner a Student B sheet. Tell them not to show these to each other.
4 Explain that each student has several weather maps which match their partner's forecasts. Their task is to find the matching pairs of weather maps and forecasts.
5 Tell them that they can read their texts aloud to each other and describe their weather maps. When they think they have found a matching pair, they should make a note of the matching number and letter.
6 When your students are ready, check through the answers with the class by asking students to call out their matching pairs of weather forecasts and maps.

Variation

This activity can also be done as an individual reading/matching exercise by giving each student a copy of both Student A and Student B sheets.

Comments

(a) You can challenge higher-level students by using weather forecasts and maps from the same time of the year (e.g. the height of summer). This will mean that the forecasts should be quite similar, and it will be more difficult to find differences between them.

(b) This activity can be recycled at various times of the year to cover different seasonal weather vocabulary.

Cross-references

For a suitable lead-in activity, see 9.1. The materials used in 9.1 can be used for the introductory stages of this activity.

9.3 Weather-map dictation

Drawing in symbols on a weather map

Level: Elementary–Pre-Intermediate
Special equipment: overhead projector (OHP)

Preparation

Select a weather forecast which includes a map and remove the text. Make an enlarged photocopy of the map and, from this, make an OHP transparency. This will later serve as an answer key. Blank out all the symbols on the enlarged photocopy of the weather map and make a copy of this for each student in the class. Keep the text of the weather forecast to read aloud during the activity.

In class

1 On the board, draw the symbols which are typically found on weather maps, making sure you include all those used in the forecast you have chosen. Elicit the meaning of each of these symbols and write them on the board. Explain any symbols your students do not know and pre-teach any new vocabulary and language in the weather forecast you are using. This may include points of the compass (e.g. *north, north-east,* etc.) and, if you are using a weather map of Britain or Europe, the names of individual countries.
2 Give each student a copy of the enlarged weather map and explain that you are going to dictate the weather forecast which accompanied this map. As they listen, they should not write the text but should draw in the appropriate symbols in the correct places.
3 Read the forecast aloud at normal speed without pausing, and repeat your dictation as often as you feel necessary to give your students adequate time to draw in the symbols.
4 At the end of the dictation, ask your students to compare their maps with a partner.

5 Finally, show your students the OHP transparency of the weather map showing the symbols and their position. Ask your students to check their own maps and make any corrections necessary. Go over any points which your students found difficult.

9.4 Temperature drills

Answering questions about temperature ratings

Level: Elementary–Pre-Intermediate

Preparation

Select a world weather guide which lists major cities in the world and indicates their maximum and minimum temperatures for the day (see Box 34 for sample world weather guide). Make one copy of this for each student in the class.

In addition, prepare a list of questions (with answers for your own reference) based on the information in the weather guide (see Box 35 for example questions).

In class

1 Give each student a copy of the weather guide and let them study it for a few moments. To help students focus on the text, ask them two or three questions to give them practice in locating information (e.g. *What's the temperature in Oslo today? Name a city where the temperature is 21 degrees centigrade*).
2 Explain that you will now ask them more questions (e.g. Yes/No, Wh- and True/False) based on the weather guide. As soon as they find the answer, they should call it out.
3 Begin asking your questions. When one student has called out the correct answer to a question, give the other students time to find where the answer was located.
4 Continue this procedure until you have run out of questions, or until your students have run out of steam.

Extension

Ask your students to prepare their own questions to put to other students using a different weather guide. This will give them useful practice in producing these structures.

Variation

A similar activity can be made using other types of tabular information such as football match results or stock-market prices.

Comment

Questions based on a table of temperatures can give useful practice in comparative and superlative structures. As in a language drill, a particular structure can be used over and over again by simply sub-stituting the names of different cities each time.

Box 34 **Sample world weather guide**

WORLD YESTERDAY
(LOCAL LUNCHTIME REPORTS)

	C	F			C	F
Algiers .....F	14	57		Luxor ......S	21	70
Amsterdam ..F	9	48		Madrid C	9	48
Athens .....F	13	55		Malaga ......F	16	61
Barcelona ...F	12	54		Malta ......F	17	63
Beirut .....F	15	59		Mecca ......F	30	86
Belfast .....F	6	43		Melbourne ...S	19	66
Belgrade ....S	15	59		Miami ......F	19	66
Berlin ......F	7	45		Milan ......R	5	41
Biarritz .....T	13	55		Montreal n/a-17		1
Bombay .....S	31	88		Moscow SN-2		28
Brussels ....R	9	48		Nairobi ....F	24	75
Budapest ...F	10	50		New Delhi ...S	16	61
Cairo ......F	18	64		New York ...S	-3	27
Cardiff .....F	9	48		Nice C	12	54
Casablanca ..S	17	63		Oslo ....R	3	37
Copenhagen .R	5	41		Palma ......F	14	57
Corfu ......F	14	57		Paris C	9	48
Dublin ......S	7	45		Peking ......S	8	46
Dubrovnik ...C	11	52		Perth ......S	26	79
Edinburgh ...S	8	46		Prague .....F	3	37
Faro ....S	17	63		Rhodes .....S	15	59
Florence ....F	11	52		Rome ......T	11	52
Geneva .....F	10	50		Singapore ...F	32	90
Gibraltar ....F	16	61		Stockholm ..R	2	36
Guernsey ...R	10	50		Sydney .....S	29	84
Helsinki C	-3	27		Tangier .....F	15	59
Hong Kong ..C	22	72		Tel Aviv ....F	16	61
Innsbruck ...S	12	54		Tenerife C	20	68
Istanbul .....S	10	50		Tokyo C	10	50
Jersey ......F	10	50		Toronto ....F	-2	28
Johan'burg ..R	15	59		Tunis ......F	17	63
Larnaca ....S	15	59		Vancouver ..C	3	37
Las Palmas ..C	21	70		Venice C	6	43
Lisbon ......R	15	59		Vienna C	1	34
London C	9	48		Warsaw .....S	3	37
Los Angeles .S	18	64		Wellington ..n/a20		68

S-Sun, F-fair, C-Cloud, R-Rain, Fg-Fog, Sn-Snow, T-Thunder

from the *Daily Mail*

Box 35   **Example questions**

Yes/No questions

Is Beirut hotter/colder than Corfu?
Is it (nearly) the same temperature / as hot / as cold in Athens as in Nice?
Are both Vienna and Warsaw as hot / cold as Vancouver?
Are both Malta and Mecca hotter/colder than Innsbruck?

Wh-questions

Where is it hotter/colder? London or Berlin?
Which is the hottest/coldest city today?
Which place is as hot/cold as London?

True/False questions

London is hotter/colder than Berlin.
Paris is not as hot as Vienna.
It's (nearly) the same temperature in Milan as in Peking.
Neither Warsaw nor Dublin is as hot/cold as Venice.
Neither Cairo nor Lisbon is hotter/colder than Wellington.
Both Algiers and New York are as hot/cold as Toronto.
Both Istanbul and Athens are hotter/colder than Nice.

9.5 Writing forecasts

Writing weather forecasts

Level: Intermediate–Post-Intermediate

Preparation

On a sheet of paper, paste a weather forecast with its map and make one copy of this for each student in the class. You will use this to introduce the activity.

In addition, find another weather forecast with accompanying map. Remove the forecast and make one copy of the weather map only for each student. Keep the forecast for the final stages of the activity.

If possible, you should choose weather forecasts from the same newspaper, as each newspaper has its own 'house' style.

For this activity, you will also need several marker pens and sheets of A3 paper.

In class

1 Give each student a copy of the complete example weather map and forecast sheet, and go through it carefully with your students, pointing out the main features of this type of text, e.g. the use of tenses, choice of vocabulary, sentence length and structure, and the use of linking words.

2 Next, give each student a copy of the weather map and ask them to write a weather forecast to accompany it. Tell them that they should use the example text as a model, and they should make sure that their own text is about the same length.

3 When your students have finished this writing stage, pair students and ask them to compare their versions. Tell them that they should try to agree on one version.

4 When your students are ready, put two pairs together and again ask them to compare their forecasts and agree on one final, polished version.

5 When all the groups have each agreed on one text, ask a representative from each group to copy their forecast onto a sheet of A3 paper, large enough for everyone to read clearly.

6 Display all the forecasts and discuss each one with the class in terms of its correctness, i.e. in terms of the weather map it accompanies and in terms of its grammatical accuracy. Try to decide with the class which forecast they think is the best according to these criteria.

7 Finally, write the original matching forecast on the board for your students to compare with their own texts. Ask them to look particularly closely for any information contained in this forecast which they failed to include in their own versions.

Cross-references

For a suitable lead-in activity, see 9.1. A quick oral version of 10.4 can serve as a suitable lead-in activity. The materials used in 9.1 can be used for the introductory stages of this activity.

10 The whole newspaper

10.1 Newspaper reading corner

Creating a newspaper reading corner to encourage reading for pleasure

Level: Elementary–Advanced

Preparation

Compile a collection of short items (e.g. headlines, sports results, horoscopes, cartoons, short articles, recipes, etc.) from all different sections of the newspaper. Choose items that will be of interest to your students, appropriate for their level and take no more than two or three minutes to read.

Pin up the items you have chosen on part of a wall in the classroom which you designate (and label) as the Newspaper Reading Corner.

This is an on-going activity; the Newspaper Reading Corner can be regularly updated by changing one or two items every day.

For a class of lower-level students, it will help if you add a gloss (a translation or an explanation) for key vocabulary and language which may cause problems.

In class

1 On the day you choose to begin the Newspaper Reading Corner, arrive in the classroom a few minutes before your students to have it set up and ready. As your students enter the classroom, invite them to visit the Newspaper Reading Corner and read the items on display.
2 Tell your students that there will be new items there every time they come to the classroom, and they should remember to look there when they have a few spare moments.
3 You should also encourage your students to add other English-language newspaper items which they find and think may be of interest to the rest of the class.

Comment

This is an ideal way of occupying early finishers or students who arrive for the lesson early, and your students should soon get into the habit of going to this spot to see what new items there are to read. The key to its success is to choose items which are light and of real interest and relevance to your students, and to keep reminding them to check it every day for new additions until it does, indeed, become a habit and something they look forward to reading.

Cross-references

Many of the items you include in the Newspaper Reading Corner can be used in other activities in this book. The benefit of this is that your students should already be familiar with the materials when you come to use them in an activity.

10.2 Where's the story about ...?

Fast reading to answer general content questions

Level: Elementary–Intermediate

Preparation

On walls or desktops around the classroom, display ten or more separate pages from different sections of one or more newspapers. You should number these pages clearly with a bold marker pen, and all the pages should be spaced well apart to avoid bottlenecks during the activity.

In addition, make up one question for one item on each page you are using. Your questions should focus on understanding the general content of the items you choose, and your questions should be worded in the following way:

1 Where's the story about a famous painting that has been stolen?
2 Where's the story about an American golfer winning an international competition?
3 Where's the story about a bank which is in financial trouble?

For your own reference, you should also make up an answer key showing the relevant page number and article headline.

In class

1 Ask your students to walk around the classroom for a few minutes looking at all the pages on display. Their aim is to get a very general idea of the content of each page and to try to remember where these pages are located in the classroom.
2 Bring all your students into the centre of the room, or any point where the newspaper pages are too far away to be read. Divide the class into teams, with between three and four students in each team.
3 Explain that you will call out a question on the general content of the articles, and the first person in each team should run to the newspaper pages and try to find the matching article. They should call out the page number and read out the headline. The first person to get the correct answer scores two points for their team.
4 Explain any key vocabulary in each question before you read it aloud.
5 Begin the activity, keeping each team's score on the board. Make sure that all team members take turns at trying to answer your questions. You can allow fellow team members to call out any help to the searching students as this will add excitement and impetus to the activity.
6 If a question is causing real difficulty, call back the searchers after allowing them a reasonable amount of time to find the answer, and repeat the question later in the activity. By then, your students will be more familiar with the materials and will stand a better chance of locating the answer.
7 At the end of the activity, add up each team's points to find the winners. Deal with any questions which your students were unable to find the answers to.

Cross-references

The same materials can be used in 10.3.

10.3 Find someone who ...

Fast reading to answer *Find someone who...* questions

Level: Post-Elementary–Intermediate

Preparation

Select ten or more newspaper pages and make up a *Find someone who ...* question sheet (suited to the level of your students) with between ten and twenty questions based on the people mentioned in the newspaper pages (see Box 36 for example questions). Make one copy of this sheet for each student in the class, as well as an answer sheet for your own reference.

For lower-level students, you may wish to renumber the newspaper pages with a bold marker pen and include on the question sheet the page number where each answer can be found. Display the newspaper sheets around the classroom on walls or desktops.

In class

1 Give each student a copy of the *Find someone who* ... question sheet and read through it with your students to check that they understand the questions.
2 Tell your students that the answers to these questions can be found somewhere on the newspaper pages displayed around the classroom.
3 Set a reasonable time limit and tell your students that they should answer as many questions as they can within this period.
4 At the end of the time limit, check your students' answers and deal with any questions they could not find the answers to.

Extension

Ask your students to make up their own questions for other students to answer. Rather than getting your students to use a *Find someone who* ... format, ask them to write a mixture of Yes/No and Wh-questions (e.g. *Can shoppers buy British beef now? How much do university students in Britain pay for their tuition? Which pop star sold his London home recently?*). This will give your students valuable practice in forming questions. You should insist that they produce an answer sheet so that they can check other students' answers quickly and easily.

Variation

If you are dealing with a particular topic in your lessons, ask questions about news items which are related to that topic. This can be an interesting way to introduce the subject. If, for example, you are dealing with the topic of law and order, you might ask questions such as the following:

1 What crime was Thomas Harding convicted of?
2 Have the police caught the man who mugged a shopper in Luton on Thursday?

3 Who was sentenced to three years in prison for his part in an armed raid on a High Street bank?

Cross-references

The same materials can be used in 10.2.

Box 36 Example questions

1 Find someone who smokes long, thin cigars.
2 Find someone who scored two goals against Manchester United.
3 Find someone who won £2.6 million on Saturday.
4 Find someone who married the son of 1960s pop star Donovan.

10.4 Vocabulary race

Fast reading to answer vocabulary questions

Level: Elementary–Advanced

Preparation

Fill a sheet of paper with extracts from various different sections of a newspaper, using as wide a selection of materials as possible, e.g. horoscopes, articles, advertisements and cartoons. It is not necessary to use complete items but it is important to fill the sheet with text. You will need one copy of this sheet for each student in the class.

In addition, make up twenty vocabulary questions based on lexical items in the newspaper extract (see Box 37 for example questions). You should also make up an answer sheet for your own reference.

The higher your students' level, the more demanding you can make the questions by including idioms, colloquialisms, phrasal verbs and so on. If you wish, you can also include vocabulary items in your students' mother tongue and ask them to find the English equivalents.

In class

1 Write the vocabulary questions on the board and read through them with your students to check that they understand them.
2 Give each student a copy of the newspaper text sheet and ask them to look through it quickly.
3 Tell your students that this is a vocabulary race and that they have

225

ten minutes (or other reasonable amount of time) to find answers to as many of the questions on the board as they can. The person who answers the most questions correctly in the time allowed is the winner.

4 Tell your students that they are allowed to use dictionaries and that they should make a written note of their answers.

5 Stop the activity at the end of the time limit (or earlier if everyone has finished) and check the answers with the class to find the winner. Deal with any questions which caused your students problems.

Extension

In a future lesson, ask your students to make up their own vocabulary question sheets for their partner to answer, perhaps competing with each other to be the first to finish.

Variation 1

Rather than writing the questions on the board, read the questions aloud to the class. This will certainly add more urgency to the competition, and can encourage your students to look for the answers more quickly.

Variation 2

Repeat the activity in a future lesson, but instead of concentrating only on vocabulary, ask your students to look for grammatical items or features, such as an example of a Conditional sentence, a prepositional phrase or a Present Perfect construction.

Cross-references

This can also serve as a quick oral follow-up to 2.1, 2.5, 2.9, 3.4, 4.1, 4.17 and 4.19. A quick oral version of this activity can serve as a suitable lead-in to 1.1, 4.17, 4.19, 5.2, 6.3, 6.5, 6.7, 7.1, 9.5 and many of the activities in Chapter 2.

Box 37 **Example questions**

Look through the newspaper items and find . . .

1   a country in Europe
2   something you can ride
3   a way of walking
4   another word for 'expensive'
5   an animal
6   the end of this expression: 'Like a bull in a china . . .'

10.5 Matching contents

Matching newspaper extracts to different sections in the contents listing

Level: Post-Elementary–Intermediate

Preparation

From one newspaper, tear out a snippet from every section which is included in the contents listing of that newspaper. These should not be complete items – just a small extract of each should be enough for students to recognise the type of text or subject-matter. Altogether, these may fill three or four sheets of (A4) paper. Number each item for ease of reference and display the sheets around the room on walls or desktops. They should not be readable from where your students are sitting. It is wise to make several copies of each sheet you display and space them well apart to prevent bottlenecks during the activity.

In addition, cut out the contents listing from the same newspaper, enlarge it if necessary to make it easier to read, and make one copy for each pair of students in the class. Alternatively, you can write this on the board and ask your students to copy it.

In class

1   Pair students and give each pair a copy of the contents listing. Check that the meaning of each section is clear by asking your students what they would expect to find there.
2   Explain that the sheets around the room contain one small extract from each of the different sections of the newspaper mentioned in the contents.
3   Explain that one student from each pair should go to the sheets, look

227

at them quickly, return to their partner, and try to match any item they can with the appropriate section of the contents. They should write the number of the item next to the relevant section on their contents sheet.

4 Make it clear that only one student from each pair should be looking at the sheets at any one time – their partner must wait (with the contents listing) until they return. Tell them that this is a team competition: the pair that match the most items correctly within a time limit of ten minutes (or other reasonable length of time) are the winners. Tell your students that they and their partner can change roles at any time they wish.

5 Stop the activity at the end of the time limit – or before if everyone has run out of steam. Check the answers with the class to find the winning pair and to deal with any items they were unable to match.

Comment

Teachers often tell students not to read every word in a fast-reading exercise and also that it is not important to understand every word of a text to complete a given exercise. In practice, however, students often pore over a text, which runs counter to the very purpose of such exercises. The use of incomplete newspaper items in this activity is an attempt to overcome this problem by making it impossible for students to read a text from beginning to end. The competitive element also adds urgency to the activity and helps to ensure that it is done at speed.

Cross-references

This can serve as a suitable lead-in to 10.7. For a suitable lead-in activity, see 10.6.

10.6 Newspaper language race

Understanding newspaper-related language

Level: Post-Elementary–Pre-Intermediate

Preparation

Make up a vocabulary list of up to twenty items related to the language of newspapers (see Box 38 for sample vocabulary list).

For each item, you will need to find one separate page of a newspaper which contains an example of the item. For instance, for *strip cartoon* you will need to find a page which actually contains a strip cartoon – not the words *strip cartoon* themselves. You should circle the strip cartoon with a brightly coloured marker pen. In total, you will need twenty newspaper pages. Finally, number all the pages clearly for ease of reference, and display the newspaper pages on walls or desktops.

In class

1 Write your vocabulary list on the board, put your students into pairs, and tell each pair to make a copy of the list. Explain that these are all words related to newspapers, and that they will be useful words to know when talking about newspapers.
2 Tell your students that on the numbered newspaper pages around the room, you have circled one strip cartoon, one caption, one competition, and so on. Your students' task is to match these circled items with the corresponding word(s) on their list and to write the appropriate page number.
3 Tell your students that this is a race and that they have five minutes (or other reasonable amount of time) to match as many of the items as they can. The pair with the most correct answers at the end of the time limit will be the winners.
4 Stop the activity promptly at the end of the time limit and check the answers with the whole class. Award one point to each pair for a correct answer and deal with any items your students were unable to match.
5 Finally, ask each pair to add up their scores to find the winners.

Comment

It is helpful to do this activity with a class in the early stages of working with newspapers. It introduces your students to language which will be useful when doing activities with newspapers and talking about newspapers.

Cross-references

This can serve as a suitable lead-in to 10.5, 10.16 and 10.17.

Box 38 **Sample vocabulary list**

	page number
1 strip cartoon	....
2 front page	....
3 puzzle	....
4 byline	....
5 masthead	....
6 headline	....
7 paragraph ‘	....
8 gossip column	....
9 caption	....
10 column	....
11 journalist	....
12 public announcement	....
13 quotation	....
14 feature	....
15 circulation figure	....
16 article	....
17 competition	....
18 editorial	....
19 advertising slogan	....
20 weather map	....

© Cambridge University Press 1999

10.7 Page numbers

Matching sections of a newspaper to the pages where they can be found

Level: Post-Elementary–Intermediate

Preparation

Bring to class a number of different complete newspapers with their contents listings removed or covered up. You should note that broadsheet newspapers (see note in 1.1) usually have a contents listing, whereas most tabloid newspapers do not. You will need one complete newspaper for each pair of students in the class. Keep any contents listings you have removed for the final stage of the activity.

In class

1 Brainstorm with your students the titles and content of the different sections that can be found in newspapers. Write their suggestions on the board.
2 Pair students, and give each pair a complete newspaper. Tell them that they should go through their newspaper and find out on which page(s) each of the sections on the board can be found. Their aim is to produce a contents listing for their newspaper following the order of the pages.
3 Tell them that they should add to their contents listing any other sections they find in their newspapers which are not included on the board. Explain also that there may be sections on the board which their particular newspaper does not contain.
4 While the activity is in progress, go from group to group to help with any vocabulary or language problems as they arise. You should also allow your students to use bilingual dictionaries.
5 When your students have finished, give each pair the original contents listing from their newspaper to compare with their own.

Variation 1

Before giving each pair the original contents listing, ask them to exchange their newspaper and completed contents listing with another pair to check. Tell them that they should discuss and try to correct any discrepancies they find.

Variation 2

Delete or cut off the page numbers from the pages of each newspaper. Divide each newspaper into separate sheets and give a set to each pair in a jumbled order with an intact, complete contents listing from their newspaper. Their task is to reassemble the newspaper according to the listing and to write the correct page number on each page.

Cross-references

For a suitable lead-in activity, see 10.5.

10.8 Looking for numbers

Finding different types of number in newspapers

Level: Elementary–Advanced

Preparation

Bring to class one or two newspapers separated into individual pages. You will need enough for each student in the class to have at least one page.

In class

1 Brainstorm with your students all the different types of numbers they can think of (e.g. temperatures, percentages, ordinal and cardinal numbers) and write a list of their ideas on the board.
2 To demonstrate the activity, take the front page of a newspaper and show your students that here they could find a date (e.g. Thursday 19 March 1998), a circulation figure (e.g. 46,850), a price (in 51 different currencies!) and several other different types of number.
3 Now give each student one or two of the newspaper pages and explain that they should look through their page(s) and try to find as many different types of number (written numerically) as they can.
4 Tell them that they only need one example of each type of number, but they should make a note of what type of number it is (e.g. 3–1 = a football score, 23% = a percentage, 22 °C = a temperature).
5 Begin the activity. Allow about ten minutes for this number-gathering stage. While your students are working, circulate to help with any vocabulary or language problems as they arise.

6 When all your students have a collection of numbers, ask them to call out the different categories of number they found, e.g. telephone numbers, tennis scores, etc. As they do so, write each category in bold capital letters on a separate sheet of paper.

7 Now display the number category sheets around the classroom and ask your students to add the examples they found to the appropriate sheet. Ask them to write clearly using quite large lettering.

8 By the end of this stage of the activity, you should have many examples of different types of number. These sheets can be used immediately or in future classes for repetition drills, practice in reading aloud, say the number and touch activities, and number dictations with your students.

Comment

Saying, understanding and writing numbers are notoriously difficult for language students at all levels, and newspapers provide a particularly rich and varied source of numbers for language practice activities.

Cross-references

Many of the materials used in other activities in the book can be used in this activity.

10.9 Pattern banks

Finding examples of grammatical patterns

Level: Elementary–Advanced

Preparation

Make a list of grammatical words, patterns and structures your students have met but which need consolidating, new ones you are now working on, or ones which are still causing your students difficulty. For example, for lower-level students, your list might include the following: *ago*, articles (*a, the*), *some, any, going to, say, tell* and time expressions (*in, on, at*). For higher-level students, your list might include *for, during, since, while, wish, should have* and passive forms (*was reported, is said to*).

Choose one of these items and write it clearly and boldly on a sheet of A3 paper. This is the pattern-bank sheet.

In addition, bring to class a supply of newspapers, and even single newspaper sheets.

In class

1 Show your students the pattern-bank sheet and explain to them that their task is to find examples of this grammar point in the newspapers.
2 Tell your students that they should look through the newspapers and, when they find an example of the grammar point, they should copy the complete sentence onto the pattern-bank sheet clearly and legibly. They should also underline the grammar point in question in their example sentences so that it stands out.
3 Begin the activity. While your students are working, check that they are copying their examples correctly. Deal with any vocabulary or language problems as they arise.
4 Stop this language-gathering stage when your students have found several examples of the grammar point.
5 Work with the whole class and use the sheet as the basis for a grammar lesson. For example, if you have enough examples, you can ask your students to look for any underlying regularity and/or try to deduce a rule (e.g. *during* + noun clause, *while* + verb clause, *ago* + Simple Past or Past Progressive). With higher-level students, a pattern bank can be used as the basis for a discussion about the grammar point in question, e.g. the possible tenses used after *wish*.

Extension

In future lessons, work on other language points to produce pattern banks, perhaps even working on more than one in the same lesson.

As this is an on-going activity, work on the pattern banks can continue whenever you have time to fill, or could perhaps even be given as a homework. New pattern-bank sheets covering different points of grammar can be added as others are completed and dealt with.

Comment

An important aspect of this activity is that all the examples will have been taken from authentic materials and will have been found by the students themselves. Because of this investment on their part, your students may be more motivated to work with their examples than with anonymous textbook examples.

Cross-references

Many of the materials used in other activities in this book can be used in this activity.

10.10 Happy news

Compiling a happy-news sheet

Level: Elementary–Intermediate

Preparation

Bring to class a supply of old newspapers and even leftover, part-pages of newspapers. You will also need several pairs of scissors, glue and sheets of A3 paper. In addition, make a copy of the instruction sheet (see Box 39) for each student in the class.

Before you use this activity, go through a newspaper and cut out examples of what, for you, are positive items, e.g. an amusing photo, a story with a happy ending, a headline word which has a positive connotation for you, a weather forecast which predicts good weather over the coming week.

In class

1 Demonstrate the activity by showing your students the newspaper items which you have selected and explaining why you find them to be positive.
2 Spread out all the newspapers and give your students a few minutes to look through them. Tell them to make a mental note of anything positive they find.
3 Give each student a copy of the instructions sheet which explains the activity and read through this with the class, checking carefully that they understand what to do.
4 Begin the activity. Circulate while your students are working to help with any vocabulary and language problems as they arise.
5 Stop the activity when your students' sheets are relatively full and ask them to display their happy-news sheets around the classroom.
6 Ask your students to walk around and read each other's work. Many things may need explaining to the readers, and you should encourage them to ask the 'publishers' to clarify or explain anything they do not understand.
7 Finally, ask your students to decide which other students' happy-news sheets they enjoyed reading and found positive or optimistic.

Variations and extensions

In a future lesson or as an alternative to finding only happy news, this activity can be applied to gathering items which accord with many other criteria:

> anything that includes certain words (e.g. related to a particular sport);
> anything that includes information on a certain country;
> anything that is sad, amazing, shocking;
> anything that includes certain grammatical structures.

Another possibility is for your students to conduct a survey to discover how many news items in one particular newspaper are 'positive', how many are 'negative' and how many are 'neutral'. This can also be extended by comparing the news content of a tabloid and that of a broadsheet newspaper in the same terms (see note in 1.1).

Comment

Inevitably, this activity will leave the room strewn with more litter than the average waste-paper basket can cope with. It is wise to be armed with a large bin liner.

Box 39 **Happy-news instructions**

Happy news

Newspapers are often full of sad, depressing, shocking and tragic news. This is your chance to change all that and use the newspapers you have looked through to 'publish' your own one-page HAPPY-NEWS sheet!

READ THESE INSTRUCTIONS CAREFULLY BEFORE YOU BEGIN.

1 Cut out ANYTHING you find in the newspaper sheets which you find to be happy, positive or optimistic. You can use words, phrases, headlines, parts of texts, photographs, jokes, cartoons and advertisements.

2 Nothing you use should be bigger than 6cm × 10cm – about the size of an audio-cassette insert.

3 Your happy-news sheet should include at least 10 different items and these should be a mixture of text and visual material.

4 Paste the items you have chosen onto a sheet of A3 paper, making the layout as attractive and as interesting as possible.

5 Give your happy-news sheet a title and write your name on it.

YOU HAVE ABOUT . . . . MINUTES TO DO THIS.

© Cambridge University Press 1999

10.11 Personal collages

Creating a personal collage using newspaper items

Level: Pre-Intermediate–Post-Intermediate

Preparation

Before the lesson, prepare a collage about yourself on a sheet of A3 paper using different newspaper items (a mixture of text and visual material). Your collage should give personal information about yourself – your past, present and future, your hobbies and interests, things you like, things which are important to you, your lifestyle, your concerns, and so on (see Box 40 for author's personal collage and explanatory notes).

In addition, bring to class a supply of newspapers and even single newspaper sheets, as well as glue, several pairs of scissors, and sheets of A3 paper.

In class

1 To demonstrate the activity, show your students your own collage, and explain that this contains information about you. Invite them to interpret the information they see there. Each time they guess something correctly, say something more about it to give some additional background information. Encourage your students to ask you questions about any points they do not immediately understand. Finally, explain any items they were unable to interpret.

2 Explain to your students that they should now go through the newspapers and make their own personal collages, using a mixture of visuals and text from any parts of the newspaper. The most important thing is that whatever they choose to include should be true, should tell people something about them, and should be something they feel comfortable talking about.

3 As your students are working on their collages, move around the room giving help with any problems concerning vocabulary or language as they arise.

4 When your students have completed their collages, form small groups of three or four students. Ask them to talk about, explain, interpret, and ask about the items on their collages as you did with your own in the demonstration.

5 Allow some time for this exchange, and then either form new groups to repeat this discussion stage, or ask your students to display their

collages around the classroom. Invite your students to read each other's work, and tell them to ask the owners to explain anything they do not understand. The collages can then be left on display to personalise and brighten up your classroom.

Comment

This activity can work well both at the beginning of a course with a new group of students, or even with an established group.

If you feel that the preparation of the collages will take too much time in class, give each student a newspaper, and ask them to prepare their personal collages for homework and bring them to the next lesson.

Cross-references

For a similar activity using only newspaper headlines, see 1.11.

Box 40 **Author's personal collage**

1

2

3 **Is it Time for a new TV?**

4 **Is it Art? Draw your own conclusions.**

5

6

The Royal Ballet

12–16 January
Romeo and Juliet

7

8

PISCES Feb 20-Mar 20

9

24 Staunch suppor
26 She wept as I
   going round the o
27 Fellows with mode
   retreat first—it wa
   assistance in the cri
28 Make little effort to
   oneself? (4,6,4)

10

Spring in Paris

...Mongolia is largely treeles~
My evening was in Paris, indulging all the city's romantic clichés. Sunset would be enjoyed from the steps of Sacré-Cœur, with all Paris spread beneath our feet. There would be Champagne cocktails at Harry's Bar, a performance of *Madame Butterfly* at the Opéra Garnier, dinner at La Coupole, a late-night tango bar off the boulevard de Sebastopol, an even later-night dance hall in Bastille, and finally a walk along the banks of the Seine at dawn beneath the Pont des Arts and the Pont Neuf.

© The Telegraph plc, London 1995

11 # addicts of the Internet

Explanatory notes

1 This reminds me of the fact that I can't swim. I suppose I should learn, really, because I've been saved from drowning twice already. Perhaps next time there'll be nobody around, and I won't be so lucky!

2 I hate mobile phones! They are the most annoying thing I know. Worst of all is when somebody you're with receives a call and then ignores you for the next 15 minutes!

3 It was a strange coincidence to find this headline. Just the week before, my faithful old television set broke down. It couldn't be repaired, so I decided simply to live without it. I soon discovered what a telly-addict I had become. After a week of torture, I gave in and bought another one.

4 This headline reminds me of my own attempts at art over the years, and something important I discovered: I wasn't very good at it! But one Christmas I did make a collage for some friends, using labels from teabag sachets. It's still hanging there on their kitchen wall. Or, at least, it's there every time I go to see them. Aren't friends wonderful?

5 And this is how I got so many teabag sachets. I love tea. The first thing I do in the morning is crawl into the kitchen to put the kettle on. After my first cup of tea, I'm ready to face ... my second cup of tea. Facing the day comes much later.

6 Romeo and Juliet was the first ballet I ever saw, and it was a magical evening. It's something I wasn't sure I'd really enjoy very much. But I did, and I've been a fan ever since.

7 I'm not a great football fan, but it amused me to see my name on this player's shirt.

8 This is my sign of the zodiac, so it's perhaps surprising that I can't swim. I once started reading a book about Pisceans and was startled by how accurate it was. I'm not sure about their qualities, but I did seem to have all their faults!

9 I enjoy doing crosswords, and it's one of the first things I look for when I open up a newspaper. I don't like doing them in public places though, especially if someone's watching me and I can't find any of the answers.

10 Spring is the time of year when I first came to Paris, and it's where I now live. I like this extract because it mentions so many places I know, and brings back wonderful memories.

11 This is something I'm certainly not. In fact, I have a very strained relationship with technology. The overhead projector I was using in an assessed lesson for a teaching examination blew up the moment I switched it on. And it once took me half an hour to find the 'on' button for my laptop computer!

10.12 Topic banks

Collating materials related to themes and topics to be covered during future lessons

Level: Intermediate–Advanced

Preparation

Bring into class a number of newspapers plus colour supplements and magazines. Before the lesson, compile a list of the themes and topics you will be covering with your class during their lessons. You will also need several pairs of scissors and as many folders as you have topics to store the material your students find. You should also write each topic heading on the cover of a separate folder.

In class

1 On the board, write the list of topic areas your class will be covering in their coming lessons, e.g. health, education, crime, holidays, work, relationships, and so on. Spend two or three minutes on each topic, brainstorming with your students the kind of things each topic might include, and write their ideas on the board.
2 Explain to your class that newspapers can provide them with a lot of helpful and interesting background material for these lessons, and that today they are going to look through newspapers for materials related to the topics on the board.
3 Tell your students that they should go through the newspapers and magazines and cut out (carefully!) any materials they find related to any of the topics on the board.
4 You should let this materials-gathering stage of the activity continue for at least twenty minutes, but carry on for a longer period if your students' interest is still holding.
5 Finally, divide the class into as many groups as there are topics and assign one topic to each group. Give each group the folder with their topic heading and ask them to gather all the relevant materials from all the other students and file it inside their folder.

Extension

In your next lesson, bring out all the materials your students have collected. This can then be sifted by you and your students and checked for its interest, relevance and appropriateness.

Comments

(a) This activity is designed for use with classes where you intend to do project work or theme- and topic-based lessons, and is best used at the beginning of the course. Depending on how much material your class are able to find this first time, it may be necessary to repeat the activity to look for more material on a given topic at a later date.

(b) By involving your students in the process of materials gathering, you enable them to take an important step towards taking some degree of responsibility for their language learning.

Cross-references

You may be able to use the materials your students have gathered for other activities in this book.

10.13 Special interest groups

Making up news sheets for special interest groups

Level: Intermediate–Advanced

Preparation

Bring to class a supply of old newspapers, colour supplements and magazines, and even single and part-pages of newspapers. For this activity, you will also need glue, several pairs of scissors and sheets of A3 paper.

In class

1 With your students, make a list on the board of their hobbies, skills and special interests, and include personal information or characteristics. Start them off with a few suggestions to help them, e.g. *nature-lover, music-lover, sportsperson, computer-user, language-learner, Italian, teenager, car-driver, house-owner, businessperson*, and so on. The important point is to translate their ideas into relatively broad categories which are not too narrow in their focus, e.g. *sportsperson* rather than *badminton player*. This may involve some negotiation with your students to find suitable category titles.

2 Put your students into groups of three and ask each group to choose one of the categories from the list on the board – this need not

necessarily be one which applies to any of the group members personally.

3 Explain that each group is an editorial team which must make up a special interest group (SIG) news sheet for the category they have chosen. To do this, they should look through the newspapers and cut out anything they think would be of particular interest to members of this SIG.

4 Tell them that they should try to fill a sheet of paper with different items – ideally, a mixture of text and visual material. They should make the layout as attractive and eye-catching as possible, and they must be able to explain and justify any item they decide to include on their page. They should also give their page a suitable title.

5 Put scissors, glue, paper and newspapers at everyone's disposal and begin the activity. Move from group to group, helping with any vocabulary and language problems as they arise.

6 When all the groups are ready, ask them to display their SIG sheets around the room for SIG members, and any other interested parties, to read. Tell your students that they should ask editorial team members to explain any items if they do not fully understand why they have been included.

7 Finally, with the whole class, invite your students to decide which SIG members were particularly well catered for.

Cross-references

You may be able to use the materials your students have gathered for other activities in this book.

10.14 Looking for repeated language

Identifying language specific to different text types

Level: Intermediate–Advanced

Preparation

For this activity, you will need to make up a number of sets of materials (containing three or four items). The items in each set should be from the same type of text and texts should deal with the same subject-matter, e.g. sets of weather forecasts, sets of advertisements selling the same type of item or offering the same service, reports of sporting events covering the same sport, articles covering the same topic area (e.g. politics, crime, disasters), Problem Page letters, charity appeals, business reports, and so on. Each group of three students in your class will need one set of materials.

In class

1 To demonstrate this activity, read aloud two weather forecasts and ask your students to note down any words, phrases or grammatical patterns or structures they hear repeated. Read the forecasts aloud two or three times if necessary, and write your students' answers on the board.

2 Make the point clear that many specific types of text and many items dealing with a specific topic will often contain a number of similar or even identical vocabulary items and grammatical structures. Ask your students to think of other newspaper items where they could expect to find a certain amount of repetition of lexis or grammar, and write their ideas on the board.

3 Now form groups of three students and give each group one of the sets of newspaper items you have prepared.

4 Explain that each group should go through their items very carefully and make a note of any similar or identical language used in their items.

5 Begin the activity. While groups are working, circulate to deal with any vocabulary or language problems as they arise.

6 When they have finished, ask each group to make a short presentation to the class to report their findings.

7 Finally, point out to your students that if they know beforehand which language is likely to occur in specific texts, this can help them in their reading. It is also a very clear indication of which lexis and grammar it would be helpful for them to learn.

Cross-references

For a version of this activity using only advertising phrases, see 4.16. Many of the materials used in other activities in this book can be used in this activity.

10.15 Newspaper reading habits

Answering and discussing questions about newspaper reading habits

Level: Post-Elementary–Advanced

Preparation

Make one copy of the questionnaire (see Box 41) for each student in the class.

In class

1 Give each student a copy of the questionnaire and explain that this is designed to get them thinking and talking about newspapers and to find out about their newspaper reading habits.
2 Go through the questionnaire with your students to deal with any vocabulary or language problems, then ask your students to work alone to complete the questionnaire. When they have finished, form groups of three or four students.
3 Explain that each group should now use their answers as a basis for a discussion about their newspaper reading habits. Allow about fifteen minutes for this discussion stage.
4 Finally, with the whole class, go through some of the questions and ask your students to tell you their answers. This will give you some useful, general information about your students' newspaper reading habits.

Extension

Ask your students to collate their information to make a poster, representing visually (perhaps in the form of a graph) the newspaper reading habits of the class as a whole.

Variation 1

Instead of asking your students to complete the questionnaire alone, ask them to work in pairs to interview each other and record their partner's answers.

Variation 2

This activity can provide interesting cultural information if your students can interview native-English-speakers or if you work with a multinational group of students.

Variation 3

As the primary aim of the activity is to find out about your students' newspaper reading habits, for very low-level classes, you may even choose to rewrite the questionnaire into your students' own language and allow them to hold their discussion in their mother tongue.

Cross-references

This can serve as a suitable lead-in to 10.16 and 10.17. For a suitable lead-in activity, see 10.18.

Box 41 **Newspaper reading habits questionnaire**

This questionnaire is designed to find out about your newspaper reading habits. Read the questions carefully and answer them as fully as you can.

1 Write the names of 3 national newspapers in your country. What reputation and/or political bias do they have?

(a)

(b)

(c)

2 What is the local newspaper in your area?

3 Which English-language newspapers do you know? What do you know about these newspapers?

4 Is there a particular newspaper you like to read? Why?

5 Do members of your family read the same newspaper as you?

6 How often do you read a newspaper?

7 Do you pay for the newspaper?

8 Is there a particular time of day when you read a newspaper?

9 Is there a particular place where you read a newspaper?

10 How long do you spend reading a newspaper?

11 Are there any sections of the newspaper you never read?

12 Do you always read a newspaper in the same order?

13 Which section of the newspaper do you read first?

14 Which sections do you read next?

15 Do you ever talk to people about things you read in the newspaper?

16 Do you think it is important for people to read newspapers? Why?

17 Do you believe everything you read in the newspaper?

18 Do you think a newspaper is good value for money?

19 What do you do with a newspaper once you have read it?

20 How do you think reading English-language newspapers can help your language learning?

© Cambridge University Press 1999

10.16 Newspaper preferences

Discovering personal newspaper preferences

Level: Intermediate–Advanced

Preparation

Bring into class as many different, complete, English-language news-papers as you can, including even duplicate copies and different editions of the same newspaper.

In class

1 On the board, write a list of the names of all the different newspapers you have brought to the lesson and tell your students to make a copy of this list. Ask your students if they are familiar with any of these newspapers and invite them to tell the class anything they know about them.

2 Spread out the newspapers and explain to your students that they are going to look through English-language newspapers to find out which one(s) they prefer.

3 Tell your students that they should each take one newspaper and spend about five minutes looking through it from beginning to end. They should not spend too long on any one section or item, but should try to gain an overall impression of the whole newspaper.

4 Explain that you will stop them at the end of the five minutes. They should then give the newspaper a score from zero to ten (the top score) and write this score next to that newspaper on their list. This score should reflect how much the newspaper appeals to them. Tell them that they should also make brief notes about what they like or dislike about the newspaper.

5 Begin the activity. After five minutes, tell each student to stop reading their newspaper, award it a score and write brief notes about it. They should then choose a different newspaper.

6 When each student has seen several newspapers, bring this part of the activity to a close and hold a feedback session with the class. Ask your students to call out the score they gave each newspaper they saw, and write these on the board. When all the scores have been recorded, add them up. The final score should reveal which news-paper the class as a whole prefers.

7 Finally, invite comments from your students about what they liked or disliked about each newspaper and the reasons why. It will probably

interest your students if you also tell them which of the newspapers you prefer and why.

Comment

This activity introduces students to some of the different English-language newspapers which are available and puts them in a much better position to know which paper they would be interested in reading should they decide to buy one.

Cross-references

For suitable lead-in activities, see 10.6, 10.15 and 10.18. For a suitable follow-up activity, see 10.17.

10.17 Comparisons

Comparing English-language newspapers with newspapers from your students' own country

Level: Intermediate–Advanced

Preparation

Bring to class complete copies of different English-language newspapers as well as complete copies of different newspapers from your students' own country. You will need one copy of both types of newspaper for each pair of students in your class.

In class

1 Give each student any one of the newspapers you have brought to the lesson and ask them to look through these for two or three minutes.
2 After they have had time to skim through their newspapers, ask your students to suggest what points they could focus on if they were trying to get an overall impression of a newspaper. Write their ideas on the board. This list could include allocation of space to particular sections (e.g. home news, international news, features, sport, business, etc.), number, size and type of photographs and advertisements, general presentation and appearance (e.g. use of colour, style, print, layout etc.), space given to entertainment (e.g. TV and radio, crosswords, horoscopes, quizzes, etc.), and so on.

3 Now put your students into pairs and give each pair one English-language newspaper and one from their own country. These should be two broadly similar types of newspaper such as two tabloid newspapers or two broadsheets (see note in 1.1).
4 Explain that they are going to compare their two newspapers to look for similarities and differences between them. Tell them that they should make notes of their findings, and that they will need these notes to give a short presentation of their newspapers to the class.
5 Begin the activity, setting a reasonable time limit for this stage of the activity. While your students are working, be available to deal with any vocabulary or language problems that arise.
6 When your students are ready, ask each pair in turn to present their two newspapers to the class, describing and explaining in which aspects they are similar and where they differ. If you are short of time, this reporting stage can be done between pairs.

Comment

This activity is most practical with a monolingual group of students whose national newspapers are readily available. It can be done, however, with a multinational group perhaps studying in an English-speaking country. Language students abroad often buy or have sent to them newspapers from their own countries to keep up with home news. If you give them a few days' warning before trying this activity, you can ask them to bring copies of their newspapers to the lesson.

Cross-references

This can serve as a suitable follow-up to 10.6. For suitable lead-in activities, see 10.6 and 10.15.

10.18 And I quote

Discussing quotations about newspapers

Level: Intermediate–Advanced
Special equipment: overhead projector (OHP)

Preparation

Make an OHP transparency of the quotations sheet (see Box 42).

In class

1 Read one of the quotations aloud to your students and ask them for their reactions to it using suitable prompt-questions, e.g. *What does it mean? Do you agree with it? Do you disagree with it? Do you think it is true or fair? Why did the person say this?*
2 Form groups of three students, tell them to look at the other quotations and help them with any problem vocabulary or language.
3 Tell them that one student should choose one of the quotations for their group to discuss, and begin the discussion by giving their own reactions to the quotation.
4 When they have finished their discussion, another student in the group should choose another quotation and begin another discussion.
5 Continue this procedure for as long as your students' interest holds.
6 Finally, with the whole class, ask each student to choose one quotation which they particularly liked, and ask them to explain briefly why.

Cross-references

This can serve as a suitable lead-in to 10.15, 10.16 and 10.20.

Box 42 **Quotations about newspapers**

Newspapers are owned by individuals and corporations, but freedom of the press belongs to the people.

Anonymous

Newspapers are unable, seemingly, to discriminate between a bicycle accident and the collapse of civilisation.

George Bernard Shaw

The fact that a man is a newspaper reporter is evidence of some flaw of character.

Lyndon B. Johnson (US President 1963–1968)

Whenever you find hundreds and thousands of sane people trying to get out of a place and a little bunch of madmen trying to get in, you know the latter are reporters.

H. R. Knickerbocker

Newspapermen ask you dumb questions. They look up at the sun and ask you if it's shining.

Sonny Liston

All day long, Hollywood reporters lie in the sun, and when the sun goes down, they lie some more.

Frank Sinatra

Always grab the reader by the throat in the first paragraph, sink your thumbs into his windpipe in the second, and hold him against the wall until the tag line.

Paul O'Neil (American writer)

The first duty of the press is to obtain the earliest and most correct intelligence of events of the time and instantly, by disclosing them, to make them the common property of the nation.

Editor of *The Times*, London, 1852

Reference: Randall (1996)

10.19 Newspaper puzzles

Playing newspaper puzzles, word games and quizzes

Level: Post-Intermediate–Advanced

Preparation

From a selection of newspapers, compile a sheet of puzzles, word games and quizzes. Some weekend newspapers have children's sections with puzzles and, as these are based on a more limited vocabulary, they are ideal for this activity. Deal with any problem vocabulary or instructions by adding a gloss (a translation or an explanation) where necessary. Make one copy of the games sheet for each student in the class. Keep any answers printed in the newspaper for the final stages of the activity.

In addition, bring to the lesson a number of dictionaries for your students to use during the activity, and give them advance warning to bring their own. If you include non-cryptic crossword puzzles in this activity, it would also be helpful to have a thesaurus available.

In class

1 To demonstrate the activity, choose one of the newspaper puzzles and write it on the board, e.g. a nine-letter grid where the aim is to make up as many words as possible using only these letters (see Box 43 for sample grid). The most important rules here are that each word must contain three letters or more, and must always include the letter in the middle of the grid.

2 Play the game with the whole class and write their answers on the board. When they have exhausted their ideas, tell them some of the words they were unable to find and explain the meaning of any new words.

3 Explain to your students that puzzles like this are very popular in many English-language newspapers. Give each student a copy of the puzzles sheet you have compiled and allow them a few moments to look through the puzzles and games.

4 Tell your students that they should each choose a puzzle they would like to do. They should also decide whether they would like to work alone, with a partner, or in a small group, perhaps making it into a competition.

5 When all your students have chosen a puzzle and decided whether they wish to work alone, in pairs or in groups, begin the activity. Make sure that dictionaries are within everyone's reach. While your

students are working, move around the class giving help where necessary.

6 As the activity draws to a close, help your students check their answers.

7 Finally, ask your students if they have enjoyed this activity. If they have, encourage them to try some of the other puzzles at home.

Comment

Some newspapers print the answers to puzzles, word games and quizzes in the same edition on another page or upside down below the game. Other newspapers give the answers in the next day's edition, or, if it is a weekend paper, in the following weekend's edition.

Box 43 Sample nine-letter grid

G	A	N
E	T	I
H	C	S

10.20 Ethics

Discussing ethical dilemmas facing journalists

Level: Post-Intermediate–Advanced

Preparation

For this activity, you will need to refer to the list of ethical questions (see Box 44).

In class

1 On the board, write one of the questions and explain to your students that this is an ethical question facing journalists today. Check that your students understand it, and hold a short open discussion with your students on this question. You should add your own opinions on the matter.

2 At the end of this discussion phase, ask your students to suggest other ethical dilemmas facing journalists today.

3 Put your students into groups of three or four and explain that you will read aloud another ethical dilemma facing journalists today. Each group will then have five minutes to discuss the question before they have to report back to the class.
4 Choose another question which you think will interest your students, pre-teach any key vocabulary, and read the question aloud. Remind your students that they now have exactly five minutes to discuss this issue.
5 Stop the discussion promptly after five minutes, then ask groups to report back to the class the general feelings of their group members concerning the question.
6 Repeat this procedure for other suitable questions for as long as your students' energy and interest holds.

Extension

If you can arrange it, it would be very interesting for your students if you could invite a local journalist to a future lesson to discuss some of these questions. It would also be interesting to know what s/he considers to be the most important ethical issues facing journalists today – at a local, national and international level.

Cross-references

For a suitable lead-in activity, see 10.18.

Box 44 **Everyday ethical dilemmas facing journalists**

Here are a number of everyday ethical issues that can confront journalists:

- Should journalists ever lie or use deceit in the pursuit of a story?
- Should they ever edit a direct quotation?
- Is it legitimate to tape a conversation and not inform the interviewee of this?
- Should journalists accept freebies? Should they do so only on certain conditions? Are there any significantly different ethical issues in being offered a book for review, a free ticket to review a play and a free trip to the Seychelles for a travel feature?
- What is the impact of the plethora of awards on standards?
- What considerations should a journalist have when interviewing children?
- Should a reporter contact the parents of a student who has committed suicide at university?
- Should newspapers carry columns by local Christian leaders but not by those of other faiths?
- To what extent should newspapers provide readers with the right to reply to inaccuracies?
- What special consideration should a journalist have when dealing with the mentally ill?
- How important is it for journalists to protect their sources?
- Is cheque-book journalism (paying sources) justified?
- Is it legitimate to invade someone's privacy for a story? Do different standards apply to public figures and to members of the general public?
- To what extent does overt commitment to a political party or campaigning movement interfere with professionalism and notions of fairness?
- Should newspapers carry government misinformation during times of war (and peace)?
- Is it legitimate ever to break an embargo?
- Is it possible to provide guidelines on questions of taste and the use of 'shocking' photographs or obscene language?
- To what extent does newspaper language reinforce militarist and ageist stereotypes and how can journalists confront this issue?

Reference: Keeble (1994), pp. 26–27

Appendix 1 Stylistic and structural features of newspaper headlines

Stylistic features

Alliteration

Alliteration is the repetition of the same initial sound in a group of words.

> Wives' war of waiting and writing
> Spice Girls feel the fickle finger of fame

Assonance

Assonance is the repetition of one particular vowel sound in a group of words.

> Wotto lotto bosh on lotto dosh

Cliché

The word *cliché* is used in a pejorative sense to refer to a word or expression that is considered to be over-used, or used indiscriminately. Clichés come in several different forms, including alliterative phrases, over-dramatic adjectives, metaphors and single words.

> Skiers safe and sound
> Proud parents win coveted title
> Tower of strength
> Fairy-tale romance
> Soap star in love-child mercy dash

Euphemism

Euphemism is the use of a particular word or expression which is considered more acceptable or pleasant, or less controversial, than certain other words or expressions. It can be used as a way of being vague and unclear, or to cover up the truth or reality of a situation.

> Minister threatens air support [i.e. bombing]

BA reports passenger underflow [i.e. very few passengers]
IBM announces job rationalisation [i.e. job cuts]

Irony

Irony in newspaper headlines can be used for news events in which a person seems mocked by fate or events. Although frequently tragic, there is often an element of black (graveyard) humour to be found in such headlines.

Bike crash kills flying phobia man
Bull savages anti-bloodsport campaigner

Metaphor

Metaphor is when a phrase or expression usually used to describe one thing is used to describe something else.

Ministers read the riot act by PM
[i.e. the Prime Minister was angry with his ministers]

New hospital put on ice
[i.e. the building of the new hospital has been suspended]

Pun

A pun is a play on a word which has several meanings or which sounds like another word. It is a feature frequently used in tabloid newspapers for humorous effect.

Fisherman nets lotto jackpot
Xerox present the fax to shareholders [i.e. the facts]
Car-makers drive up profits

Repetition

Repetition of words in headlines is for emphasis and very strong, dramatic effect.

Out Out Out
Why, Oh Why, Oh Why?

Shared knowledge

Many headlines assume shared cultural knowledge and shared general knowledge between the headline writer and the reader. This includes the use of only first names or surnames of people who are considered so well-known that stating their full name, position or title or reason for prominence is considered unnecessary.

> Kiss for Harry as he meets pop idols
> [reference to Prince Harry, the son of the Prince of Wales]

> You cannot be serious
> [reference to the exact words used by an American tennis star in an
>   angry outburst]

> Where in the world is our poor kidnapped Tinky Winky?
> [reference to a popular children's TV programme character]

> Odd couple who longed for a Mary Poppins life
> [reference to a film character and the type of person she represents]

> Tragedy of A-level girl on joyride
> [reference to a public examination in the British school system]

Simile

Simile is describing one thing by likening it to another.

> Crash scene like a battlefield
> Villagers sick as a parrot

Structural features

Abbreviations and acronyms

Abbreviations and acronyms are often used in headlines to save space.

> Razor-sharp legal star beaten by the OJ factor
> NATO envoys bring peace hope
> Organ donor in CJD shock
> NHS faces a terminal lack of faith
> AIDS clinic to close
> Sea birds could help set EU fishing quotas

Omission

Articles and other determiners, possessive adjectives and parts of the verb 'to be' (particularly in passive constructions) are frequently omitted in newspaper headlines.

Pound falls
Biker loses arm in crash
Man stabbed after rail row

Tenses

1 The infinitive is used to refer to future events.

Minister to quit
France to sell 20% of Telecom

2 The *-ing* form of the verb, representing the Present Progressive, is used to refer to events that are happening at the moment.

Au pair agency facing huge damages claim
Authorities failing child ME sufferers

3 The *-ing* form of the verb, representing the Present Progressive, is also used to refer to future events.

Women facing poverty in old age

4 The Simple Present is often used to refer to events which happened in the past.

Beatles' PR man dies aged 65
Elephants kill 7 in rampage

5 The Simple Present can also be used to refer to events happening at the moment.

France prepares for World Cup mania
Bank expects high rate of interest in open day

Short headlines

Many short news reports, particularly News in Brief items, are accompanied by headlines made up of only two or three words. Although a number of different variations are possible, there are several fairly common combinations.

1 noun + noun

Tunnel death
Birthday rat

2 adjective + noun

Lethal attack
Lucky numbers

3 noun + verb

> Sailors rescued
> Trains withdrawn
> Pound falls

4 noun + noun + noun

> Poison case wait
> Briton arrest fear
> Ferry fire payout

5 noun + verb + noun

> Animals left fortune
> Court delays crucifixion
> Racer loses title

Reference: Hicks (1993)

Appendix 2   Web sites

England

Daily Mirror	http://www.mirror.co.uk
Electronic Telegraph	http://www.telegraph.co.uk
European	http://www.the-european.com
Evening Standard	http://www.thisislondon.co.uk
Financial Times	http://www.ft.com
Guardian	http://www.guardian.co.uk
Independent	http://www.independent.co.uk
Observer	http://www.observer.co.uk
Telegraph	http://www.telegraph.co.uk
Sunday Times	http://www.sunday-times.co.uk
The Times	http://www.the-times.co.uk

Ireland

Belfast Morning News	http://www.irishnews.com
Belfast Telegraph	http://www.belfasttelegraph.co.uk
Examiner	http://www.examiner.ie
Irish Independent	http://www.independent.ie
Irish News	http://www.irishnews.com
Irish Times	http://www.irish-times.ie
Limerick Post	http://www.limerickpost.ie

Scotland

Electronic Herald	http://www.dcthomson.co.uk/ mags/tele
Evening Times	http://www.cims.co.uk/ eveningtimes
Scotsman	http://www.scotsman.com/ index.html
Scottish Daily Record	http://www.record-mail.co.uk/rm
Sunday Mail	http://www.record-mail.co.uk/rm

USA

International Herald Tribune	http://www.iht.com
Los Angeles Times	http://www.latimes.com/HOME
New York Times	http://www.nytimes.com
USA Today	http://www.usatoday.com
Wall Street Journal	http://www.wsj.com
Washington Post	http://www.washingtonpost.com

This is only a very small selection of newspapers which are on the Internet. Teachers may also be interested in visiting the following web sites:

CNN Interactive	http://www.cnn.com
The Economist	http://www.economist.com
Electronic Newsstand	http://www.enews.com
ISN KidNews	http://www.vsa.cape.com/ ~powens/KidNews.html
Newsweek	http://www.newsweek.com
Newspapers on the Web	http://www.intercom.com.au/ intercom/newsprs/index.html
OneWorld Magazine	http://www.envirolink.org/ oneworld/index.html
Reuters	http://www.reuters.com
Time Magazine	http://www.time.com
The Ultimate Collection of News Links	http://pppp.net/links/news

Reference: Sperling (1997)

Cartoons and strip cartoons

The Born Loser	http://www.unitedmedia.com/ comics/bornloser
Cartoon Stock	http://www.cartoonstock.com
The Comic Strip	http://www.unitedmedia.com/ comics
The Dilbert Zone	http://www.unitedmedia.com/ comics/dilbert
Garfield Online	http://www.garfield.com
Rob Thacker's Calvin and Hobbes Page	http://fermi.phys.ualberta.ca/ ~thacker/cal.html

Appendix 3 Abbreviations used in classified advertisements

Abbreviation	Full form
a/phone; an/phone	answerphone
appt	appointment
att; attract	attractive
avail	available
balc	balcony
bath; b/room	bathroom
BB; B&B	bed and breakfast
bed(s); bedrm(s)	bedroom(s)
bldng	building
brkfst rm	breakfast-room
b/w; b&w	black and white
c.	circa (e.g. *c. £30,000*)
c	chest (e.g. *c 36″* = chest size 36 inches)
cc	credit card(s)
cent	century
ch; c/h	central heating
charm	charming
clkrm	cloakroom
c/o	care of (e.g. *Write c/o The Manager*)
cols	colours
concs	concessions (e.g. *student concs*)
CV	curriculum vitae
dble	double
dep	deposit
det	detached
din rm	dining-room
DIY	do it yourself
d/g; d/glazing; d/glz	double glazing
educ	educated
ent	entrance

Abbreviation	Full form
ent'ment	entertainment
e/phone	entry phone
est	established/estimate
eves	evenings
ex con; ex cond	excellent condition
excl	excluding
ext	extension
F	female
f/k; f/kit; f/kitchen	fitted kitchen
flr	floor
fr	from
fsh	full service history
f/ship	friendship
ft	foot/feet
f/t	full-time
gch	gas central heating
gdn	garden
gf; g/f	ground floor
gfch	gas-fired central heating
gge; grge	garage
g/con	good condition
grnd	ground
gsoh	good sense of humour
g/tee; guar	guarantee
gwo	good working order
hrs	hours
h/some	handsome
immed	immediately
in(s)	inch(es)
inc; incl	included/including
indpt	independent
ins	insurance/inches
int	international
ints	interests
k	thousand (e.g. £15*k*)
kit	kitchen
l	length (e.g. *l* 24″ = length 24 inches)

Abbreviation	Full form
lnge	lounge
l/r; liv/rm	living-room
lrg	large
lux	luxury
M	male
max	maximum
min	minimum/minute
mins	minutes
mnth	month
mod cons	modern conveniences
mpg	miles per gallon
'n'	and
new dec; new decor	newly decorated
no.	number
nr	near
n/s	non-smoker
nt	night
OAP	old age pensioner
ono	or near(est) offer
ovno	or very near offer
pa	per annum
pat	patio
pcm	per calendar month
ph; pr hr	per hour
poss	possibly
p+p	postage and packing
pppn	per person per night (e.g. £25 *pppn*)
prof	professional
prog	programme
prop	proprietor
p/t	part-time
pw	per week
p/x; p/exchange	part-exchange
rec rm	reception-room
ref	refund/reference
refs	references
reg	registered (e.g. *reg childminder*)

Abbreviation	Full form
reg	registration (e.g. *Saab V-reg*)
req; reqd	required
res	reservation
rm(s)	room(s)
RRP	recommended retail price
r/ship	relationship
sae	stamped addressed envelope
s/c	self-contained
sep	separate
s/h; sec hand	second hand
shwr	shower
slp	sleeps (e.g. *slp 2–6* = sleeps 2–6 people)
sngle	single
sq	square
tel	telephone
tdh	tall dark (and) handsome
tlc	tender loving care
v	very
VAT	Value Added Tax
VCR	video cassette recorder
VDU	visual display unit
vgc	very good condition
w	waist (e.g. *w 36″* = waist size 36 inches)
wc	water closet (i.e. toilet)
w/d; w/day	weekday
w/e	weekend
wk(s)	week(s)
wltm	would like to meet
yo	years old (e.g. *32 yo* = thirty-two years old)
yr(s)	year(s)

Bibliography

Baddock, B. 1988. *Scoop*, Prentice Hall
Berne, E. 1964. *Games People Play*, Penguin
Chiaro, D. 1992. *The Language of Jokes*, Routledge
Davis, P. & Rinvolucri, M. 1988. *Dictation*, Cambridge University Press
Dick, J. 1991. *Freelance Writing for Newspapers*, A & C Black
Fowler, R. 1991. *Language in the News*, Routledge
Grellet, F. 1981. *Developing Reading Skills*, Cambridge University Press
Hartley, J. 1982. *Understanding News*, Routledge
Hedge, T. 1985. *Using Readers in Language Teaching*, Modern English Publications
Hicks, W. 1993. *English for Journalists*, Routledge
Hill, D. 1982. Matching Activities, *Modern English Teacher* Vol. 10, No. 2
Keeble, R. 1994. *The Newspaper Handbook*, Routledge
Land, G. 1988. *Behind the Headlines*, Longman
Metcalf, F. (compiler) 1986. *The Penguin Dictionary of Modern Humorous Quotations*, Guild Publishing
Nunan, D. 1989. *Designing Tasks for the Communicative Classroom*, Cambridge University Press
Randall, D. 1996. *The Universal Journalist*, Pluto Press
Sanderson, P. 1994. Problem Page Letters, *Modern English Teacher* Vol. 3, No. 4
Sanderson, P. 1994. Weather Forecast, *Standpoints* No. 35
Sperling, D. 1997. *The Internet Guide for English Language Teachers*, Prentice Hall Regents
Waterhouse, K. 1993. *Waterhouse on Newspaper Style*, Penguin

Index